WOOLMAN ON CONTRACT

WOOLMAN ON CONTRACT

Fifth Edition

Gillian Black, LLB (Hons), PhD, Solicitor
Senior Lecturer in Law, University of Edinburgh

Consultant Editor:
The Hon Lord Woolman

W. GREEN

 THOMSON REUTERS

Published in 2014 by W. Green, 21 Alva Street,
Edinburgh EH2 4PS
Part of Thomson Reuters.
Registered in England & Wales, Company No 1679046.
Registered Off ce and address for service:
5 Canada Square, Canary Wharf, London, E14 sAQ

Typeset by YHT Ltd, London
Printed and bound in Great Britain by CPI Group (UK) Ltd, Croydon, CR0 4YY

ISBN 978-0-414-01910-2

A catalogue record for this title is available
from the British Library

No natural forests were destroyed to make this product; only
farmed timber was used and replanted.

PREFACE TO FIFTH EDITION

Contract disputes continue to keep the Scottish courts busy, and this new edition of *Woolman on Contract* has been updated to take account of the myriad developments that have occurred in the last four years. In preparing and revising this text, I have been fortunate to have the support of Lord Woolman, whose advice and guidance has been invaluable, as ever. In addition, I wish to record my thanks to Professor Laura Macgregor, David Cabrelli, and Lorna Richardson of Edinburgh Law School, and Dr Dot Reid of Glasgow University. Professor Hector MacQueen and Charles Garland of the Scottish Law Commission have also been very generous with their time in relation to the current work of the SLC. Thanks also to Alisdair MacPherson and Amy Pairman, whose research assistance has helped ensure the appendix and statutory material are up-to-date. I have endeavoured to state the law as at June 1, 2014.

Gillian Black
Old College, Edinburgh
June 1, 2014.

CONTENTS

TABLE OF CASES

TABLE OF STATUTES

TABLE OF SCOTTISH STATUTES

TABLE OF STATUTORY INSTRUMENTS

SCOTTISH STATUTORY INSTRUMENTS

CHAPTER 1

INTRODUCTION

Contracts feature in many areas of our lives. Each day we may be **1–01** involved in a variety of different contracts: buying goods online, travelling by bus, going to the cinema or having clothes dry-cleaned. Some of our most important long-term relationships—those concerning how we earn a living and where we reside—are based upon contracts. Nor can we fail to be aware that the business world is rooted in contract. Sale, auctions, hire, share-dealing, insurance and commercial leasing are just a few examples. The list could be extended almost indefinitely. What links together these different contractual arrangements? Let us consider a few explanations.

One answer that suggests itself is that every contract effects an exchange. The exchange may take different forms: services for money, goods for money or goods for goods. The exchange may take place at the time the contract is made or it may be postponed to sometime in the future. Most contracts possess this element of exchange. Exchange, however, cannot be the whole answer because in some contracts no such element is present. There is no legal objection to a confidentiality agreement whereby a prospective investor consents not to disclose confidential information about a company. The agreement can be enforced even though the prospective investor is not paid nor receives any other benefit for signing the agreement. So while exchange is a common factor in most contracts, it is not a necessary ingredient.

Another suggested link between the different types of contract is the **1–02** concept of promise. It is possible to reduce every contract to the form "X promises the following" and "Y promises the following". Consider a contract of employment. The employee's main promise is to carry out the work he is instructed to do. The employer's main promise is to pay the employee's salary. Defining contracts in terms of promise is useful because it emphasises the obligatory nature of the transaction. The moral precept that we must abide by our promises enables us readily to accept that people who break their legal promises must face the consequences. So if the employee breaks his promise and does not perform his duties, the employer has the option of terminating the contract of employment. Equally if the employer breaks his promise, the employee is entitled to refuse to carry out his duties and to sue to recover the salary.

There are, however, two reasons why it is inappropriate to define contract in terms of promise. The first is that, as we have seen, the majority of contracts actually do involve an element of exchange. One thing is given in return for another. The concept of promise does not truly

1

explain this reciprocity which is at the core of most contracts. Viewing a contract as two distinct promises distorts the picture by failing to reflect that the promises are the counterparts of one another. A look at a simple contract of sale of goods may help to illustrate this point. The customer who purchases a newspaper can be viewed as promising to pay the price. Similarly the newsagent can be seen as promising to transfer the newspaper. These promises are not given in isolation, however. Such an analysis therefore seems artificial—it does not square with the *reciprocal* nature of the purchaser's and seller's acts.

The second reason for not defining contracts in terms of promise is because in Scots law there is a separate category of obligation which is actually called promise.[1] This category is distinct from that of contract. A promise is an obligation where only one party undertakes to be legally bound and the obligation arises by an act on his part alone. Suppose a newspaper runs a promotional campaign in which it states that £50,000 will be paid to the first person to paddle around the Scottish coastline in a kayak.[2] A person who performed this feat might enforce this obligation as a promise. The newspaper would be bound to pay over the sum to anyone who satisfied this condition. In Ch.4, below, we shall see that the dividing line between contract and promise is narrow. Nonetheless it is preferable to avoid defining the one, contract, in terms of the other, promise.[3]

1–03   The discussion so far shows how difficult it is to find a definition of contract which will overcome all objections. Some jurists have given up the search as a lost cause. Most, however, have come to the conclusion that a definition can best be framed in terms of the notion of agreement. It may involve the construction of an oil tanker, the provision of an overdraft, or the purchase of a bar of chocolate. In each case the parties agree on the nature of their particular bargain and how it is to be performed. A contract can be said to be an agreement between two (or more) parties. However, it is a particular type of agreement: it is one which is legally enforceable. Two points need to be made about this definition. First the term "enforceable" is used here in a special sense. It can mean that the parties are made to fulfil their contractual obligations, if necessary with recourse to the courts. Alternatively, it can mean that the parties are entitled to exercise certain remedies in the event of the other's failure to perform as agreed. If a builder fails to turn up on the due date to erect an extension to a house, the owner could litigate to make the builder come and actually build the extension. It is much more likely, however, that he will claim damages instead—and the contract may

---

[1] For a detailed review of the relationship between promises and contract law, see M. Hogg, *Promises and Contract Law: Comparative Perspectives* (Cambridge: Cambridge University Press, 2011).

[2] In 1985, Brian Wilson paddled from Southerness Point near Dumfries to Seacliff Beach near North Berwick, thereby nearly achieving this feat.

[3] The Anglo-American approach to contract views contract as a mutual exchange of promises, and is sometimes referred to as the promissory approach. In contrast, the approach in Scotland and Civilian jurisdictions focuses on the agreement of both parties, using a consensual analysis.

provide for a limit on the amount of damages to be paid. Secondly, agreement may be more apparent than real. Does an individual really "agree" to the terms of a car-hire contract? The customer usually signs the form put in front of him without attending in any detail to its terms. If he does read the small print, he may not understand its meaning. Even the most battle-hardened solicitor may sign such an agreement on the footing that she is in no position to negotiate more favourable terms. Defining contract as an enforceable agreement therefore may not satisfy the jurist, but it does provide a working definition.

A query may be put. Even if agreement does link all the different types **1–04** of contract, surely the truth is that the principles relating to each contract form a separate branch of law? There are, for example, special rules relating to marine insurance which are not mirrored in other types of insurance contract, far less in contracts of lease or partnership. Why do lawyers not speak of a law of contracts rather than a law of contract? Paradoxically, the answer to this question stems precisely from the great variety of contracts which exist. The range of contractual arrangements which people can enter into is so vast that it is not possible to lay down specific rules to cover every situation that may arise. Accordingly, when a contractual dispute arises, there is often no special rule to resolve the issue. Recourse must then be made to the general law of contract, because it is a system of general principles rather than particular rules. A new or unusual situation can be resolved by reference to a principle even where the special rules are silent. So in looking at a particular legal problem, it is always necessary to have in mind both the general principles of Scots contract law and any special rules relating to the contract in question.

The interaction of the special rules and the general principles is illustrated by the contract of employment. Over the past five decades there has been a colossal growth in employment law. Parliament has enacted a great deal of legislation concerning, for example, equality, discrimination on grounds of age, sex, race or disability, maternity and paternity leave, and the right to strike. In addition, employment tribunals and the courts have produced a large volume of case law interpreting that legislation. But that has not eclipsed the role of the law of contract entirely. Questions concerning whether a contract of employment has been formed and, if so, on what terms, continue to depend in large measure on the general law of contract. Likewise questions relating to who can sue on the contract and what the measure of damages for breach ought to be. In some rare instances different solutions may be provided. An employee who is sacked may present a complaint of unfair dismissal to an employment tribunal. That is a statutory remedy of the law of employment. But it is still open to an employee to bring the older contractual action of wrongful dismissal in the sheriff court or the Court of Session. This might be advantageous to the employee who has not worked for a sufficient length of time to claim unfair dismissal, or who feels that the financial limits on the awards made by employment tribunals are too low.

In this book we shall discuss the general law of contract. In passing, we shall also consider the law of promise. The principles of contract law will be illustrated by reference to the many different varieties of contract. As is demonstrated by the example of employment, the law of contract provides a framework of principles into which each individual contract fits. We begin by looking at the development of contract and shall then consider some aspects of contract theory.

DEVELOPMENT

1–05   In early societies there was no great need for a law of contract. Individuals tended to live in fixed social and economic positions. Contracts would be relatively simple and would usually involve simultaneous exchange—barter or sale. In such cases, there is not much scope for disputes to arise. Both parties can see and touch the commodities with which they are dealing, whether they be gold or grain or animals. Ownership usually depends on an individual's status—as chief, slave or child—rather than on the contracts which he makes. The role of custom is more important in individuals' lives than their ability to make contracts. So whether a person owns a particular parcel of land will depend on several factors: on whether land can be owned by an individual in that community; on that person's right to the land by virtue of inheritance or marriage. His ownership will not, however, be determined by reference to his having bought the land from the previous owner. Court actions, when they developed, focused on recovering debts, such as a failure by one party to pay the other for their performance. There was no principled body of law governing "contracts". A law of contract, including appropriate remedies, comes to be required when there is a development from simultaneous to future exchange. Sometimes this is referred to as the change from "executed" to "executory" contracts. The Romans were the first to work out in detail the legal consequences of contractual obligations. As Rome developed in commercial and in political importance, there was a need to devise laws to regulate the great increase in business transactions which occurred. Originally it was a rather rigid system. Contracts could in general only be enforced if they were real or formal. Real contracts were those which required something more than mere agreement. At first some ceremony would have to be gone through. Later what was required was transfer of the item in question. The transfer could be actual or symbolic. So far as formal contracts were concerned, a set of formalities had to be observed for the transaction to be effective. Instead of two parties merely agreeing that A should sell B a slave, or that X would lease a room in the urbs from Y, formal contracts required that some set pattern of words had to be gone through, or some special writing used. In the later period the jurists succeeded in making the law much more flexible, but it remained a law of contracts rather than contract. This meant that if a dispute occurred, it would be resolved by reference to the rules of the particular contract in question, not by reference to some general body of principles.

1–06   The continental jurist Grotius (1583–1645) is generally regarded as the author of the modern law of contract. His achievement was to take the principles laid down by the Romans in their several species of contract and to bind them together into a coherent body of law, animated by the general notion that all obligations should be binding. In other words, failure to comply with formalities and real requirements should not prevent a contract from being enforceable against the parties to it.

The architect of modern Scots law, Viscount Stair (1619–1695), borrowed from a number of sources when writing his magisterial work, the *Institutions of the Law of Scotland*, published in 1681. As well as drawing heavily on Roman law, Grotius and other continental writers, Stair relied on the canon law and the common law of Scotland as it existed in his time. There are two important points to note about Stair's treatment of contract. The first is that his account is a much more substantial, developed treatment than is to be found in contemporaneous English works. Blackstone, for example, hardly devoted any pages to contract law and it can be fairly said that the English did not have a law of contract until the nineteenth century. The second point is that Stair was even more radical than Grotius in his desire to remove formal and real impediments from the law. He adopted the maxim of the canon law: "every paction produceth action". Loosely translated, this means that every seriously intended engagement is binding on the parties, irrespective of the form in which it is couched.

The eighteenth and nineteenth centuries were periods of great social **1–07** and economic change. The shift from agriculture to industry and the urbanisation of the population saw a large increase in the number and range of transactions which took place. Manufacturers bought materials, hired workers, subcontracted work and sold the goods produced; all on a scale hitherto unknown. Law was not immune from this change. Courts had to attempt to deal with a variety of new types of transaction. They responded by fashioning new law to meet the new conditions.

Two interlinked ideas came into prominence: freedom of contract and sanctity of contract. Freedom of contract means that everyone, unless underage or lacking mental capacity, can exercise choice. They can choose (a) whether or not to enter a particular contact and (b) to determine the terms on which it is made. Sanctity of contract is the corollary of freedom of contract. It simply means that all contracts freely entered into are binding upon the parties. In an age of expansion, when Britain's pre-eminence in many spheres, military, economic, and scientific, was at its height, there was a natural reluctance to tamper with the established order of things. While things were going so well for the country as a whole, the argument ran, any intervention might seriously hamper continued prosperity and development. In economic matters this led the government to pursue a laissez-faire policy. It did not attempt to regulate markets or manufacturers except in the case of extreme abuses. This was reflected in the legal context, where the courts were unwilling to interfere with the contracts coming before them. Workers were bound by their contracts, however long their working hours or poor their remuneration. It was not for the judges to relieve someone of a bad bargain. Freedom of contract was an application of the utilitarian philosophy that everyone was the best judge of their own interests. Bentham stated that:

"... no man of ripe years and of sound mind, acting freely, and with his eyes open, ought to be hindered, with a view to his advantage, from making such bargain, in the way of obtaining money as he thinks fit, nor ... anybody hindered from supplying him, upon any terms he thinks proper to accede to".[4]

1–08 Freedom of contract should not be overemphasised in the Scottish context. A study of the contract cases decided by the courts presided over by the greatest Scottish judge of the nineteenth century, John Inglis, successively Lord Justice-Clerk and Lord President of the Court of Session, suggests that the concept never reached the same zenith in Scotland as it did in England. The courts did in general seem more willing than their English counterparts to step in to correct obvious unfairness when circumstances warranted it. However, freedom of contract was and remains an important strand in contract thinking. If the parties are of equal bargaining strength and wish to tailor a contract to their individual wishes, the law has always given them wide scope to accomplish their aim. A successful recording star, for example, might negotiate a contract with a promoter of rock concerts. It may allow for a very high fee to be paid and contain a variety of unusual terms and conditions. Perhaps it is stipulated that champagne will be available in the star's dressing room and that a private jet will convey the star's entourage between cities. Suppose that audience attendance at the concerts is very low and it becomes uneconomic for the promoter to continue with the contract. The court will be very reluctant to interfere with the bargain. It presumes that the parties are the best judge of their own interests and should adhere to the arrangements which they made. If the nineteenth century can be viewed as a century of laissez-faire, however, then the twentieth century can be seen as one of intervention. Even in the nineteenth century the notion of freedom of contract was largely a juristic abstraction rather than a reality of everyday life. A traveller from Edinburgh to London would have to go by train, by coach or by ship. By the end of the century the train would almost certainly be his preferred mode of travel. As only one company operated the railway line between the two capitals, the traveller had accordingly no choice about the party with whom he contracted. Moreover when he went to the booking desk to buy his ticket, the opportunities for negotiating the terms of travel were non-existent. He either bought the ticket on the railway company's terms or he did not travel. Freedom of contract in such a situation was a myth.

1–09 With the growth of monopolies in various fields, whether government or private, freedom of choice in deciding with whom to enter contracts has been eroded. Likewise the opportunity to negotiate terms. Many businesses fix their contractual terms in advance by the use of printed forms or online terms and conditions. Suppose an individual wishes to buy a television, hire a car or borrow money from the bank. In each case, he normally has to sign a form which already has the terms of the

---

[4] *Jeremy Bentham's Economic Writings*, edited by Werner Stark (London: Royal Economic Society, 1952), i, 129.

contract printed upon it or, where contracting online, check the box to state that he accepts the website's terms and conditions. There is no opportunity to vary the terms; they must be taken as they stand or left. French lawyers refer to such a contract as a *contrat d'adhesion*—one either adheres completely or not at all. The recognition that all contracts were not freely entered into and freely negotiated led to the development of new doctrines and new principles. But these developments have occurred in the context of a widely held belief that an important feature of the law of contract is its tendency to promote stability by having certain legal rules. People must be able to predict how their contracts will be enforced. And what they themselves have agreed will usually determine their legal rights. So the presumption is to enforce the arrangements that the parties themselves have arrived at. Interference by the courts will only occur in strictly defined circumstances.

CONTRACTUAL THEORY

It is helpful to obtain a mental fix on the place of the law of contract **1–10** relative to other areas of law. On p.8 a broad division of the law is given.

Public law and private law

It can be helpful to think of law regulating two different forms of rela- **1–11** tionship. Public law is that area of law which concerns the relationship of the state with private persons, or of different organs of the state with one another. Thus taxation is part of public law because in matters relating to tax, whether income, corporation or value added tax, the Crown in the shape of Her Majesty's Revenue and Customs ("HMRC") is always involved. In administrative law, a government department or other public authority is always one side of the equation. In criminal cases the state, in the guise of the Lord Advocate or procurator fiscal, prosecutes those who are alleged to have committed an offence. Private law is that body of law dealing with the relationships of private persons. A person in law can be a natural person, i.e. an individual, or a juristic person, such as a partnership, voluntary association or company. So when two neighbours have a dispute about an overhanging branch, or a customer queries the quality of an item he has bought in a shop, or a shareholder wishes to take action against the directors of a company, these are all within the sphere of private law. The Scotland Act 1998 which established the Scottish Parliament defines "Scots private law" as referring to a number of "areas of the civil law of Scotland", (a) the general principles of private law; (b) the law of persons; (c) the law of obligations; (d) the law of property; and (e) the law of actions.[5]

This distinction between private and public law can appear more **1–12** important in English law than in Scots law. The history of Scots law indicates that, for certain purposes, the courts have been reluctant to

---

[5] Scotland Act 1998 s.126(4).

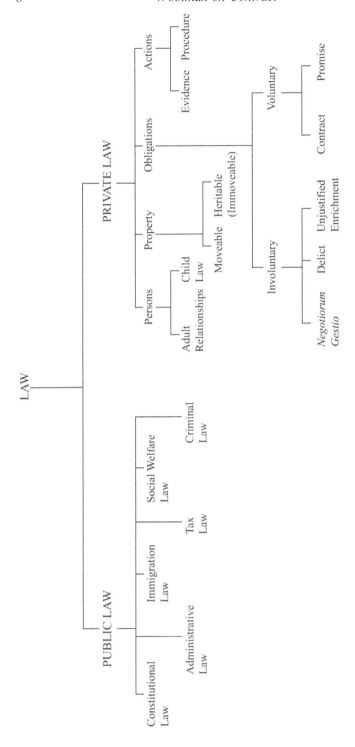

differentiate between the two forms of relationship.[6] In any event the boundaries between the two often dissolve. It is still possible, although rare, for an individual to raise a private prosecution. Public authorities are subject to private law. A contract made by a local health board to build a hospital or to be supplied with laundry is just as much governed by private law as any similar contract made by a private person. This is so even where the contractual dispute may have profound political and social consequences. For example, *Attorney General v Blake*[7] involved litigation for breach of a contract of employment between the UK Government and an ex-spy, turned traitor. The Government was awarded damages for breach of contract. Although it was a highly unusual case, the litigation was ultimately a question of contract and governed by private law. It has since influenced other contract disputes between private parties.

Property and obligations

More detailed consideration must be given to the relationship between **1–13** the law of property and the law of obligations. These two branches of private law often interact, because property is often transferred or affected by a contract such as sale, hire or lease. Property is concerned with ownership, which gives rise to a real right (*jus in re*) on the part of the owner. Obligations, on the other hand, only give rise to a personal right (*jus in personam*). The difference between real and personal rights can best be explained by an example:

When a house is sold in Scotland, the first step is for the purchaser and seller to complete missives. The missives are the contractual letters exchanged between the parties' respective solicitors setting out the property to be sold, the purchase price, the date of entry and so on. Subsequently, the seller grants the purchaser a document known as a disposition in return for the price.

Once the missives are completed, the purchaser has a personal right against a particular person, the seller. This is the contractual stage of the process. Should the seller default in transferring the house, the purchaser can sue him for delivery of a valid title. But if the seller goes bankrupt or sells the house to someone else, the purchaser's right to the house may be defeated. His only remedy may be to attempt to recover damages from the seller. When the purchaser receives the disposition and his title to the property is registered in the Land Register, however, he becomes the owner. As owner he has a right of property, a right which is "good against the whole world". He can prevent anyone from defeating his title. A real right involves the idea of a right to a thing, whereas a personal right connotes a right against a person.

A personal right can only exist if someone has a correlative duty or **1–14** obligation. Although we term this branch of the law the law of

---

[6] See in respect of judicial review *West v Secretary of State for Scotland*, 1992 S.C. 385; 1992 S.L.T. 636.
[7] *Attorney General v Blake* [2001] 1 A.C. 268. See further discussion of this case in Ch.10.

obligations, it would be equally possible to call it the law of personal rights. Viscount Stair explained the relationship between rights and obligations as follows:

> "Obligation is a legal tie by which we may be necessitate or constrained to pay or perform something. This tie lieth upon the debtor; and the power of making use of it in the creditor is the personal right itself, which is a power given by the law, to exact from persons that which they are due."[8]

Accordingly the feature of an obligation is that there is always a correlative right to enforce it.

Non-voluntary (obediential) obligations

1–15 Some obligations are imposed by law, rather than voluntarily assumed, and are termed obediential obligations. There are three types of such obligation: delict, unjustified enrichment and *negotiorum gestio*. The law of delict obliges persons to compensate others for any harm which they have caused to them either deliberately or negligently. This is sometimes called the obligation to make reparation. Suppose a worker is injured in the course of employment, or a pedestrian is knocked down by a car, or a politician is defamed. Any subsequent court action which is brought is an attempt by the person injured to satisfy a personal right. He seeks a court decree requiring the other person to fulfil the obligation of compensation which the law has placed upon him.[9] The second class of obediential obligation, unjustified enrichment, relates to situations where one person has benefited at the expense of another. Here the obligation is to restore the parties to the position where neither can be said to be "unjustifiedly enriched". This obligation comes into play, for example, where one person is paid money by mistake, or builds a house on another's property believing it to be his own. Here the respective obligations which arise are for the recipient to repay the money and for the owner of the ground to pay to the extent to which he is enriched. From these examples it can be seen that unjustified enrichment is based on equitable considerations.[10] *Negotiorum gestio* is the doctrine whereby one person (the *gestor* or manager) manages the affairs of another who is absent. There is no official appointment or contract of mandate for the *gestor*. Nonetheless, the person who benefits from the actions of the *gestor* may be obliged to compensate him for his expenses and outlays.

---

[8] Stair, I, 3, 1.

[9] For further details, see Joe M. Thomson, *Delictual Liability*, 4th edn (Haywards Heath: Tottel, 2009); Gordon Cameron, *LawBasics: Delict*, 4th edn (Edinburgh: W Green, 2011).

[10] For further details, see Hector L. MacQueen, *LawBasics: Unjustified Enrichment*, 3rd edn (Edinburgh: W. Green, 2013).

Voluntary obligations

Voluntary (or conventional) obligations, by contrast to obediential **1–16**
obligations, arise through choice. Unless a monopoly exists, a person can
choose with whom to contract, or whether to make a promise. An
individual is not bound to buy cheese in a particular shop, to go on
holiday with a particular travel firm, or to take out insurance with a
particular company. Any contract entered into is the choice of the parties
concerned. It arises out of the parties' own volition. So the difference
between voluntary and involuntary obligations is the difference between
imposition and assumption. Obediential obligations are imposed,
voluntary obligations are assumed.

There are two types of voluntary obligation: promise and contract.
Stair suggested that voluntary obligations arose through the exercise of
will. In the case of promise (a unilateral obligation) it is the will of the
person making the promise. In the case of contracts (bilateral obligations) it is the will of both parties to the transaction. For this purpose
Stair divided acts of the will into three categories: desire, resolution and
engagement.[11] One might conceive a desire, and even resolve to carry it
out, but neither of these states of mind gives rise to a legal obligation. It is
only when there is some definite purpose to do something, manifested by
words or conduct, that there could be said to be engagement and consequently that legal rights and duties arise.

This notion of voluntary obligation resting on the idea of will plays an
important role in contract law and ties in very closely with the notion of
freedom of contract. It will come as no surprise that in England, will
theory had its heyday in the nineteenth century. The basic rationale is
fairly straightforward. A person has free will and can do what he likes so
far as he is not restrained by law. By choosing to engage with someone he
voluntarily relinquishes part of his independence by granting that person
a right against him. As he has chosen to assume this obligation he should
be bound by it.

There are powerful objections to this theory. Adam Smith was one of **1–17**
the first writers to criticise the idea that obligations sprung purely from
the exercise of the will. He noted that if someone engaged to do something in the future and subsequently changed his mind then the logical
consequence, according to will theory, should be that he was relieved of
his obligation, yet this was not the case. A person who made a contract
could not slip out of it by changing his mind. It was therefore not, Smith
suggested, the will of the person engaging which gave rise to the obligation but rather "the expectation and dependence which was excited in
him to whom the contract was made".[12] This difference of theoretical
approach is of considerable importance. Smith's view was that the law is
really concerned with protecting the person to whom the undertaking is
made, rather than binding the other person to his statement. It is

---

[11] Stair, I, 10, 2.
[12] Adam Smith, *Lectures on Jurisprudence*, edited by Ronald L. Meek, David D. Raphael
and Peter G. Stein (Oxford: Clarendon Press, 1978), ii, 56.

erroneous to consider the two views as opposite sides of the same coin. If the foundation of the law of contract is the inquiry, "Has a declaration of will been made?" that is very different from the inquiry, "Should we protect the interest of the person who relied upon the other's statement?" In our discussion of the various topics of contract law we shall see that there is a continuous interplay between the consensual approach of Stair and the reliance approach of Smith. In general, the reliance view prevails, but occasionally it is the consensual view which is emphasised.

SCOTS LAW AND ENGLISH LAW

1–18 In many areas of contract law the Scots and English approach is broadly similar. Sometimes, however, the detailed rules differ markedly north and south of the border. Examples are the law relating to formalities, illegality, collateral contracts, capacity, frustration and assignation. Two important pieces of legislation apply solely to Scotland: the Requirements of Writing (Scotland) Act 1995 and the Contract (Scotland) Act 1997. A well-known illustration of the difference between the two countries' laws relates to house purchase agreements. In Scotland the parties are bound at the stage of completion of the missives, rather than when the disposition (the title document) is delivered. In England the stage at which the parties are bound comes later, when formal documents are exchanged. One other major point of difference is consideration. This is part of English but not Scots law. Consideration is the requirement that a contract is only binding if there is some element of bargain or reciprocity in the arrangement. Scots and English differences will be considered more fully in the appropriate chapters of this book. This does not mean that the solutions to problems which arise differ. It would be odd if a large retailer trading in both England and Scotland found that its ordinary contracts were dealt with in a completely different fashion by the two legal systems. Rather, the solutions are often the same but arrived at by a different route. English authorities must accordingly be used with care. It is as if one is translating from one language into another. The elegance of French poetry can never be matched by a translation into German. So with Scots and English law. A sentence of the great legislative draftsman Sir M.D. Chalmers seems apposite. In relation to the English Statute of Frauds 1677 he noted "it has ... never applied to Scotland and Scotsmen never appear to have felt the want of it".[13] The contortions which English law developed to get round the more unhappy applications of that Act would likewise not be welcomed in Scotland. One other point about the difference between the two legal systems concerns procedure. Until the late nineteenth century, the common law courts in England administered different remedies from the Chancery courts, which were courts of Equity. Despite the nineteenth century reforms, English lawyers persist in talking about "common law" and "Equity" rules and remedies. Scottish

---

[13] *Chalmers' Sale of Goods Act*, edited by Ralph Sutton and N.P. Shannon, 12th edn (London: Butterworth & Co, 1945), p.26.

courts have always had an inherent equitable jurisdiction (with a small "e") and the different procedural approaches in England find no counterpart in our law.

Nevertheless the greater size of England and the fact that London is **1–19** the commercial hub of the United Kingdom means inevitably that there are a far higher number of reported decisions on contractual issues there. Many English decisions have either been accepted into Scots law or are of high persuasive value. Accordingly we shall refer to a number of English cases in this book. Differences between the two systems will be pointed out where appropriate.

THE EUROPEAN DIMENSION

Future development of Scots contract law is likely to be further affected **1–20** by European influences. We can already see changes brought about by European Directives, most notably in the field of consumer protection.[14] However, a recent project may bring about more fundamental changes. The draft Common Frame of Reference (or "dCFR") was published in 2009 after years of collaboration and research between European scholars. It is a set of model rules which seeks to provide uniform rules on private law, including contract. These model rules set down principles for governing all areas of contract law, including formation, breach and remedies. The dCFR does not have the force of law, but could be used as a "toolbox", to allow parties to a contract to choose the rules which govern their contract. One advantage of the dCFR is that it harmonises the contract rules applicable throughout Europe. The potential for implementing parts of the dCFR in Scots law is currently being considered by the Scottish Law Commission.

CURRENT LAW REFORM

In its Eighth Programme of Law Reform, published in 2010, the Scottish **1–21** Law Commission announced that it was undertaking a review of Scots contract law, prompted by the publication of the dCFR the previous year. Since then, the SLC has published the following papers:

- Discussion Paper on Interpretation of Contract, February 2011 (DP 147).
- Discussion Paper on Formation of Contract, March 2012 (DP 154).
- Discussion Paper on Third Party Rights in Contract, March 2014 (DP 157).

---

[14] These will be discussed in Ch.9.

- Report and draft bill on execution in counterpart, April 2013 (SLC 231)—this report and draft bill arose from the work in the Discussion Paper on Formation of Contract.

There is also a Discussion Paper on Remedies for Breach of Contract forthcoming.

These papers will be referred to below as appropriate, and further review of Scots contract law is awaited with interest. Of the work undertaken by the SLC so far, the Report on execution in counterpart has led to the Legal Writings (Counterparts and Delivery) (Scotland) Bill being introduced to the Scottish Parliament in May 2014.

CHAPTER 2

FORMATION OF CONTRACT—CONCLUDING AN AGREEMENT

When does a contract come into existence? Often the answer will be clear. **2–01** By their conduct, or by means of the written or spoken word, or by a combination of these methods, the parties will make it plain that a binding contract exists between them. Setting out contract terms in a written document and signing it is the clearest method of concluding a contract. It is, however, far from the only method. At the corner newsagent, for example, contracts are commonly made without any words being exchanged. The customer tenders his money, together with the newspaper, magazine or sweets he wishes to purchase. By taking the money and placing it in the till, the newsagent concludes the bargain. Oral contracts may be struck involving much larger sums of money. A typical illustration concerns second-hand cars. The prospective purchaser expresses an interest in a particular model in the showroom. The seller indicates a price. The purchaser suggests a different price. After haggling about this and the other terms of the contract, whether, for example, a tax disc or a full tank of petrol is included, the purchaser pays the price which is finally agreed and drives the car out of the showroom. Sometimes it may be difficult to determine with precision when, or if, a contract has been concluded. Suppose Valerie is interested in going on holiday to Denmark. She finds a suitable deal online and decides to book it. Is the contract complete when she adds the holiday to her online shopping basket, when she completes the online booking form, when the completed form is received electronically by the company, when the company acknowledges the booking, or when the price of the holiday is paid? No clear-cut answer can be given. It will depend on the travel website's terms and conditions, any further communications between the parties, their subsequent actions and the context in which these occur. In this chapter we shall consider the relevant principles which apply to these issues.

THE BASIC RULE—AGREEMENT

As was discussed in Ch.1, contract is usually analysed in terms of **2–02** agreement. Formation occurs when the parties reach agreement as to the essential features of their transaction. This is sometimes referred to as *consensus in idem* (a meeting of the minds). Agreement does not mean that the parties' minds have coincided on every point. A person cannot

know the inner thought processes of another individual. Accordingly it is
not necessary that there is full *subjective* agreement. Suppose a musician
flags down a taxi in the street and is carried to his desired destination. At
the end of the journey he refuses to pay the fare unless the taxi driver
carries his heavy instrument up three flights of stairs. The taxi driver
refuses on the basis that their agreement concerned carriage by vehicle
alone. A tribunal asked to resolve the dispute would find in favour of the
driver unless the musician could prove that there was a specific agreement
to carry the instrument upstairs. The law adopts an *objective* approach in
testing agreement, one which is concerned with the "external indicia of
agreement". Instead of looking at what the parties to the contract were
actually thinking at the time of contracting, the law looks for those
outward indications which evince consensus. The question is, would it
appear to a neutral third party that agreement had been reached? In other
words, would such a person infer from the contracting parties' words and
deeds that a proposal had been assented to?

2–03   Sometimes, parties may have different beliefs at the relevant time. In
Muirhead and Turnbull v Dickson[1]:

> The manager of a Glasgow piano shop called on Dickson and his
> wife at their home. Dickson agreed to take a piano from the shop at
> the price of £26, payment to be made by way of monthly instalments.
> No written document was signed. A few days later the piano was
> delivered. Dickson began paying the instalments but after five
> months stopped paying. The piano shop raised an action to recover
> the piano from him. It argued that Dickson had received the piano
> under a contract of hire-purchase. Under such a contract, ownership
> of the piano did not pass until all the instalments were paid. Alter-
> natively, the shop contended that the parties had never reached
> agreement at all, so there was no contract. In either case, the shop
> would be entitled to return of the piano. Dickson maintained that he
> had bought the piano on credit sale. A credit sale contract would
> have made Dickson owner of the piano and left the piano shop to
> attempt to recover the balance of the price, rather than the piano
> itself.

It was held that, viewed objectively, the evidence disclosed that a contract
of credit sale had been entered into. A factor of some importance in the
case was the relative novelty of hire-purchase. The court thought that the
onus was on the piano shop to make it plain that it was this new type of
contract which had been entered into. The point to emphasise is that the
parties had not agreed as a matter of psychological fact about the terms
of the contract they had entered into. Nevertheless they were bound, for
even where parties honestly differ, "commercial contracts cannot be
arranged by what people think in their inmost minds. Commercial contracts are made according to what people say."[2] Accordingly, Dickson

---

[1] *Muirhead and Turnbull v Dickson* (1905) 7 F. 686; (1905) 13 S.L.T. 151.
[2] *Muirhead and Turnbull v Dickson* (1905) 7 F. 686, per Lord President Dunedin at 694.

was the owner of the piano and the shop could not recover it from him. The shop's remedy was to seek payment of the outstanding instalments.

The corollary is that even if parties themselves believe there is a binding **2–04** contract, the courts will not enforce it if they find that in fact agreement has never been reached:

> "It is not enough for the parties to agree in saying there was a concluded contract if there was none, and then to ask for a judicial decision as to what the contract in fact was. That would be the same thing as asking us to make the bargain when our sole function is to interpret it."[3]

In the case in which that statement was made, equipment was provided and some work was carried out on a garden pond. When the contractor asked for payment for the work the householder refused, claiming that the work was defective. Both in the sheriff court and in the Court of Session the contractor's claim for damages for breach of contract was successful. Nevertheless, on appeal it was decided by the House of Lords that in truth there was no contract between the parties. The contract documents showed that the contractor had offered to hire the equipment. But the householder had purported to accept an offer to hire the equipment and to operate the equipment to clear the pond. There had been an offer of hire, and a purported acceptance of hire and services. As the offer and the acceptance had not met, there was no consensus and no contract. Accordingly, the contractors had no contractual claim to recover the cost of the work done on the pond. Instead, their remedy lay in the law of unjustified enrichment. This decision is perhaps an extreme application of the objective approach. Where work or performance has followed on an apparent contract which the parties themselves believe to be binding, the courts will normally give effect to that belief. That is because performance is often treated by the courts as indicative that consensus has been reached.

THE OFFER/ACCEPTANCE ANALYSIS

If contract can be described in terms of agreement, it is essential to have a **2–05** means of determining when the necessary agreement has been reached. Most contracts can be analysed in terms of **offer** and **acceptance**: "an offer accepted is a contract".[4] The person making the offer is known as the offeror. The offeree is the person to whom the offer is made and, if he accepts the offer, he becomes the acceptor. A contract requires at least two parties, since it is not possible to contract with one's self. In terms of the offer/acceptance analysis, a contract is formed when an offer is met with an unqualified acceptance. If a person who has received an offer replies by saying that he agrees to the offer but wishes to add conditions

---

[3] *Mathieson Gee (Ayrshire) Ltd v Quigley*, 1952 S.C. (HL) 38; 1952 S.L.T. 239.
[4] Stair, I, 10, 3.

of his own, that reply is a **qualified acceptance**. A qualified acceptance does not conclude a contract. It amounts to a rejection of the offer. It is also a **counter-offer**, which, in turn is open for acceptance. A neat illustration of these points is provided by the case of *Wolf and Wolf v Forfar Potato Co Ltd*[5]:

> A Forfar company offered by telex to sell a quantity of Désirée potatoes to a firm of Amsterdam potato merchants. The offer was open for acceptance by 5pm the following day. The potato merchants sent an "acceptance" by telex the following morning. In this telex various new conditions were set out. When the Dutch merchants learned from a telephone call to Forfar that these new conditions were not acceptable, they sent a second telex. This second telex was also received before the 5pm deadline had expired. It purported to accept the original Forfar terms but reiterated that the Dutch merchants would be glad if their earlier conditions were given consideration by the Scottish company. No further communication was made by the Forfar company and no potatoes were sent. The Amsterdam merchants raised an action of damages for breach of contract. They argued that they had received an offer which they had accepted before the time-limit had expired.

It was held that no contract existed. The first acceptance amounted to a counter-offer which "killed" the original offer. It was, accordingly, no longer capable of acceptance by the second telex. As the counter-offer (the first telex) had not been accepted by the Scottish company, there was no contract.

2–06   Slightly different circumstances occurred in *Findlater v Maan*[6]:

> Mr Maan advertised his house for sale. By letter dated March 25, 1988, Mr and Mrs Findlater offered to purchase the property. A qualified acceptance was given by the seller on March 28, 1988. By letter dated March 29, 1988 the purchasers accepted the conditions contained in the seller's qualified acceptance and inserted one further condition. On March 30, and without referring to the letter of March 29, the seller intimated one further condition. On April 6, the purchasers withdrew the condition contained in their letter of March 29, accepted the condition specified in the seller's letter of March 30, and purported to conclude the bargain. By this stage, the seller had changed his mind and did not wish to proceed with the sale. An action of declarator of contract was raised by the purchasers. The Second Division held unanimously that a contract existed.

In distinguishing the case from that of *Wolf and Wolf*, Lord Justice-Clerk Ross stated:

---

[5] *Wolf and Wolf v Forfar Potato Co Ltd*, 1984 S.L.T. 100.
[6] *Findlater v Maan*, 1990 S.L.T. 465; cf. *Rutterford v Allied Breweries Ltd*, 1990 S.L.T. 249.

Morton's Trustees v T

"In my opinion the true approach to be made in the present case is as follows. The letter of 29 March and the letter of 30 March were two offers which existed at the same time, one at the instance of the seller and the other at the instance of the purchaser. They were not written under reference to one another and neither of them super-seded the other. They both co-existed. In that situation I am of opinion that it was open to the pursuers to accept the offer contained in the letter of 30 March 1988."[7]

Whether or not an acceptance has been qualified is a question of con- **2–07** struction. The response may simply be hesitant or under reservation or a mere request for further information. In such instances the acceptance will be valid and will not amount to a counter-offer. Where an acceptance contained the phrase "the usual conditions of acceptance apply" and there were no such conditions, the contract was held binding and the phrase ignored as meaningless.[8]

Where the parties negotiate over a period, there will often be a series of **2–08** offers and counter-offers before agreement is finally reached. In such cases, the person who was the original offeror may become the eventual acceptor. For instance, A offers to hire B's concert venue for one night at a price of £500. B replies that he is prepared to hire out the venue to A for two nights at a price of £750. A accepts this suggestion. On this scenario, A is the acceptor as well as being the original offeror.

Because of the importance of offers and acceptance it is necessary to examine the key features of each in more detail.

Offers

The distinction between offers and invitations to treat

An offer may be express—"I offer you £50 for your old lawnmower"—or **2–09** implied, for example, handing over money for a theatre ticket. The key feature of an offer is that it contemplates acceptance. No further nego-tiation is contemplated. Instead, a contract is formed as soon as the offer is accepted.

In some cases, however, there is no intention to be bound by the other party's purported acceptance. Rather the person is merely indicating his bargaining position. In effect, he is saying "these are the terms upon which I am willing to negotiate further". Statements of this second type are known as invitations to treat. The difference between the two is important. If a statement constitutes an offer, it is in the hands of the offeree to form the contract. If the statement is merely an invitation to treat, then the person making the statement will not be bound by the other party's simple assent. If a statement is circulated widely—such as in a hoarding advertisement, newspaper or website—and amounts to an

---

[7] *Findlater v Maan*, 1990 S.L.T. 465 at 468.
[8] *Nicolene Ltd v Simmonds* [1953] 1 Q.B. 543.

offer rather than an invitation to treat, the person making the statement may find themselves in contracts with many more people than they anticipated. An example indicates how important the distinction between offers and invitations to treat can be. In *Carlill v Carbolic Smokeball Co Ltd*[9]:

> The Carbolic Smokeball Co placed an advertisement in the *Pall Mall Gazette* in November 1891. It stated that the company would pay £100 to anyone who caught one of a number of specified diseases after using one of their smokeballs in the prescribed manner for two weeks. The company claimed to have deposited £1,000 in the Alliance Bank to show its "sincerity in the matter". Mrs Carlill bought one of the balls and used it three times daily for two weeks. She caught influenza (one of the specified diseases) and requested payment of the £100 sum. The company refused to pay. Accordingly, an action was raised by Mrs Carlill.

The Carbolic Smokeball Co put up several arguments in its defence to the action. One argument was that the advertisement was merely an invitation to treat. This was rejected. The wording of the advertisement went beyond an indication of the company's bargaining position. As Bowen L.J. put it: "It is an offer to become liable to anyone who, before it is retracted, performs the conditions." The court awarded Mrs Carlill her £100 reward.

2–10   It is not always easy to distinguish invitations to treat from offers. The touchstone, here as elsewhere in contract law, is that of apparent intention, objectively discerned. If the person's statements or actions disclose an intention to be bound, it is an offer. If not, it is an invitation to treat. In *Carlill*, the fact that money had been deposited with the Alliance Bank was an objective indication of the company's intention to be bound. Questions of intention provide the courts with difficult problems. The intention of the alleged offeror must be gathered from the whole circumstances surrounding the parties' communications. In *Dawson International Plc v Coats Paton Plc*[10]:

> The defenders, a large Scottish textile company, thought that they were vulnerable to a hostile takeover. In early 1986, representatives of the board of directors met with the pursuers' board to discuss a possible offer from them. It was agreed by the defenders to recommend the pursuers' offer to their shareholders and this was done. Subsequently, the defenders withdrew their recommendation. The pursuers claimed there was a contract in terms of which the defenders would recommend their offer. They sought damages for the abortive costs of their takeover bid. It was held that no such contract existed.

---

[9] *Carlill v Carbolic Smokeball Co* [1893] 1 Q.B. 256.
[10] *Dawson International Plc v Coats Paton Plc*, 1993 S.L.T. 80.

Lord Prosser stated:

> "Speaking generally, I would accept that when two parties are talking to one another about a matter which has commercial significance to both, a statement by one party that he will do some particular thing will normally be construed as obligatory, or as an offer, rather than a mere statement of intention, if the words and deeds of the other party indicate that the statement was so understood, and the obligation confirmed or the offer accepted so that parties appeared to regard the commercial 'deal' as concluded. But in considering whether there is indeed a contract between the parties, in any particular case, it will always be essential to look at the particular facts, with a view to discovering whether these facts, rather than some general rule of thumb, can be said to reveal consensus and an intention to conclude a contract."[11]

Two further cases illustrate the narrow distinction between offers and **2–11** invitations to treat. In the first case a dispute arose as to whether there was a concluded sale of a property in Jamaica called "Bumper Hall Pen".[12] A telegraphed to B: "Will you sell us BHP? Telegraph lowest cash price." B telegraphed in reply: "Lowest cash price for BHP £900." Following this, A telegraphed: "We agree to buy BHP for £900 asked by you. Please send us your title deed in order that we may get early possession." No further correspondence took place. It was held that no contract had been formed. In the second case a merchant in Leith wrote to a firm in Largo, Fife as follows: "I am offering today Plate Linseed for Jan./Feb. shipment to Leith, and have pleasure in quoting you 100 tons at 41s. 3d., usual Plate terms. I shall be glad to hear if you are buyers, and await your esteemed reply."[13] The Largo firm purported to accept, but a dispute then arose as to whether there was a valid contract. The court decided that a contract had been formed. The distinction to be drawn between the two cases is that in the first, the party was merely indicating the price at which he was prepared to contract, and could be regarded as "merely an opening of negotiations"[14]; whereas in the second the word "offer" was actually used, a definite quantity and price were mentioned and the letter looked to the conclusion of the contract by reply.

In several common situations English law has adopted presumptions as **2–12** to whether some statement or action amounts to an offer or an invitation to treat. Scots law has fewer authorities on this branch of the law, but it is probable that in most instances we would approach the matter in the same way. These are only presumptions, not rules of law. Accordingly they can be displaced if the contrary intention is proved.

---

[11] *Dawson International Plc v Coats Paton Plc*, 1993 S.L.T. 80 at 95.

[12] *Harvey v Facey* [1893] A.C. 552.

[13] *Alexander Philp & Co v Knoblauch*, 1907 S.C. 994; 15 S.L.T. 61.

[14] *Alexander Philp & Co v Knoblauch*, 1907 S.C. 994; 15 S.L.T. 61, per the Lord Justice-Clerk's comments on *Harvey v Facey*.

Shop displays

2–13   There is no recent Scottish authority in point on shop displays. In one old case it was accepted that such displays were invitations to treat.[15] In England, the two leading authorities which analyse the issue are unusual. Each concerned prosecutions in respect of alleged offences by shop-keepers. Accordingly they were criminal rather than civil cases. The first case concerned the sale of drugs without the supervision of a qualified chemist[16]; the second, offering an offensive weapon for sale.[17] In each case the display was held to be an invitation to treat rather than an offer. A factor stressed by the court was that a shop is a place for bargaining, not for compulsory sales.

The presumption that a display is merely an invitation to treat can be displaced. In one case an individual took a deckchair from a stack on the beach.[18] He was injured because it was defective. The display of deck chairs was held to constitute an offer. The man had then concluded a contract by removing the deckchair and sitting on it: that was the acceptance. It may be that the court was more inclined to reach this result because personal injury was involved.

Websites

2–14   Online shops, and their websites, are analogous to shop displays: goods advertised for sale online are presumed to be invitations to treat unless this presumption is displaced.[19] Thus, where a website erroneously prices TVs for sale at a fraction of their true price, the seller will not be obliged to honour orders placed, since the order will be regarded as an offer rather than an acceptance. Judicial authority has been critical of "pre-datory" attempts by customers to snatch at a bargain in this way.[20] However, the true interpretation in every case will depend on the website's terms and conditions. To protect the online seller, the website's terms should make it clear that the purchaser's online order is an offer, which the trader is free to accept or reject.

Auction sales

The three stages of an auction sale can be analysed as follows:

(a) exposure of the item for sale—invitation to treat
(b) the bid—offer
(c) the fall of the auctioneer's hammer—acceptance

---

[15] *Campbell v Kerr*, 24 Feb. 1810, F.C.
[16] *Pharmaceutical Society of Great Britain v Boots Cash Chemists (Southern) Ltd* [1953] 1 Q.B. 401; [1953] 1 All E.R. 482.
[17] *Fisher v Bell* [1961] 1 Q.B. 394.
[18] *Chapelton v Barry Urban DC* [1940] 1 K.B. 532.
[19] *Chwee Kin Keong v Digilandmall.com Pte Ltd* [2004] 2 S.L.R. 594.
[20] *Chwee Kin Keong v Digilandmall.com Pte Ltd* [2004] 2 S.L.R. 594.

Until the hammer falls, the bidder is entitled to withdraw his bid.[21] No **2–15**
contract exists until that moment. Individuals who feel nervous about
making inadvertent gestures in salesrooms may be comforted by this
knowledge. What of the seller? Like the buyer he too may wish to
withdraw after the bidding has commenced. To accomplish this he may
put a reserve price on the article to be auctioned. This ensures that the
item is not sold below a certain sum, although it is not a complete right to
withdraw.

Advertisements

Advertisements, whether on television, hoardings, online, or in the press **2–16**
are presumed to be invitations to treat. The position is analogous to that
of shop window displays. An advertiser is granted the right to determine
the person with whom it contracts. If an advertisement was an offer, the
advertiser might be contractually bound to persons which it was unable
to supply. Suppose a company advertising beds was faced with unusually
heavy demand. It would be unfortunate if it were held liable in damages
to all persons who ordered online in response to the advertisement,
irrespective of the availability of the beds. In appropriate circumstances,
however, the general presumption can be displaced. For this to occur, the
advertisement must clearly indicate that the advertiser intends to be
bound upon acceptance. This was the case in *Carlill*.[22]

Vending machines

These present particular difficulties. Who makes the offer: the machine or **2–17**
the customer? In one English case involving a ticket machine at the
entrance to a car park, it was argued that the machine made a standing
offer because it had to deliver the ticket to any person who put the correct
money in the slot.[23] It had no discretion to accept or reject a particular
person. This is probably the correct analysis, even if it may seem rather
surreal to apply the concept of intention to machines. That objection
loses force when it is remembered that it is not the intention of the
machine itself which is relevant, but rather that of its owner who chose to
place it there.

Tenders

A tender or quotation to carry out work is an offer. For example, a letter **2–18**
from a plumber which states that a new bathroom will be installed at a
specified price is converted into a contract by simple acceptance. In some
instances, for example in relation to car repairs, the repairer may be

---

[21] *Fenwick v Macdonald Fraser & Co* (1904) 6 F. 850. This analysis of invitation to treat/
offer/acceptance can also apply to goods for sale through eBay, although eBay is not a
true auction since there is no involvement of an auctioneer. Further, eBay's standard
terms and conditions disapply many of the common law rules on auctions: for example, it
is not possible to retract a bid on eBay simply because the bidder has changed his mind.
[22] *Carlill v Carbolic Smokeball Co* [1893] 1 Q.B. 256.
[23] *Thornton v Shoe Lane Parking Ltd* [1971] 2 Q.B. 163; [1971] 1 All E.R. 686.

unwilling to give a definite quotation. Then the parties must reach some agreement as to the manner in which the price is to be fixed. It is common to stipulate that express authorisation is required for repairs beyond a certain maximum cash limit, or that the car owner will pay for all costs reasonably necessary to obtain an MOT certificate. An invitation to tender, however, will be classed as an invitation to treat.

Features of offers

2–19   An offer must be sufficiently definite in its terms to allow the other party to accept it outright. Where an offer lacks an essential detail,[24] it will not be an offer capable of being accepted.

Who may accept

2–20   In some instances, albeit rare, an offer is made to the world at large. Such offers are capable of acceptance by anyone who sees or hears the offer. The case of *Carlill* is a good example. The offer of reward was addressed to everyone who happened to read the advertisement. Normally, however, an offer is made to a particular person and the rule is that only that person can accept the offer. A purported acceptance by another person is accordingly invalid.[25]

Revocation

2–21   An offer may be withdrawn at any time before acceptance. This is an important feature of offers. The opportunity of withdrawing (*locus poenitentiae*) exists up to the moment the acceptance is given. Apart from express revocation, an offer is impliedly withdrawn by the death, insanity or bankruptcy of the offeror.

To take effect, the revocation must actually be communicated to the offeree. This can be done orally.[26] It is not necessary for the retraction of the offer actually to be brought to the attention of the offeree. Doing all that is reasonable to bring it to his notice, such as delivering it to his normal business address, is enough.[27]

In some cases, the offeror may have made a promise to keep the offer open for a certain period. It is possible in Scots law for a person to bind himself to keep his offer open. Suppose X writes to Y on Monday stating: "I offer to sell you my house for £300,000 and will keep this offer open until Friday at 12 noon". This is analysed as an offer with a promise to keep the offer open, and X may be liable to pay Y damages if he breaks this promise and withdraws the offer on Thursday.

---

[24] The essential terms of a contract are discussed at para.2–34 below.

[25] Discussed in *Fleming Buildings Ltd v Forrest* [2010] CSIH 8.

[26] *McMillan v Caldwell*, 1991 S.L.T. 325, per Lord Kirkwood at 329L.

[27] *Burnley v Alford*, 1919 2 S.L.T. 123; *Carmarthen Developments Ltd v Pennington* [2008] CSOH 139.

Termination

Another method by which an offer comes to an end is termination. **2–22**
Where a time limit for acceptance is attached, the offer automatically falls
on the expiry of that time limit. Of course, the offeror can waive the time
limit if he so wishes. Where no time limit is stated, an offer only remains
open for a reasonable time. An early American case provides a colourful
example.[28] In May 1837 an offer of reward for the "apprehension and
conviction of incendiaries" was issued. Relevant information was given
to the authorities in 1841. It was held that no obligation to pay the
reward remained, as the time lapse was unreasonably long. What
amounts to a reasonable time will depend upon the circumstances of the
case. Where the contract concerns the sale or supply of a commodity for
which there is a ready market, acceptance will usually require to be by
return of post. In *Wylie and Lochhead v McElroy and Sons*,[29] a delay of
five weeks in accepting an offer to carry out ironwork at new stables was
held to be unreasonable. At the time the price of iron was fluctuating
from day to day. To allow the client to wait and accept the offer when the
price of iron changed in his favour would be unfair. It would allow him to
speculate at the expense of the offeror. Where an offer asked for a
response within 2–3 weeks, this was held not to be a valid or enforceable
time limit, but nevertheless indicated that a speedy response was required.
The purported acceptance nine months later was not effective as the offer
had lapsed.[30]

Referential bids

A fixed bid is one in which a definite price is mentioned. A "referential **2–23**
bid" is one where the bidder offers a certain sum in excess of any other
bid made. An example is: "I offer £500 more than the highest bid you
receive from any other party." Sometimes the two are combined, as in: "I
offer £500,000 or whatever is offered by party B plus £5,000, whichever is
the greater." The House of Lords has held that such bids are only valid if
reasonable notice is given to all parties that such bids may be used.[31]
Otherwise the person making the referential bid would always succeed
against a rival bidder making a conventional fixed bid. This would be
plainly unjust. A further problem which could arise if referential bids
were widely used would be that it might lead to no valid bids being
submitted. Such bids depend upon at least one person using a fixed bid,
so in the absence of such a bid there would be no reference point upon
which the other bids could be based.

---

[28] *Loring v City of Boston* (1844) 7 Metcalf 409.
[29] *Wylie and Lochhead v McElroy and Sons* (1873) 1 R. 41.
[30] *Flaws v International Oil Pollution Compensation Fund*, 2002 S.L.T. 270 IH.
[31] *Harvela Investments Ltd v Royal Trust Co of Canada (CI) Ltd* [1986] A.C. 207; [1985] 3
W.L.R. 276; [1985] 1 All E.R. 261.

2–24 An acceptance is a final unqualified assent to an offer. Like offers, acceptances can be express or implied. The action of a check-out assistant in taking a customer's basket and scanning the items through the till indicates implied acceptance of the customer's offer to buy. Silence does not generally, however, constitute acceptance. A man who sends a letter offering to sell beehives to a neighbour cannot assume that a binding contract has been formed simply because he does not receive a reply to the contrary. The neighbour's silence does not amount to acquiescence. Nor is it possible to stipulate that silence on the part of the offeree is to be regarded as effective. An offeror cannot say: "I offer to purchase your stamp collection for £400 and if I do not hear from you by Wednesday I shall take it that you agree." If this rule did not exist persons could have contracts imposed upon them without their consent. Despite this principle, certain unscrupulous traders can try to take advantage of unsuspecting "customers", by sending unsolicited items through the post and demanding payment if the goods are not returned within a specified time. People who are unsure of their legal rights may think they are bound to pay for these items. To deal with this problem, Parliament enacted legislation that provides that recipients of unsolicited goods can treat them as their own if they are not reclaimed by the sender within a specified period.[32] There is no obligation upon the recipient to return them.

Exceptionally, however, silence may amount to valid acceptance. This might happen where there is a history of dealing between the contracting parties, or where there have been prolonged negotiations. In the beehives example, there may have been several prior transactions and on each occasion the neighbour has omitted to give any positive acceptance but has simply paid for the beehives when delivered. Alternatively, silence may be sufficient if the offeror waives the need for acceptance.

One must be careful to distinguish situations where the offeree is silent, from situations where an offer is followed by actings by the other party. An express offer followed by actions by the offeree consistent with acceptance is enough to infer the existence of a contract.

COMMUNICATION OF OFFERS AND ACCEPTANCES

2–25 In general, offers and acceptances do not take effect if they are not communicated to the other party: "An offer is nothing until it is communicated to the party to whom it is made."[33] This seems obvious. Imagine that a promoter had typed up, but not emailed, an offer to book a particular musician for one of his venues. If the musician surreptitiously found out about the offer he is not entitled to accept it. The same is true in respect of acceptances. The offeror cannot divine when the offeree mentally assents to the offer. He requires communication of the

---

[32] Unsolicited Goods and Services Act 1971, as amended.
[33] *Thomson v James* (1855) 18 D. 1, per Lord President McNeill at 10.

acceptance before a binding contract exists. Communication requires that the offer or acceptance be received by the other party. It may be that receipt at that party's premises is sufficient, even if the recipient has not actually read the offer or acceptance. The exercise of an option to purchase was held to be effective when the letter was received at the seller's solicitor's office and not when it was read later in the day.[34]

As with many rules, there are exceptions to the need for actual communication. An offeror may waive the need for express communication of the acceptance. In *Carlill*, the contract was formed when the smokeballs were purchased. Mrs Carlill did not require to write to the company intimating that she accepted the company's offer of reward should she succumb to one or other of the specified diseases. The terms of the advertisement demonstrated that no communication of acceptance was required.

Formality of language

In most contracts, there is no requirement for formal wording to be used. **2–26** An email exchange stating "go ahead" and "it's on the way" has been held to be sufficient to conclude a contract, regardless of its brevity and informality.[35] While many commercial contracts may be concluded in this way, there are specific requirements for contracts relating to land, and these will be examined in Ch.5.

Mode of communication

An offer may be intimated by any mode of communication. The offeror **2–27** can, however, prescribe the manner in which the acceptance is to be communicated. He may stipulate that communication is to be made by letter, by telephone, by email or by facsimile. Where that occurs, communication of the acceptance by other means is invalid. In one case the exercise of an option to purchase a piece of land was required to be "by notice in writing to the intending vendor."[36] It was held that notification by telephone to the vendor's solicitors did not satisfy this requirement. What was required was written intimation to the vendor himself. If the offeror does not prescribe the mode of communication, the acceptance can be given in any competent manner. However, it must be delivered to the offeror. Where the contract must be in writing and signed,[37] then an acceptance by fax will not be sufficient since the original writing will not have been delivered to the offeror. That is because "as long as a writing remained in the granter's own custody, he was free to change his mind and to destroy it or at least not to deliver it."[38] Accordingly, only actual delivery to the offeror will be sufficient to conclude the contract.[39] An

---

[34] *Carmarthen Developments Ltd v Pennington* [2008] CSOH 139.

[35] *Baillie Estates Ltd v Du Pont (UK) Ltd* [2009] CSIH 95 at [25].

[36] *Holwell Securities Ltd v Hughes* [1974] 1 W.L.R. 155.

[37] For example, a contract for the sale of land.

[38] *Park, Petitioners* [2009] CSOH 122 at [23].

[39] The proposed Legal Writings (Counterparts and Delivery) (Scotland) Bill will enable a traditional document to be delivered electronically, if it is enacted.

alternative to actual delivery is constructive delivery. This would happen where the sender of the faxed letter states that the sending solicitor will hold the original letter in trust for the receiving solicitor.[40]

2–28   There is nothing inherently different about concluding contracts by email, rather than by fax or by letter. Contracts concluded by email will therefore be valid, unless there is a requirement for formal writing. It is still possible to analyse the email correspondence to identify the offer and acceptance. However, there is one significant difference with email as a mode of communication: the use of email disclaimers. This is wording which is automatically attached to an email as it is sent. This wording will disclaim the sender's liability for any loss caused by the email and it may also contain wording which says that the email is not to have contractual effect. In the only Scottish case to consider the point so far, the court was not inclined to enforce the disclaimer, since both parties had proceeded on the basis that their email communications were contractually binding, irrespective of this wording.[41] Whether an email disclaimer would be upheld is therefore likely to turn on the facts of each case.

It is sometimes said that an acceptance should be given in the same mode as the offer. Accordingly, an offer made in writing should be accepted in writing. There is a measure of common sense to be applied here. Whilst an emailed acceptance to an offer posted by second class post is likely to be legally effective, the converse probably does not hold. This is because an offer sent by email suggests that a speedy response is sought. By contrast, the use of second class post indicates a more leisurely mode of proceeding.

When is a contract concluded?

2–29   The answer to this question depends upon when the acceptance takes effect: only then will there be a concluded contract. The general rule is that an acceptance only takes effect when it is received by the offeror. That is the case in respect of telephone,[42] telex[43] and fax communications, unless the contract is one which requires a formal written document, in which case the contract will be concluded when the original signed acceptance is received by the offeror.[44] Email and voicemail are analogous to telephone communications and it is likely that emails or voicemails must actually be received by the offeror to take effect. The burden is upon the offeree to ensure that his words are communicated and understood. Should, accordingly, a telephone line go dead during the

---

[40] *Park, Petitioners* [2009] CSOH 122 at [23].
[41] *Baillie Estates Ltd v Du Pont (UK) Ltd* [2009] CSOH 95. This point was not raised on appeal. See also G. Black, "Formation of contract: the role of contractual intention and email disclaimers" (2011) Jur. Rev. 97.
[42] See *Entores Ltd v Miles Far East Corp* [1955] 2 Q.B. 327.
[43] *Brinkibon Ltd v Stahag Stahl und Stahlwarenhandels GmbH* [1983] 2 A.C. 34; [1982] 1 All E.R. 293. Note that telexes are no longer widely in use.
[44] *Park, Petitioners* [2009] CSOH 122; reversing *McIntosh v Alam*, 1998 S.L.T. (Sh. Ct).

course of negotiations, it is up to the offeree to ensure that his acceptance has been heard. If he does not call back to check matters, and any dispute arises, no contract will have been concluded.[45]

There is a different rule for postal communications. In *Dunlop v Higgins*[46] the House of Lords held that the acceptance was made when the acceptor put it in the post.[47] This rule only applies to unqualified acceptances,[48] and it can have startling consequences. For instance:

(1) Where an offer is only open for a specified period, acceptance is effective when the acceptance is posted within the time limit, even if it is not received until some days later. So, where an offer to purchase goods stated: "This for reply by Monday, 6th inst."[49] a letter posted on the evening of the 6th, which only reached the offeror the following day, was held to be timeous acceptance.

(2) In one English case, the rule was taken to its logical conclusion and a contract was held to have been concluded even though the acceptance went missing in the post and was never received.[50] One Scottish judge, Lord Shand, doubted whether the same solution should be applied in Scotland.[51] His view is surely the better one. It is one matter for an offeror to be contractually bound for a day or two before the offer is actually received, quite another when the acceptance is never received at all.

(3) We have seen that an offer can always be withdrawn before acceptance but that the revocation must be brought to the attention of the offeree if it is to take effect. If the acceptance is posted while the revocation of the offer is in transit a contract will come into being before the revocation takes effect.[52] A contract may thereby be formed even though there is never a point in time when the parties have reached *consensus in idem*.

In essence this rule of acceptance "effective on dispatch" is an arbitrary **2–30** one. It means that in the interval of time between one party knowing that the contract is concluded and the other finding out, the law favours the acceptor. He can rely on the contract at the moment of posting. If, of course, the offeror does not wish this to occur, it is open to him to prescribe another method of communication or to stipulate that any letter of acceptance must be received by him to be effective. In this way, he can "contract out" of this rule should it not suit him.

---

[45] *Entores Ltd v Miles Far East Corp* [1955] 2 Q.B. 327.
[46] *Dunlop v Higgins* (1848) 6 Bell's App. 195.
[47] *Dunlop v Higgins* (1848) 6 Bell's App. 195, per Lord Chancellor Cottenham at 207. See also *Thomson v James* (1855) 18 D. 1.
[48] It has been held that the postal rule does not apply to the exercise of an option under a contract: *Carmarthen Developments Ltd v Pennington* [2008] CSOH 139.
[49] *Jacobson, Sons & Co v Underwood & Son* (1894) 21 R. 654.
[50] *Household Fire Insurance Co v Grant* (1879) 4 Ex. D. 216.
[51] *Mason v Benhar Coal Co* (1882) 9 R. 883 at 890.
[52] *Thomson v James* (1855) 18 D. 1.

The logical consequence of the postal rule should be that once the acceptance is posted, it cannot be revoked by the sender. After all, that acceptance is the point at which the contract comes into being. Surprisingly, in the only case upon the issue, *Countess of Dunmore v Alexander*, it was held that the postal acceptance might be revoked.[53]

Consumer protection

2-31 In certain contracts, legislation provides extra protection for consumers. Although the basic principles of contract law still apply, consumers may benefit from additional statutory protection, especially when contracting online. Measures include implied terms relating to the quality of the goods bought, a right of cancellation which allows them to withdraw from the contract (which would not usually be possible after the contract has been concluded), and a right to receive a written record of the terms and conditions of the contract. These measures supplement the standard principles, but they do not change the rules as to creation of a contract by means of offer and acceptance.[54]

CONSIDERATION

2-32 In England obligations are enforceable only when supported by "consideration". In essence, consideration means that there must be some reciprocity, or element of bargain, in the transaction. Consideration is therefore an additional technical requirement beyond offer and acceptance which must be satisfied before obligations are upheld in English law. Since most contracts contain a consideration this is not usually a problem. Where, for example, X offers to buy Y's bike for £100, the consideration given by X for the bike is £100. In some cases, however, the parties may agree that one will provide goods or services but the other will not pay for them. This is known as a gratuitous contract. For example, if Audrey enters into a contract with a telecoms company for telephone and broadband services at a fixed monthly rate, she may need cables and equipment installed to allow her to receive these services. The installation is carried out free of charge, to allow her to enter into the primary contract, but it is carried out by a third party, the telecoms company's supplier. In this case, there would be a gratuitous contract between Audrey and the telecoms company's supplier for the provision and installation of cables: Audrey would have rights and remedies against the supplier in the event the installation was sub-standard. Such a

---

[53] *Countess of Dunmore v Alexander* (1830) 9 S. 190.
[54] The relevant legislation includes the Sale of Goods Act 1979, the Electronic Commerce (EC Directive) Regulations 2002 (SI 2002/2013), the Consumer Protection from Unfair Trading Regulations 2008 (SI 2008/1277) and the Consumer Contracts (Information, Cancellation and Additional Charges) Regulations 2013 (SI 2013/3134). See further W.C.H. Ervine, *Consumer Law in Scotland*, 4th edn (Edinburgh: W. Green, 2008); G. Black (ed), *Business Law in Scotland*, 2nd edn (Edinburgh: W Green, 2011).

contract would be enforceable in Scots law, since there is no requirement in Scots law for a consideration. In English law, however, a "gratuitous contract" for the installation of cables would not be enforceable.

Over the years, however, the concept of consideration has become somewhat elastic. The English courts have been prepared—rather artificially—to "find" consideration in many instances. A promise in return for a promise is good consideration. So is an act in return for a promise. In determining whether or not there is consideration, no inquiry is made into the value of the other party's performance. It is enough that something is given in return, no matter how low in value. That is why the term "peppercorn rent" can be literally as well as figuratively true. If a landlord stipulates that the rent for premises shall be three peppercorns, this will be binding. It follows that in practice, the difference between the two legal systems is often not very great.[55]

Even where consideration is absent, a person can make a binding obligation under English law by way of a deed, which means that the document must bear the word "deed" or other indication on its face that it is intended to be a deed, and that it is signed by the maker of the deed, together with a witness. The signed deed must then be "delivered", which requires the maker to show that he intends to be bound by the deed.

INCOMPLETE AGREEMENTS

Sometimes it is not easy to tell when the parties have completed their **2–33** negotiations and have concluded a contract. The parties may be discussing several different aspects of their proposed relationship—some which are critical to determine the obligations they are willing to undertake and others which are less important to them. On some occasions there may be one particular aspect of the contract which remains outstanding after *consensus in idem* has been reached on all the other points. When this occurs disputes may arise as to whether or not there is a contract. A number of factors can help to determine whether or not there is an enforceable agreement. For example, it is important whether the parties can demonstrate an intention to be legally bound, and this will be considered in the following chapter. Other factors include whether the outstanding term is essential, whether the parties have commenced performance of the contract, and whether a term can be implied into the contract to complete it.

Essential terms

In some instances, agreement on certain key matters is required. The **2–34** classic instance is the contract of lease. The essential elements are (a) the identity of the parties, (b) the property to be leased, (c) the rent and (d) the duration of the lease. In other contracts, it is usually essential to

---

[55] See, for example *Williams v Roffey Bros & Nicholls (Contractors) Ltd* [1991] 1 Q.B. 1; [1990] 2 W.L.R. 1153; [1990] 1 All E.R. 512.

identify the parties, the subject matter and the price. If an essential term of a contract is not agreed, then the contract cannot be enforced. Two examples may help to illustrate this principle. (1) Suppose Humphrey agrees to buy Greta's car. Until they settle upon the price neither could force the other to go through with the bargain. (2) Ginger negotiates with Fred to rent his holiday cottage on Shapinsay for £500 per week. Until they have agreed the dates of the proposed let, it would not be possible to enforce any agreement.

2–35   Apart from the question of whether it is possible to enforce a contract which is missing an essential term, that absence may indicate that the parties were still negotiating and had not reached the point of concluding a contract. In certain circumstances, however, this may not be decisive. Rather than agreeing the price, for example, the parties may agree how it is to be calculated. Where the parties agreed expressly that "the prices [are] to be mutually settled at a later and appropriate date" and then went on to perform their obligations under the agreement, it was held that a contract had been formed.[56]

Performance

2–36   The parties may indicate that they had in fact moved beyond negotiation and concluded an agreement.[57] For example, despite the fact that a key part of the contract has not been agreed, one party may start to perform its obligations under the contract and the other party may permit this. This is illustrated in *Avintair Ltd v Ryder Airline Services Ltd*[58]:

> Avintair agreed to introduce Ryder to new clients who would pro-vide Ryder with work. No agreement was reached regarding the commission that Avintair would receive from Ryder for its intro-duction services. Later Ryder contacted Avintair and said that it did not wish to proceed. Avintair raised an action against Ryder seeking payment for the introduction services it had already provided. Ryder defended the action on the basis that there was no concluded con-tract as the parties had still been negotiating about the price.

The court held that Avintair was entitled to reasonable remuneration. The services provided to Ryder were not intended to be free of charge. There was therefore a contract with an implied term that Avintair would be paid a reasonable sum. A contract was not excluded merely because the parties had continued to carry on negotiations. While it might appear odd to impose a term as to payment when the parties were still nego-tiating about that very matter, it is clear that what happened was fair in that Ryder had benefited as a result of Avintair's work. Where the parties

---

[56] *R&J Dempster Ltd v Motherwell Bridge & Engineering Co*, 1964 S.C. 308; 1964 S.L.T. 353.
[57] *Neilson v Stewart*, 1991 S.L.T. 523.
[58] *Avintair Ltd v Ryder Airline Services Ltd*, 1994 S.L.T. 613.

have performed some of their obligations under the contract, the courts will usually be unwilling to find that there is no contract.

Implied terms

In cases where an express term is missing, a term may need to be implied 2–37 if the contract is to be enforced. In *Avintair* the implied term was that Ryder would pay reasonable remuneration for the services they received. Some other examples of terms that are implied in such situation are:

> (a) in a contract of sale of goods, if no price is specified, then the buyer must pay a reasonable price[59]; (b) in a contract of lease, if no period is specified, a period of one year will be presumed[60]; (c) in a contract of loan, it is presumed that the money is repayable on demand[61]; and (d) in a contract to carry out works, if no remuneration is specified, an entitlement to reasonable remuneration will be implied. The general rules for implied terms are considered in Ch.7.

LIMITS OF THE OFFER/ACCEPTANCE APPROACH

Although most agreements can be analysed into a sequence of offer, 2–38 counter-offer, acceptance, and so on, it is not always possible to do so. Hiring a taxi, buying a newspaper and many of the other common transactions of everyday life are, on one view, only capable of such an analysis by adopting an artificial approach. Few people think in terms of offers and acceptances when they make agreements. It is only in relation to a small number of contracts that the offer/acceptance analysis is readily apparent. But in general, such an analysis is helpful. It enables us to break down and isolate each component part of the transaction to determine what the respective rights and duties of the parties actually are at any particular stage. Some specific situations call for comment.

Identical cross-offers

If A emails B offering to sell B his car for £2,500 and simultaneously B 2–39 emails A offering to purchase the car at the same price, then it would appear that consensus has been reached. The parties' minds are *ad idem* with regard to the essential features of the bargain. Normally of course, the parties will be delighted to go through with the bargain in such circumstances. However, if one of the contracting parties changes his mind and refuses to go through with the transaction, an offer/acceptance analysis suggests that there is no contract. Neither party has received an acceptance and therefore neither can be bound.[62] This may appear a

---

[59] Sale of Goods Act 1979 s.8(2).
[60] *Gray v University of Edinburgh*, 1962 S.C. 157; 1962 S.L.T. 173.
[61] *Neilson v Stewart*, 1991 S.L.T. 523.
[62] *Tinn v Hoffman* (1837) 29 LT 271.

rather rigid adherence to the requirement of offer and acceptance at the expense of the true issue in question, namely whether the parties are in agreement.

Members of a club

2–40 When individuals join a club or society, few legal rights or duties will normally arise. Often the only obligation on members is to pay a subscription. But what is the position if individuals voluntarily submit to some legal liability in relation to other club members? It is difficult, applying an offer and acceptance analysis, to unravel the legal relationship of club members with one another. In one case, competitors in a yacht race agreed under club rules to pay full compensation to any other boat which they damaged during the event.[63] This waived the statutory rule which limited the liability of boats by reference to the tonnage of the yacht in question. While there was no doubt that the competitors had agreed to full liability, it was difficult to identify any process of offer and acceptance which had occurred between the individual entrants. The contract (if any) appeared to be between each competitor and the club. Nevertheless the court held that there was indeed an offer by one competitor to the next. It has been pointed out that, even if the analysis holds in relation to later competitors, it cannot logically explain the position of the first entrant who had not received any offer.

The "Battle of the Forms"

2–41 Businesses typically contract on printed forms which contain all their standard terms and conditions. When a new contract is concluded, only a few specific details need to be added, such as the parties' names, the goods in question and the price. These forms are prepared in advance by legal advisers and amount to "package contracts". When each party uses its own standard form and neither form refers to the other, it may appear that there is no consensus. If, however, performance follows and a dispute arises it seems inappropriate to hold that there is no contract. Accordingly the trusty offer/acceptance analysis has been pressed into service in this arena as well, although it may not appear the most suitable approach. An example is provided by the case of *Continental Tyre and Rubber Co Ltd v Trunk Trailer Co Ltd*[64]:

> Company T ordered a quantity of tyres from company C. The order was placed on company T's standard printed purchase form. No written acceptance was given, but company C proceeded to supply tyres in a number of consignments. Each consignment was accompanied by a "delivery note" and several days after each delivery, company C sent an invoice to company T. Both the "delivery note" and the invoice sought to incorporate the sellers' terms into the contract. Those terms were materially different from the buyers'

---

[63] *Clarke v Earl of Dunraven (The Satanita)* [1895] P. 248, affirmed [1897] A.C. 59.
[64] *Continental Tyre and Rubber Co Ltd v Trunk Trailer Co Ltd*, 1987 S.C.L.R. 58.

terms. A dispute arose regarding the quality of the tyres supplied. The sellers sought to rely on a term which operated in their favour and was included in their own standard form. It was held that the buyers' terms ought to prevail. The contract was complete when the first batch was delivered in response to the purchasers' order. The purchasers had made the offer which the sellers had impliedly accepted. Accordingly, the delivery note and the invoice came too late to be the basis of the contract. Thus, the courts typically apply a "last shot" analysis: whichever set of terms are provided last, before acceptance through performance or agreement, is held to be the applicable terms governing the contract.

In an earlier English case, Lord Denning M.R., noted the difficulty of applying an offer, counter-offer, acceptance analysis in such cases and suggested that:

> "... the better way is to look at all the documents passing between the parties and glean from them, or from the conduct of the parties, whether they have reached agreement on all material points, even though there may be differences between the forms and conditions printed on the back of them."[65]

Nonetheless, the courts find the offer and acceptance analysis a useful tool in relation to contract formation.

---

[65] *Butler Machine Tool Co v Ex-cell-o Corp (England)* [1979] 1 W.L.R. 401; [1979] 1 All E.R. 965.

CHAPTER 3

FORMATION OF CONTRACT—ENFORCEABLE AGREEMENTS

3–01 The presence of *consensus in idem* is necessary to form a contract but it is not sufficient. Various other features must be present. These include an intention to create legal relations, capacity, and compliance with formalities.[1]

INTENTION TO CREATE LEGAL RELATIONS

3–02 Not all agreements are contracts. A contract is only formed when a serious offer is accepted. In the words of Stair:

> "... in the act of contracting, it must be of purpose to oblige, either really or presumptively, and so much be serious, so that what is expressed in jest or scorn makes no contract."[2]

If the offer and acceptance are not seriously intended, there cannot be a contract. Thus, for an agreement to be legally enforceable, the parties must intend to be legally bound by their agreement. When taken to its logical conclusion, there will be some cases where the parties have reached full agreement on all terms of their "contract" but it will not be legally enforceable because there is no intention to be legally bound. An example of this is *WS Karoulias SA v Drambuie Liqueur Co Ltd (No.2)*[3]:

> Parties to a distributorship agreement had agreed all the terms of their relationship and had reduced it to writing. However, they had not signed the written document. Since distributorship agreements do not need to be signed in Scots law, it appeared that the parties had reached full agreement and had therefore entered into an enforceable contract. However, Drambuie attempted to walk away, arguing that there was no contract.

The court held that the "contract" was not in fact enforceable:

---

[1] Capacity and formalities will be considered in Ch.5.
[2] Stair, I, 10, 6; I, 10, 13.
[3] *WS Karoulias SA v Drambuie Liqueur Co Ltd (No.2)*, 2005 S.L.T. 813.

"The evidence in this case ... persuaded me that the intention of the parties was that they would only become bound by the terms of that document only when it was signed on behalf of them."[4]

The lack of signature proved a lack of intention to be legally bound. There was therefore no contract.

In the English case of *RTS Flexible Systems Ltd v Molkerei Alois* **3–03** *Müller GmbH & Co KG*, the Supreme Court reached a different conclusion. The draft contract contained a clause stating that the parties would not be bound until they had both signed the contract. However, the Supreme Court held that the unsigned draft terms did constitute a binding contract. How can these two cases be reconciled? The difference is that, in *RTS Flexible Systems*, the parties had both performed part of the contract. Their actings were taken to be a waiver of the need for a signature.[5] In *WS Karoulias*, there was no performance, and therefore no evidence that the parties waived the need for signature.

To determine whether there was an intention to be bound by the agreement, Lord Hodge has identified four different elements that are relevant: (i) whether the parties manifested an intention to be immediately bound; (ii) the importance of what the parties said and did, when assessed objectively: the court will ask what reasonable and honest men in the position of the parties would have understood by their communications; (iii) whether any light can be shed on the matter by looking at the parties' behaviour after the moment of alleged formation; and (iv) the need for the court to adopt a neutral stance when considering whether or not the parties intended to enter into a contract.[6]

In many cases, the parties' intention to be legally bound can be presumed. There is a presumption that the parties to a commercial agreement intend it to be legally binding. However, this presumption can be rebutted if the parties can show that they did not intend their agreement to be a contract. This was the case in *Karoulias*. Conversely, there are situations where the law presumes that the parties did not intend to create binding relations. No legal rights and duties flow from such agreements and they cannot, accordingly, be enforced. Again this can be overturned if the parties prove that they *did* intend their agreement to be a contract. In considering these presumptions it is important to remember that these are not "watertight compartments".[7] Each case will depend on its facts. Commercial agreements are presumed to be legally binding. What situations are presumed not to be legally binding on the parties?

---

[4] *WS Karoulias SA v Drambuie Liqueur Co Ltd (No.2)*, 2005 S.L.T. 813, per Lord Clarke at [53].
[5] *RTS Flexible Systems Ltd v Molkerei Alois Müller GmbH & Co KG* [2010] UKSC 14, per (a different) Lord Clarke at [86].
[6] *Morgan Utilities Ltd v Scottish Water Solutions Ltd* [2011] CSOH 112, per Lord Hodge at [52].
[7] *Robertson v Anderson*, 2003 S.L.T. 235, per Lord Reed at [13].

Social agreements

3–04 In the host of everyday arrangements made by individuals, a large number are presumed not to create legal relations. An agreement to invite an acquaintance to a concert does not give rise to legal liability if broken. Of course one can figure exceptions. To request a neighbour to purchase expensive tickets for the opera on your behalf may well give cause for legal action if you fail to pay for them. The question in each case will be whether a reasonable person would have assumed that legal consequences would flow from the agreement. One notable case where the presumption was overturned was *Robertson v Anderson*[8]:

> The pursuer and the defender were close friends. On November 21, 1997 they went to play bingo together at the Mecca Bingo Hall in Drumchapel. They had done so many times before. That night, the defender won over £100,000 on the national jackpot. The pursuer claimed that there was a long standing agreement between her and the defender that they would split their winnings. This was disputed by the defender, who claimed that if any agreement existed it was an informal or social agreement only.

The Inner House therefore had to address the following question:

> "... the critical issue is whether what was said by each party amounted to a serious undertaking of the kind to which the law attributes binding effect, or was, for example, merely light-hearted banter between friends, or a statement of future intention of a nonbinding character."[9]

The evidence of the pursuer persuaded the court that the agreement to share the bingo winnings was an enforceable contract:

> "Although this was undoubtedly an informal arrangement made between friends, the Lord Ordinary was nevertheless entitled to conclude that it was an agreement which gave rise to legal consequences ... an intention to create legal relations can be inferred."[10]

Domestic agreements

3–05 The courts are reluctant to uphold domestic agreements as contracts. A wife who looks after her husband during an illness is presumed not to do so under an implied contract.[11] However, it is always possible for the presumption to be displaced where it is clear that the parties intended to

---

[8] *Robertson v Anderson*, 2003 S.L.T. 235, per Lord Reed at [13].
[9] *Robertson v Anderson*, 2003 S.L.T. 235, per Lord Reed at [12].
[10] *Robertson v Anderson*, 2003 S.L.T. 235, per Lord Reed at [15].
[11] *Edgar v Lord Advocate*, 1965 S.C. 67. Compensation in respect of such services is, however, now available under statute in certain actions of damages for personal injuries, Administration of Justice Act 1982 s.8.

put their relationship on a legal footing. A specific type of domestic agreement is a separation agreement, whereby a couple agree a division of assets on their separation. These can take the form of pre- or post-nuptial agreements. An agreement between the parties to a marriage is enforceable but can be set aside by the courts if it was not fair and reasonable at the time it was entered into.[12]

Commercial agreements binding in honour only

Moral obligations do not always bring legal obligations in their train. A **3–06** debtor compromised a sum which he owed by paying one half.[13] In granting a receipt, the creditors stated that it was "understood that [the debtor] will pay the balance of 10s. per pound whenever he is able to do so." On the same date the debtor wrote to the creditor and stated: "I beg to assure you that I will pay up the deficiency as soon as I am able to do so". It was held that the arrangement to make payment of the balance was an "honourable understanding" which did not import any legal obligation. Similarly, a "letter of comfort" from a parent company stating that it was their policy to ensure that one of their subsidiaries was in a position at all times to meet its liabilities did not render them liable for a £10 million bank loan when the subsidiary went into liquidation.[14]

In the above situations the court inferred that the agreement was not binding from the terms of agreement and the circumstances. The parties themselves may stipulate that their agreement is not to be legally binding. In the leading English case on the matter, *Rose & Frank Co v JR Crompton & Bros Ltd*, a clause stating that the agreement was to be "binding in honour only, and not subject to the jurisdiction of the courts", was upheld.[15] Actual deliveries which had taken place under the agreement were, however, to be paid for on the basis that they formed individual contracts of sale. Clauses of this nature could enable parties to evade their normal legal liabilities. Happily the use of such clauses is rare. The cases that have come before the courts have shown that judges do not approve of these arrangements. In one case, an agreement was made in terms of which a government department agreed to make ex gratia payments in respect of harbour dues.[16] Although the Lord Ordinary recognised that agreements could be entered into which were not legally enforceable, he held that the department were bound to pay the dues. The words "ex gratia" were not in his view enough to remove the intention to effect legal relations. While agreements which are binding in honour only are rare, agreements which remove the jurisdiction of the courts are more common. Commercial agreements may provide that the parties will not litigate in court, but will bind themselves to resolve the dispute through

---

[12] Family Law (Scotland) Act 1985 s.16.
[13] *Ritchie v Cowan & Kinghorn* (1901) 3 F. 1071.
[14] *Kleinwort Benson Ltd v Malaysia Mining Corp Bhd* [1989] 1 W.L.R. 379; [1989] 1 All E.R. 785.
[15] *Rose & Frank Co v JR Crompton & Bros Ltd* [1925] A.C. 445.
[16] *Wick Harbour Trustees v The Admiralty*, 1921 S.L.R. 109, cf. *Edwards v Skyways Ltd* [1964] 1 All E.R. 494.

arbitration, adjudication, mediation or some other form of dispute resolution.

Agreements to agree

3–07 In some cases, commercial parties will reach an agreement that they will work together but there will be many complex terms still to be finalised. The process of negotiating and drafting the written contract can easily take several months. In this situation, the parties may choose to note their intended future agreement in a brief written document, to provide reassurance to the other about their long-term relationship. Such agreements may be referred to as letters of comfort, heads of agreement, heads of terms, or agreements to agree. In most cases, the parties will not intend them to be legally binding, but only to provide an outline of their future relationship. Where there is genuinely an agreement to agree, then this will be unenforceable from lack of certainty. Some purported agreements to agree are, however, drafted in sufficiently certain terms that they are proper agreements and are therefore capable of being enforced. The question then arises, will a document entitled "agreement to agree" or "heads of agreement" be enforceable or will it be presumed that the parties did not intend it to be legally binding? The courts have held that such agreements will be enforceable where they bear all the "hallmarks" of an agreement intended to be legally binding. Relevant factors will be whether it has been typed, signed and witnessed, and whether it is an expression of consensus.[17]

Collective agreements

3–08 Agreements between employers and trade unions are known as collective agreements. Often they are of great length and cover every aspect of pay, conditions and work practices. For a long time the status of such agreements was unclear, but in the late 1960s it was decided by an English court that collective agreements were not presumed to effect legal relations.[18] Breach of the terms of such an agreement could not therefore be remedied by litigation. This principle is now enshrined in Trade Union and Labour Relations (Consolidation) Act 1992 s.179. Unless the collective agreement is in writing and has an express stipulation that it is to have legal force, no action will lie if one side defaults in its obligation under the contract. The collective agreement is a statement of aspiration and an indication of good faith, rather than a legal document. If the collective agreement is in writing and has an express stipulation that it is to have legal force, then it is conclusively presumed to be a legally enforceable agreement. Even if the collective agreement is of no legal effect however, it may be expressly or impliedly incorporated into an employee's contract of employment. In such a case, its terms will legally bind the employee and employer concerned.

---

[17] *Latta v Burns* [2004] ScotCS 27 at [10].
[18] *Ford Motor Co Ltd v Amalgamated Union of Engineering and Foundry Workers* [1969] 2 Q.B. 303; 2 All E.R. 481.

Voluntary organisations

It is presumed that persons join clubs, whether sporting, political or **3–09** recreational, for mutual association, not to assume legal rights or liabilities. So long as such bodies conduct their affairs according to the canons of natural justice and within the provisions of the race and sex discrimination legislation, no legal rights arise. The law will not intervene to say who is properly entitled to enter a particular competition or uphold the right of a sportsman to play a particular game. But the law will intervene when it is clear that the parties have intended legal relations, as in the case of *The Satanita*,[19] where all the competitors had signed a carefully worded document. An intention to effect legal relations will also be deemed to be present where a member's financial (or "patrimonial") interest is affected by the action of the club or voluntary association.

A patrimonial interest is a property interest: one that can be valued in money terms. This question of patrimonial interest concerns persons who hold offices in voluntary associations and in particular, ministers of religion. In many cases, internal church matters will not be of the sort that give rise to a legally binding relationship. Matters of employment are different, however. While the earlier view was that the spiritual nature of a clergyman's calling ousts the temporal, a recent House of Lords decision held that a minister of the Church of Scotland was an employee of the Church. Consequently, the minister was entitled to the protection of the Sex Discrimination Act 1975 and the jurisdiction of the courts.[20]

UNCERTAINTY

Even where there is consensus between the parties and an intention to be **3–10** bound, an agreement (or a specific term in the agreement) will not be enforceable if it is lacking in certainty. For example, Frank Plc wishes to license software to be developed by Sammy Ltd. The parties have been discussing exactly what the software should do, when it is to be delivered and what licence fee should be payable. In order to get the contract signed, they agree that "the customary level of support will be provided during reasonable hours for the usual remuneration". If a dispute arises as to the level of support it is unlikely that a court could enforce this term. It is simply too vague. The test that the courts use to determine whether an agreement is too uncertain is to ask whether it would be possible to frame a decree of specific implement requiring a party to perform its obligations under the contract.[21] If this cannot be done, the contract—or part of it—is said to be void for uncertainty. In the words of Lord President Dunedin: "A contract which cannot be enforced by specific implement ... is no contract at all, and cannot form the ground of an

---

[19] *Clarke v Earl of Dunraven (The Satanita)* [1895] P. 248; affirmed [1897] A.C. 59.
[20] *Percy v Board of National Mission of the Church of Scotland*, 2006 S.C. (HL) 1.
[21] Specific implement is considered in more detail in relation to breach of contract in Ch.10.

action for damages".[22] It is nevertheless common for such imprecise expressions as "reasonable remuneration", "reasonable endeavours" and "best practice" to feature in contracts. Sometimes it is the very fact that they are imprecise that makes these terms attractive to the parties—each assumes that the term will have the meaning that best suits them. The courts recognise that these terms are used by parties and will attempt to give effect to them, rather than be the "destroyer of bargains".[23] For example, where there is an objective standard against which to measure the "reasonable endeavours", then the court will assess the conduct of the party against that standard.[24] If there is no such objective standard, then the obligation is not enforceable.

3–11 Uncertainty may strike at only part of the contract. If that is so, the issue of whether the contract as a whole may survive will depend on the importance within the contract of the terms rendered void. If it touches the core of the agreement it is likely that the whole agreement will be considered void. If the term in question is more peripheral, it may be ignored and the remainder of the agreement may be given effect.

WHEN IS THE CONTRACT BROUGHT INTO OPERATION?

3–12 In some instances the parties to the contract may wish to postpone its legal enforceability. It is competent for the parties to provide that the contract shall not take effect until a particular date or event occurs.

> *Example*: A may agree to buy B's car provided that the car passes an MOT test. A is not bound to buy the car unless and until the car passes the test.

This is an example of a conditional contract. Not all conditions have the effect of postponing or suspending the operation of the contract. The legal effect of a particular condition will depend on a number of factors. If the condition refers to a future certain event such as a particular date, or the death of a named individual, then the obligation is constituted immediately: "In truth such an obligation is a present obligation which is to be discharged in the future".[25] So if A agrees to pay a debt when A's grandfather dies, that obligation exists from the moment it is entered into. It is only performance which is postponed. But where the condition refers to a future uncertain event—that X will reach the age of 18, or that Y will swim the Channel—its effect will either be suspensive or resolutive. Suspensive if the obligation only becomes enforceable when the uncertain event occurs; resolutive if the obligation exists immediately, but is to

[22] *McArthur v Lawson* (1877) 4 R. 1134 at 1136.
[23] *R&D Construction Group Ltd v Hallam Land Management* [2009] CSOH 128, per Lord Hodge at [39].
[24] *Scottish Coal Co Ltd v Danish Forestry Co Ltd* [2010] CSIH 56; also *R&D Construction Group Ltd v Hallam Land Management* [2010] CSIH 96.
[25] Thomas B. Smith, *A Short Commentary on the Law of Scotland* (Edinburgh: W. Green, 1962), p.617.

come to an end if and when the uncertain event happens. An example of a suspensive condition would be where a job is offered subject to a medical examination being passed. Only when a satisfactory medical report is received does a contract of employment arise. But an offer of employment subject to documentary proof that the individual held the academic qualifications which he claimed, would be a resolutive condition. The contract of employment would arise when the individual accepted the offer. If, however, he could not confirm his qualifications the employment would be deemed never to have arisen. These two examples demonstrate that sometimes, there is no more than a hair's breadth between the two types of action.

A common expression in English law is that the agreement will be **3–13** "subject to contract". Its effect is to suspend the operation of the contract until written documents are signed by the parties. A "subject to contract" clause can, however, be waived by the actions of the parties.[26] Most agreements for house transfers in England include such a clause. This has led to the practice of "gazumping". A seller who has agreed to sell to a particular person subject to contract may renege on his agreement and decide to sell to someone else. As there is no legally enforceable obligation the seller is entitled to do this. Under Scots law there is no conclusive answer regarding the effect of a "subject to contract" clause.[27] It will always be a question of construction. Should it be clear that the parties did not intend to be bound until a formal writing is signed, then the contract does not come into existence until that condition is satisfied.

---

[26] *RTS Flexible Systems Ltd v Molkerei Alois Müller GmbH & Co KG* [2010] UKSC 14.
[27] *Erskine v Glendinning* (1871) 9 M. 656; *Stobo Ltd v Morrisons (Gowns) Ltd*, 1949 S.C. 184.

CHAPTER 4

PROMISE

4–01 Scots law recognises a second type of voluntary obligation known as promise. Stair described a promise as "that which is simple and pure, and hath not implied as a condition the acceptance of another".[1] A clear case of promise is an undertaking to make a gift.

> *Example:* Rudolph, a wealthy philanthropist, visits an exhibition of watercolours by Zeke. Two days later Zeke receives a signed letter from Rudolph. It states that Rudolph is impressed by Zeke's paintings and that he promises to send Zeke £2,500 to assist him in his work.

Rudolph is legally bound to honour this obligation. He has incurred the obligation despite the fact that Zeke has done nothing. Indeed Zeke may be completely unaware of Rudolph's intention until he receives the letter. But once Rudolph declares his intention, Zeke acquires a personal right—a right to sue Rudolph for £2,500. If Rudolph does not send the cheque, he can be obliged to do so by Zeke.

PROMISE OR CONTRACT?

4–02 When is a particular obligation analysed as a promise rather than a contract? In particular, what are the differences between promise and offer? They can be listed as follows:[2]

> (1) A contract arises out of the will of two parties: it is bilateral. A promise is the product of one person's intention alone: "it acquires its binding force by reason of the declarant's expression of his will to be bound".[3] Accordingly, promises are sometimes referred to as unilateral obligations.[4]

---

[1] Stair, I, 10, 4. For a review of the historical Scottish sources on promise, see M. Hogg, *Promises and Contract Law: Comparative Perspectives* (Cambridge: Cambridge University Press, 2011), pp.147–151.

[2] For a recent statement of these legal consequences, see *Regus (Maxim) Ltd v Bank of Scotland plc* [2013] CSIH 12, per Lord President Gill, at [33]–[41].

[3] *Regus (Maxim) Ltd v Bank of Scotland plc* [2013] CSIH 12, per Lord President Gill, at [33].

[4] The Requirements of Writing (Scotland) Act 1995, refers to promises as "unilateral obligations" and "gratuitous unilateral obligations", s.1(2)(a)(i), (ii).

(2) Offers must be accepted, but promises do not require an acceptance. The acceptance of an offer must be made with reference to the original offer. In contrast, a condition in a promise can be fulfilled even where the promisee did not know of the original promise.

(3) An offer is revocable until it is accepted. Because a promise does not require an acceptance, it is binding and irrevocable from the moment it is made.

(4) A promise places an obligation on one person alone. By contrast, contracts place obligations on both parties to the contract. In theory this is true even of gratuitous contracts. For instance, if A offers to gift a statue to his local council and it accepts, the council is under an obligation to take the statue. In the case of a promise the council would always have a right to reject the statue.

The apparent simplicity of this analysis is belied by the problems which occur in practice in attempting to distinguish a promise from a contract. A person giving an undertaking will not normally have in mind the relevant legal rules. The words used will not be particularly precise or technical. There is no requirement to use specific words (such as "I promise") in order to create a promise. In some instances there will be no words at all but simply acts or a mixture of words and acts. It is then necessary to analyse the circumstances to determine the exact nature of the obligation in question. This is not always an easy task. One distinction is to ask whether the person making the statement intended to be bound immediately or whether he expected an acceptance from the other party. Where there is an intention to be bound immediately, this is indicative of a promise. Nevertheless, the problem of classification can be illustrated by reference to two cases. In the first, *Morton's Trustees v The Aged Christian Friend Society of Scotland*[5]:

> Morton wrote to a committee which was promoting a charitable society. He offered to pay the society £1,000 by 10 annual instalments of £100 if certain conditions regarding its constitution were observed. Morton's offer was accepted by the committee, the society was formed and the conditions in the offer complied with. During his lifetime Morton paid the instalments every year, but he died leaving two instalments unpaid. A dispute arose as to whether his estate was bound to pay the remaining instalments. It was held that the society were entitled to recover the outstanding sum from Morton's estate. There was a binding contract between Morton and the society.

By contrast in *Smith v Oliver*[6]: **4–03**

---

[5] *Morton's Trustees v The Aged Christian Friend Society of Scotland* (1899) 2 F. 82; (1899) 7 S.L.T. 220.
[6] *Smith v Oliver*, 1911 S.C. 103; 1910 2 S.L.T. 304.

During the course of her life Mrs Oliver had given money from time to time toward the cost of certain structural alterations to a church in Dalry, Edinburgh. After her death the trustees of the church raised an action against her executor, claiming that Mrs Oliver had promised to provide £7,000 in her will for the remainder of the outlay involved. No such provision in the will had been made. The trustees said that they had relied on the assurances that Mrs Oliver had given in arranging for the work to be undertaken.

There was held to be no contract here, only a promise. As the trustees did not have a signed statement from Mrs Oliver to prove the promise, their action failed.

The substance of the transaction in each case was the same. Both Mr Morton and Mrs Oliver wished to make a gift, one to a charity, the other to a church. Can we explain why different legal analyses were applied? The answer lies in the circumstances in which the obligation was undertaken. Mr Morton had actually used the word "offer" several times in his letters to the committee. It was not disputed that they had accepted the offer. Mrs Oliver's case was different. She had not committed her thoughts to writing. The church trustees could only point to various oral statements which she had made. No offer could be inferred from these statements, nor had there been any definite acceptance: "There is in truth no contract at all averred here, but merely a promise to pay".[7] Without a signed statement from the promisor, the promise was unenforceable.

The guidance to be derived from these two cases has not proved particularly helpful. Where possible, courts have avoided committing themselves to one analysis or the other. In *Bathgate v Rosie* a young boy broke a shop window while out playing one evening.[8] His mother told the shopkeeper's wife that she would pay for the cost of a replacement. However, when the window was installed, the mother refused to pay. The sheriff held that the mother was bound to pay the replacement cost because she had given an unqualified undertaking to do so, but he did not specify whether it was a promise or a contract. What is clear is that a promise cannot be converted into a contract. In the old case of *Miller v Tremamondo* it was alleged that a man had married a lady on the strength of certain financial assurances made by her father.[9] When these assurances were not realised, the husband sued his (now) father-in-law to fulfil his promises. It was decided that the alleged assurances were promises. The mere fact that the husband-to-be had acted on the faith of the promises did not convert them into a contract.

A presumption in favour of contract

4–04   There is no doubt that through time there has developed a general presumption in favour of an analysis in terms of contract rather than in terms of promise. Several cases can be cited in support of this

---

[7] *Smith v Oliver*, 1911 S.C. 103; 1910 2 S.L.T. 304, per Lord President Dunedin.
[8] *Bathgate v Rosie*, 1976 S.L.T. (Sh Ct) 16.
[9] *Miller v Tremamondo* (1771) Mor. 12395.

proposition. In *Malcolm v Campbell* a lady signed a document before witnesses which said, "I have agreed to sell my house for £150 to Miss Malcolm" and delivered the document to Miss Malcolm.[10] The court decided that the lady was not bound by the document as it was only one side of a bilateral arrangement. The circumstances of *A&G Paterson Ltd v Highland Railway Co* took place during the First World War. Various railway companies undertook to maintain freight rates for timber at a fixed rate while an arrangement they had with the government remained in force.[11] The companies sought to increase the rates before the arrangement had terminated. It was held that the undertaking did not amount to a contract and was therefore unenforceable. In *Muirhead v Gribben* an assurance was given by one firm of solicitors to another.[12] They stated that the second firm's fees would be paid if they transferred to the first firm papers belonging to a particular client. This was held to be a contract rather than a promise.

Three factors have had a bearing on this preference for a contractual analysis. First, many situations which might possibly be regarded as a promise involve the satisfaction of a condition. The condition is that some act be performed. Let us take an example. Suppose a wealthy businessman makes the following statement: "I promise to pay £150 to the first person to climb Ben Nevis wearing roller skates." The businessman does not receive a return promise for his own obligation. No one is bound to fulfil the condition. But it is clear that if performance is made he must pay the sum stipulated. Now an offer can be viewed as a promise to perform, subject to a condition being satisfied, viz. that acceptance be given. It is not therefore difficult to view fulfilment of the condition by performance as implied acceptance. This is the line that the courts have tended to adopt.

Secondly, there is a strong presumption against donation in the law. **4–05** The law is reluctant to hold that a person intended to benefit another without receiving anything in return, unless clear evidence of that intention is present. All promises appear on their face to be gratuitous and, therefore, to be treated with caution. In a contract, even a gratuitous contract like the one in *Morton*, both parties know of and assent to the creation of the obligation. Clear evidence of both parties' intention is therefore present and it is expected that the person benefited will rely on the obligation. The presumption against donation is particularly the case in commercial transactions. In *Regus (Maxim) Ltd v Bank of Scotland plc*,[13] the court rejected the claim that the defender had made a promise to the pursuers to release funds for fitting out commercial premises. The relevant letter from the bank was not addressed directly to the pursuer, and the final sentence noted that the release of funds was "subject always to agreement of wider commercial terms with the incoming tenant". Moreover, the court noted that it was improbable that a bank, whose

---

[10] *Malcolm v Campbell* (1891) 19 R. 278.
[11] *A&G Paterson Ltd v Highland Railway Co*, 1927 S.C. (HL) 32.
[12] *Muirhead v Gribben*, 1983 S.L.T. (Sh Ct) 102.
[13] *Regus (Maxim) Ltd v Bank of Scotland plc* [2013] CSIH 12.

obligations are owed to its customers, would make a binding promise in favour of a third party.

4–06   The third factor which has led to a presumption in favour of contract rather than promise is the influence of English law. As discussed in Ch.2, English law requires there to be a consideration in order for an obligation to be enforceable. This means that English law will not enforce a bare promise where the promisor receives nothing in return. Consideration is therefore an additional technical requirement beyond offer and acceptance which must be satisfied before obligations are upheld. It also means that all obligations in English law must be bilateral or multilateral, not unilateral. A classic example of consideration in English law occurs in *Stilk v Myrick*[14]:

Nine seamen had been engaged to sail a ship on a return trip from London to the Baltic. Two of the crew deserted at Kronstadt. The captain promised the remainder of the crew extra wages if they would work the ship home shorthanded. However, when the ship arrived back in Britain, the owner refused to pay the extra amount and an action was brought by one of the seamen for the increased wage. He was unsuccessful. It was held that there was no consideration for the captain's promise—the crew were under an existing contractual duty to bring the ship home. The captain's promise to pay them extra was unsupported by consideration. He received nothing in return for his promise which he was not already due.

In Scots law, the promise given by the captain could be enforceable as a unilateral obligation, despite the lack of consideration.

THE PRACTICAL APPLICATION OF THE CONCEPT OF PROMISE

4–07   Promises can be very useful in a number of situations. There is no specific form of words required to create a promise, so long as the promisor uses words which demonstrate a serious intention to be bound immediately. Where it appears that the promisor is still considering matters or has not yet engaged himself, the court will be unlikely to recognise an enforceable promise.[15] Further, an expression of intention followed by actings in accordance with that intention does not constitute a promise.[16] Although there is no need for acceptance, the promise must be communicated to the promisee or a third party, to signify the promisor's engagement.[17] The Requirements of Writing (Scotland) Act 1995 requires that all unilateral obligations must be made in formal, i.e. signed, writing to be enforceable. The important exception to this rule is a promise made in the course of business.[18]

Promises may also be conditional. For example, a grandparent can

---

[14] *Stilk v Myrick* (1809) 2 Camp. 317; (1809) 6 Esp. 129.
[15] *Cawdor v Cawdor* [2007] CSIH 3; 2007 S.L.T. 152.
[16] *Cawdor v Cawdor* [2007] CSIH 3; 2007 S.L.T. 152.
[17] *Cawdor v Cawdor* [2007] CSIH 3; 2007 S.L.T. 152.
[18] Requirements of Writing (Scotland) Act 1995 s.1(2)(a)(ii).

promise to give a grandchild £1,000 in the event of the grandchild's marriage. There is no obligation on the grandchild to get married but, if he chooses to, he has fulfilled the condition and is therefore entitled to enforce the grandparent's promise. In commercial situations, the ability to make conditional promises can be important, as we will see below.

Firm offers

The first situation where the concept of promise is useful is in connection **4–08** with promises to keep an offer open. In *Littlejohn v Hadwen* the estate of Renniston was being sold.[19] In a postscript to a letter containing details of the estate, the seller's solicitor wrote, "it is understood that Mr Littlejohn has the offer of the estate of Renniston for ten days from this date". Lord Fraser regarded this as, "an obligation, no doubt unilateral, but still binding upon the offeror during the appointed period". Thus, a promise to keep an offer open for a specified period will be enforceable.

Third party rights

The concept of promise has allowed Scots law to develop the principle **4–09** that third persons may acquire rights under a contract to which they were not parties. Two contracting parties can bind themselves in favour of a third. This is known as *jus quaesitum tertio* and will be discussed in Ch.11.

The reward cases

Those cases where a promise to pay a reward in the event of a condition **4–10** being fulfilled are referred to generally as "the reward cases". Before the late nineteenth century, the precise analysis of such cases in Scotland was unclear. This can be seen by examining the case of *Petrie v Earl of Airlie*[20]:

> The Earl of Airlie did not vote in support of the great Reform Bill which extended the franchise for the House of Commons. Subsequently, a poster appeared accusing the Earl of Airlie and others of conduct amounting to treason by not supporting the measure in Parliament. The Earl stated that he would pay 100 guineas reward for information leading to the detection of the author and printer of the placard. The reward was to be payable on conviction. Petrie informed the Earl that his brother and another person were the printers. When the Earl passed this information to the authorities, however, they declined to prosecute and he himself did not initiate a private prosecution (which was more common then). Accordingly, there was no conviction and the Earl refused to pay the reward. Petrie was successful in recovering the reward money when he sued the Earl. The opinion of the Lord Ordinary (Corehouse) was affirmed by the Inner House without their giving reasons.

---

[19] *Littlejohn v Hadwen* (1980) 20 S.L.R. 5.
[20] *Petrie v Earl of Airlie* (1834) 13 S. 68.

Professor Smith regarded the case as being one of conditional promise.[21] Professor Walker states that it could have been dealt with on this basis, but in fact it was treated as a case of contract.[22] It is not clear from the opinion of Lord Corehouse which view is correct. He did not distinctly analyse the basis upon which the obligation was founded.

4–11   In the early twentieth century there were several Scottish cases dealing with rewards.[23] All proceeded on the basis of contract rather than promise, probably because of the influence of *Carlill*. The divergence between the two approaches has practical consequences. This is clearly demonstrated by considering an Australian case, *R. v Clarke*[24]:

> A reward for information leading to the arrest of certain alleged criminals was issued by the Government of Western Australia. If the information was provided by an accomplice it was further promised that he would receive a free pardon. Clarke, who was himself under suspicion of the crime provided information. Later he found out about the reward and claimed payment.

The High Court of Australia held that Clarke was not entitled to the reward. In issuing the reward, the State Government was making an offer. Clarke gave the information without reference to that offer. There was therefore no acceptance and no contract. The Australian Chief Justice (Isaacs) instanced the case of an offer of £100 to anyone who would swim 100 yards in the harbour on the first day of the year. In his view, someone who had been thrown overboard and was simply swimming to save his life was not entitled to the sum. This argument reflects a hostility to persons acquiring money on a "something for nothing" basis. As the person would have given the information or swum the distance stipulated anyway, irrespective of the reward, the other person should not be bound to pay him anything. Perhaps it ultimately depends on one's moral perspective. On one view the condition is satisfied so the undertaking should be fulfilled. A person who issues a reward but wishes to withhold it from certain persons can do so by express stipulation. If he fails to make such a qualification, then he should be bound.

4–12   Another problem of analysing the reward in terms of offers concerns the right to withdraw. When precisely is the right to cancel lost? We have seen that offers can always be withdrawn before acceptance. Does that principle apply here? Suppose a man puts a notice in his local newspaper that he will pay £50 to anyone who will return his lost kitten "Shuggie" to him. A promise analysis means that the man must pay the money to anyone who satisfies the condition by returning the kitten to him. This will be the case even if the finder returned the kitten without being aware

---

[21] T.B. Smith, *A Short Commentary on the Law of Scotland* (Edinburgh: W. Green, 1962), p.748.

[22] David M. Walker, *Law of Contracts and Related Obligations in Scotland*, 3rd edn (Edinburgh: T. & T. Clark, 1995), para.2.34.

[23] See, e.g. *Hunter v General Accident Fire & Life Assurance Corp Ltd*, 1909 S.C. (HL) 30; 1909 2 S.L.T. 99; [1909] A.C. 404.

[24] *R. v Clarke* (1927) 40 C.L.R. 227.

of the promised reward. But if it is an offer, is the right of revocation lost when someone spies Shuggie, or picks him up, or starts going towards the man's home? And can the reward be claimed where the finder was unaware of it, and consequently did not "accept" the offer of a reward? English law has been over-elaborate in its attempt to explain why the offerer should be prevented from withdrawing his offer before acceptance is made. The promissory analysis of Scots law does seem both clearer and more appropriate.

Options

A typical option occurs where there is a provision in a contract which **4–13** allows one party to acquire certain specific rights in the future by issuing a notice to the other party.

> *Example:* A agrees to lease B's estate for 15 years. Clause 3 of the lease allows A to purchase the estate after eight years have elapsed. In order to exercise the option, A must issue a notice by means of recorded delivery letter served on B. The price for the estate will be its market value as at the date the option is triggered, which will be assessed by independent surveyors.

Some contracts are exclusively about options. A contract relating to the right to film a novel would fall into this category. A studio might agree to pay an author £20,000 in return for an option to film his novel within the next two years. Lord Ross suggested that the better view is to regard options as a type of promise, rather than as an offer.[25] In effect, the granting of an option means: "I oblige myself to do such and such provided you exercise the option." In our example, B promises to enter into missives to sell the estate to A provided that the option is exercised in terms of cl.3. This overcomes the problem that arises with offer/acceptance, where an explanation must be given as to why the option is irrevocable even before any acceptance has been made.

CONCLUSION

(1) Scots law recognises the unilateral voluntary obligation of **4–14** promise. Like contract, it is not bedevilled by the notion of consideration.
(2) A promise is irrevocable from the moment it is made and does not require acceptance.
(3) There is, however, a presumption in favour of analysing situations in terms of contract, thus requiring an offer and a valid acceptance.

---

[25] See *Stone v MacDonald*, 1979 S.L.T. 288. See also *Carmarthen Developments Ltd v Pennington* [2008] CSOH 139.

(4) No specific form of words is required to constitute a promise, although a promise which is not made in the course of business must be in writing and signed.

CHAPTER 5

CAPACITY AND FORMALITIES

In order to enter into a valid contract, both parties must have capacity. **5–01**
Capacity to contract can be affected by a person's age and mental
capacity. In addition, formalities are prescribed for certain contracts.
These are set out in the Requirements of Writing (Scotland) Act 1995.

CAPACITY

The age of legal capacity in Scotland is 16. Everyone aged over 16 years **5–02**
and in full command of their faculties can make contracts. However,
there are special provisions which apply to those who are under 16; those
who are aged 16 and 17; and to those who are not in full possession of
their mental faculties.

YOUNG PERSONS

So far as age is concerned, the law is contained in the Age of Legal **5–03**
Capacity (Scotland) Act 1991 ("the 1991 Act"). The 1991 Act separates a
person's capacity to act into three periods. In general, a person under the
age of 16 is deemed to have no capacity to enter into transactions.[1] Any
important legal step will generally be taken by that person's legal
representative.[2] Parents are usually the legal representatives.[3] However,
the general principle has an important qualification.[4] Children are entitled to enter into transactions provided two conditions are satisfied. First,
the transaction must be of a kind commonly entered into by persons of
that age and circumstances. Secondly, the terms of the transaction must
be reasonable.[5] These two conditions are cumulative: if either or both are
unfulfilled the transaction is void.

---

[1] 1991 Act s.1(1)(a).
[2] 1991 Act s.5, as amended, and Children (Scotland) Act 1995 ss.1(1)(d), 2(1)(d), 7(5).
[3] Children (Scotland) Act 1995, as amended, ss.1, 2.
[4] There are two further, limited exceptions. Persons aged under 16 have capacity to act:
(1) as the legal representative for a child of their own (Children (Scotland) Act 1995 Sch.4
para.53(2)(b)); and (2) to instruct solicitors for legal proceedings (Children (Scotland) Act
1995 Sch.4 para.53(3)).
[5] 1991 Act s.2(1).

Examples: (1) Ingrid is eight years old. If she buys a bus ticket or a comic at face value, the contracts made will be binding. (2) Archie is 11 years of age. He makes a contract, in terms of which he agrees to buy one computer game per month for a 10 month period. The price of each game is £200, which is well above the retail price. There is no provision in the contract which allows Archie to cancel. The contract is void on the basis that it is not common for 11 year old children to enter contracts of this type *and* that the terms are unreasonable.

5–04 When a person reaches the age of 16 years, the position changes. Upon attaining that age, the general principle is that a person acquires full legal capacity.[6] If, however, at the age of 16 or 17, someone enters into a "prejudicial transaction" then he is entitled to apply to the court to have the transaction set aside. A prejudicial transaction is defined by the 1991 Act as one which:

    (a) an adult, exercising reasonable prudence, would not have entered into in the circumstances of the applicant at the time of entering into the transaction; and

    (b) has caused or is likely to cause substantial prejudice to the applicant.

The application must be made before the person reaches 21 years of age. The right to have a transaction set aside under this provision does not apply where the contract is made in the applicant's trade, business or profession.[7] A party may be reluctant to enter into a transaction with a person aged 16 or 17 years old, because of the possibility that the agreement might subsequently be set aside on the ground that it is prejudicial. In such a situation, a joint application can be made to have the transaction ratified by the court.[8] The court is required to scrutinise the bargain before ratifying it. Where a transaction has been ratified, it cannot be challenged on the basis that it was prejudicial.[9]

Over the age of 18 years, a person has full capacity.

Summary   *Under 16 years — Limited capacity*
                    16 and 17 years — Qualified full capacity
                    18 years and over — Full capacity

---

[6] 1991 Act s.1(1)(b).
[7] 1991 Act s.3(3)(f).
[8] 1991 Act s.4(1).
[9] 1991 Act s.3(3)(j).

MENTAL CAPACITY

People who lack mental capacity have no capacity to enter into contracts. **5–05**
The law intervenes to protect such people by making their contracts
void.[10] Where the lack of mental capacity is temporary, such as acute
psychosis, the individual has no capacity to contract while ill, but would
regain legal capacity after successful treatment. Where an adult lacks
mental capacity and cannot deal with his property, financial affairs or
personal welfare, it is possible for a person with an interest in the adult's
affairs to apply to court for an intervention order or the appointment of a
guardian to act on the adult's behalf.[11] A person can appoint someone to
deal with his affairs if, at a future point in time, he no longer has such
capacity.[12]

  A second category of persons deemed to have no capacity to contract
are intoxicated persons. Persons who are drunk or under the influence of
drugs (whether legal or illegal) can make contracts so long as they are not
totally incapacitated. Erskine summed up the position as follows:

> "Persons while in a state of absolute drunkenness and consequently
> deprived of the exercise of reason, cannot oblige themselves, but a
> lesser degree of drunkenness which only darkens reason, has not the
> effect of annulling the contract."[13]

Intoxication will not be assessed by considering how much the party in
question had consumed, but by whether or not the individual appeared to
be capable of rational actions. In one case, a 17-year-old girl[14] averred
that she had consumed a bottle of Buckfast and 15 tablets of valium
before entering into the contract. The judge stated:

> "I was invited to consider the pursuer's appearance as disclosed on
> both of the videos. This I did. While I formed the view that the
> pursuer's behaviour was immature and somewhat strange in that at
> one stage she was carrying what appeared to be a baby's dummy
> which she had put in her mouth, her speech and actions appeared to
> me to be entirely rational and coherent and not to support the
> proposition that she lacked the necessary reason to contract."[15]

---

[10] Although where a person who lacks mental capacity buys "necessaries" then, in terms of
the Sale of Goods Act 1979 s.3(2), he must pay a reasonable price for them.
[11] Adults with Incapacity (Scotland) Act 2000 Pt 6. The Act also creates the office of Public
Guardian, to supervise a guardian or any person appointed under an intervention order,
and to maintain a register of all documents relating to orders under the Act: ss.6, 7.
[12] Adults with Incapacity (Scotland) Act 2000 Pt 2. This document is known as a power of
attorney.
[13] Erskine, I, 3, 16.
[14] Her age also raised the issue of a challengeable transaction under s.3 of the 1991 Act, but
this was not decided in court.
[15] *X v BBC* [2005] CSOH 80 at [19].

Introduction

5–06 "Formalities" means that the law lays down further requirements in order for the contract to be brought into existence. How does this work in practice? In contracts where no formalities are required, the contract will be concluded where the parties reach agreement and intend to be legally bound.[16] Where there is an oral contract, a person wishing to prove that a binding agreement exists can rely on all relevant evidence. Witnesses can be heard and any documents (such as emails) examined. But should a contract fall into a class where a particular formality is required, the validity of the contract will be determined by whether or not that formality has been complied with. The most common formality is to require some form of writing.

The general principle

5–07 The general principle in Scots law is that no special formalities are required to make a valid contract. Stair said we had adopted the canon law approach by which "every paction produceth action."[17] If, accordingly, the twin elements of agreement and intention to be bound are present, the contract is complete. This means that in Scotland most contracts have legal effect no matter what their form—whether written, oral or arising by implication from the way the parties act. Accordingly a verbal bargain to sell an Aston Martin or a block of shares valued at £5 million is binding on the parties. In the next section we shall examine the exceptions to this general principle.

Reasons for requiring writing

5–08 It would be possible for a legal system to require no formalities for contractual obligations. Every contract could be made in any fashion and proved by any means. However, there are several interlinked reasons for requiring formalities for certain types of obligation:

(1) To show that the transaction is authentic

5–09 A formality demonstrates that a particular person truly intended to conclude the transaction. In the early law seals were used. Because seals could be easily lost or forged, signed writing came to be required as a better means of authenticating a person's intention. Today we regard signed documents (or digital or electronic signatures in electronic commerce) as a mark that the signatory clearly intended to enter the transaction.

---

[16] See Chs 2 and 3.
[17] Stair, I, 10, 7.

(2) To establish the identity of the contracting parties

A signature helps to establish the identity of both parties to the contract, **5–10** to avoid errors as to identity.

(3) To emphasise the importance of transaction

Formalities may impress upon the contracting parties the importance of **5–11** their acts. In some societies in the past, the requirements have been startling:

> "Herodotus tells us that the Scythians, when they desired to make a contract entirely binding, drew blood of one another into a bowl, dipt their arrows in it, and afterwards drank it off."[18]

While blood is not required in Scots law, ink may help emphasise the solemnity of the situation. By putting their contract into writing, signing it and having the signatures witnessed, the parties are made aware of the serious nature of the transaction they are undertaking. The formality should deter them from entering contracts on a whim. It allows parties to pause and reflect before entering serious undertakings. The contracting party "is awaked from his reverie by the entrance of two or more people called in to witness what is going on" and "he will be more upon his guard and deliberate more coolly upon what he is doing."[19] When confronted by a car hire contract on holiday, however, there are few of us who actually comply with this approach.

(4) To produce certainty

When negotiations have been going on for a period, there may be certain **5–12** issues which each contracting party thinks are settled. If the agreement is oral and a dispute arises, each party may find that his recollection of the terms differs from that of the other. A written contract provides a fixed record of the agreement. This allows disputes to be resolved more easily than by recourse to the parties' (or other people's) impression of the terms of the agreement.

(5) To protect one of the parties

There are some instances where it is helpful for one of the parties to have **5–13** a written record of the terms of the transaction. A tenant or an employee may find himself in a situation where it is important to have in writing a statement of the terms of the contract. This can be particularly true where there is the possibility of exploitation by the stronger party. Some legislation requires that one party's rights are to be specifically declared in a written contract. Where goods are bought with finance provided by a credit company, for example, it is incumbent upon the company to

---

[18] Smith, *Lectures on Jurisprudence*, 1978, ii, 70.
[19] *Crichton and Dow v Syme* (1772) Mor. 17047 (said in relation to signature authenticated by witnesses).

provide a written statement of the contract to the consumer. This statement must include information telling the consumer about his rights.[20] Where contracts are concluded at a distance (such as online or by mail order), consumers must be given certain information about the contract, including the identity of the trader, a description of the goods, details as to price and delivery costs, and information about the right to cancel. Importantly, this information must be provided in a "clear and comprehensible manner" and, if provided on a durable medium, it must be legible. The trader must also confirm the contract on a durable medium.[21]

THE REQUIREMENTS OF WRITING (SCOTLAND) ACT 1995

5–14 The Requirements of Writing (Scotland) Act 1995 ("the 1995 Act") sets out the general rules as to the need for formalities for contracts generally.[22] There are other statutes and regulations with rules for particular forms of contract and these continue to have effect.[23] However, as the 1995 Act provides a scheme for contracts generally, it is the only one we shall consider in detail.

When writing is required

5–15 The 1995 Act sets down the general rule and the exceptions to it. The general rule is that writing is not required to constitute a contract or unilateral obligation.[24] The exceptions for which there is a requirement for a written document in the law of contract are:

> (1) Agreements relating to land and buildings.[25] The Scottish Law Commission recognised that many contracts are made for far greater sums of money than those which relate to land. Nonetheless, the purchase of a house is still the most important contract entered into by most people. They considered it desirable to have a rule which allows time to consider the proposed contract and discourages the formation of informal contracts without legal advice.
>
> (2) A gratuitous unilateral obligation other than an obligation undertaken in the course of a business.[26]

---

[20] Consumer Credit Act 1974 ss.58, 60, 61, 63, 64.
[21] Consumer Contracts (Information, Cancellation and Additional Charges) Regulations 2013 (SI 2013/3134) reg.13; the Electronic Commerce (EC Directive) Regulations 2002 (SI 2002/2013) reg.16.
[22] This Act was passed following a proposal for reform from the Scottish Law Commission, *Report on Requirements of Writing* (HMSO, 1988), Scot. Law Com. No.112. It has since been amended, and there are further amendments likely to come into effect, so it is critical to refer to the latest version of the Act in force.
[23] e.g. the Consumer Credit Act 1974 requires all hire purchase agreements to be legible, to embody all the terms of the agreement, including those prescribed by the Act, and to be signed by both hirer and creditor.
[24] 1995 Act s.1(1).
[25] 1995 Act s.1(2)(a)(i).
[26] 1995 Act s.1(2)(a)(ii). See Ch.4 on "Promises".

A variation to a contract or obligation falling within either of these categories is treated in the same way.[27]

Even where a written document is not required, however, it is perfectly valid for the parties to choose to document their agreement in a written contract. Where a contract is reduced to writing it shall be presumed that the written document contains all the terms of the contract.[28] This presumption can be rebutted by further evidence which shows additional terms are part of the contract, unless there is a specific written contract term (usually known as an "entire agreement" clause) which states that the document does contain all the terms of the contract.[29]

The requirements imposed

Where writing is required under the Act, there are a number of elements **5–16** to be fulfilled.

Writing

The first requirement is that there must be a written document.[30] This **5–17** must be an original and not a photocopy, scanned version or faxed copy.[31] However, there is a new Bill before the Scottish Parliament: the Legal Writings (Counterparts and Delivery) Bill. If passed, it will enable a traditional document to be delivered electronically, thereby enabling a faxed or scanned version of the signed document to be sent to the other party and to be legally binding.[32] The definition of "document" states that it includes an annex to a document.[33] However, there is specific mention of "electronic documents", being "a document created as an electronic communication within the ARTL system."[34] Such documents are valid for any contract or gratuitous unilateral obligation where they have been signed in accordance with the terms of the 1995 Act.

Signature

The second requirement is that the granter or granters sign the docu- **5–18** ment.[35] An individual must sign with one of the following:

    (1) the full name by which he is identified in the document or testing clause;

---

[27] 1995 Act s.1(6).

[28] Contract (Scotland) Act 1997 s.1(1).

[29] Contract (Scotland) Act 1997 s.1(2), (3).

[30] 1995 Act s.1(2).

[31] *Park, Petitioners* [2009] CSOH 122. A faxed copy would suffice if the original is then held by the sending solicitor on behalf of the receiving solicitor. This achieves constructive delivery.

[32] The Legal Writings (Counterparts and Delivery) Bill cl 4. This specifically addresses the problem faced in *Park, Petitioners* [2009] CSOH 122.

[33] 1995 Act s.12(1).

[34] 1995 Act s.1(2B). The ARTL system is the "automated registration of title to land" system operated by the Keeper of the Registers of Scotland.

[35] 1995 Act s.2(1).

(2) his surname preceded by (a) at least one forename, (b) at least one abbreviation or familiar form of a forename (e.g. "Willy" instead of "William"), or, (c) at least one initial of a forename; or

(3) a name or description or an initial or mark which is his normal method of signing documents of the type in question and is intended as a signature.

If the document consists of more than one page it is enough that it is signed on the last page.[36] It is possible for an offer to be contained in one or more documents, and for the acceptance to be contained in another document or documents, provided that each document is signed by the granter or granters thereof.[37] Digital signatures can be used where the granter's digital signature has been certified in accordance with the 1995 Act.[38] A digital signature is one which is uniquely linked to the signatory and can identify and authenticate the signatory. Importantly, it will involve an element of encryption by way of codes or private encryption keys.[39] A digital signature is therefore more complex, and more secure, than an electronic signature. An electronic signature could be any representation of the individual's name in electronic form, including a typed name or a scanned signature.

Contracts are bilateral obligations. The use made of the terms "granter or granters" in the 1995 Act is therefore odd. Where the contract is contained in one written document the 1995 Act envisages that it will be signed by all the parties and that each party to the contract will be considered to be a "granter". In a situation in which the offer is contained in one or more documents and the acceptance is contained in another document or other documents, the "granter" or "granters" is/are the person or persons making the offer or acceptance as the case may be. Once passed, the Legal Writings (Counterparts and Delivery) Bill will also make provision for a contract to be signed in counterpart, i.e. for one contract to be concluded by the execution of two separate, but identical, parts.[40] This is most commonly used in commercial transactions, where the parties may not ever meet to sign the contract. Instead, in terms of the proposed Bill, each party will be able to sign an identical counterpart and deliver it to the other party, or a nominated person.[41]

5–19   The current ability to have the offer and acceptance contained within separate documents is essential, as it enables the law to recognise as valid

---

[36] 1995 Act s.7(1). There is an exception in relation to testamentary documents, e.g. wills, which must be signed on every page: s.3(2).

[37] 1995 Act s.2(2).

[38] 1995 Act ss.2A, 3A. These sections were inserted by the Automated Registration of Title to Land (Electronic Communications) (Scotland) Order 2006 (SSI 2006/491). Note that there are prospective changes: ss.2A and 3A of the 1995 Act will be repealed and replaced by the Land Registration etc. (Scotland) Act 2012 Sch.3, when and if that Schedule comes into force.

[39] 1995 Act s.12, as amended.

[40] Legal Writings (Counterparts and Delivery) Bill cll.1–3.

[41] Legal Writings (Counterparts and Delivery) Bill cl.3.

contracts concluded by communication passing back and forwards between the parties. This includes order forms and an exchange of letters. A common example of a contract which requires writing and is constituted by means of exchange of letters is missives for the sale of a house. These letters, usually passing between the solicitors for the buyer and the seller, make it possible to adjust the terms on which the sale will take place. The original offer to purchase will normally be met by a qualified acceptance amending several of the suggested terms. This may in turn be met by a further qualified acceptance and so on until the terms are agreed. When this occurs, the final qualified acceptance will be met by a "clean" acceptance. To require the results of this exchange of correspondence to be incorporated into a further document encompassing all the terms would have been unnecessary and would not reflect the means by which the contract was concluded. Instead, to conclude the contract the final qualified acceptance refers to and incorporates the terms as agreed in the preceding correspondence. What is required for the contract to be formally valid is that the last qualified acceptance (the offer) and the "clean" acceptance (the acceptance) be signed by or on behalf of the parties making them. The advantages of a written contract must be balanced against the imposition of unnecessary obstacles to concluding a contract. This balance is reflected in the level of formality required by the 1995 Act, which is not great.[42] A signed letter from a prospective buyer of a house stating that he would like to buy the house for £350,000 and enquiring whether the owner would sell for that sum would, if met by a signed reply accepting the offer, form an enforceable contract.

Witnessing

Although simple signature is all that is required to give the contract **5–20** formal validity and render it enforceable, it is open to the parties to have their signatures witnessed. The effect of having the signature witnessed is that it is presumed that the person who bears to have signed the document did so and, if the document bears a date, that it was signed on the date stated.[43] This is known as evidential validity, or self-proving status.[44] Only one witness is required. The witness must be over 16, have full mental capacity and know the granter and must not also be a granter of the document. Both the granter and the witness must use one of the first two forms of signature set out above and the witness must sign after the granter. The process of the granter signing or acknowledging his signature[45] and the witness signing must be a continuous one. The name and

---

[42] A point made emphatically by Lord Drummond Young in *The Advice Centre for Mortgages v McNicoll* [2006] CSOH 58 at [16].

[43] 1995 Act s.3(1), (8).

[44] The older term for this is "probative".

[45] The 1995 Act provides that a person witnesses a subscription where he sees the granter sign or, where the granter has already signed, the granter acknowledges his signature to the witness: s.3(7).

address of the witness must be set out in the document or in a testing clause but this can be added any time before the document is registered or founded upon.[46]

The effects of the absence of writing

5–21 In the cases where the 1995 Act says that formalities are required, the general rule is that failure to have a written document signed by the granters means that there is no contract. This is despite the fact that the parties may have agreed on all the terms that were to regulate their relationship. This rule could produce results that would be unduly harsh for a party who believed that he or she had concluded a contract. For instance, assume that Marlon concludes an oral agreement with Cary to purchase a hotel from him. On the basis of that agreement, Marlon begins to advertise the business that he will conduct from the hotel, buys equipment for the hotel and starts to engage staff to work in the hotel. If the operation of the rules as to formal validity of contracts were applied then, even if he knew of the actions being taken by Marlon, Cary would be able to withdraw from the "contract" at any time, so long as the agreement remained oral and was not reduced to formal writing. This would be manifestly unfair. The 1995 Act therefore defines circumstances in which a party will be prevented from relying on the lack of formality in the conclusion of the contract to escape their obligations.[47] These rules replace and, to some extent, repeat the old doctrine of *rei interventus* which formerly addressed this problem.[48]

5–22 For a person to be prevented from relying on a lack of formality all of the following requirements must be satisfied:

(1) The contract or obligation[49] must fall within s.1(2)(a) of the 1995 Act, i.e. it must relate to the constitution of a contract relating to an interest in land, rather than the creation, transfer, variation or extinction of an interest in land itself. This difference can be illustrated by comparing missives, which constitute a contract relating to an interest in land, with the disposition, which creates an interest in land. A lack of formality in a disposition (such as a lack of signature) could not be cured by the provisions in s.1(3)

---

[46] 1995 Act ss.3(1), 7(5), 10.

[47] 1995 Act s.1(3), (4).

[48] Section 1(5) of the 1995 Act states that the statutory rule "replaces" the doctrines of *rei interventus* and homologation. Judicial authority has confirmed that *rei interventus* can no longer be used, as a result of the wording in s.1(5): *Advice Centre for Mortgages v McNicoll* [2006] CSOH 58 at [52]. The statutory rule is broader than that which existed under the doctrine of *rei interventus* in that it includes refraining from acting as well as acting on the basis of the contract. In contrast, the doctrine of homologation (which looked to the acts of the party seeking to escape from the contract to render it enforceable) is not provided for under the 1995 Act.

[49] This principle applies to gratuitous unilateral obligations too, so a promise which is not in writing could still be enforced by virtue of this provision.

and (4), whereas failure to reduce the missives to writing could be overcome by relying on s.1(3) and (4).[50]

(2) The party seeking to uphold the contract or unilateral obligation must have acted or refrained from acting in reliance on it. It is necessary that what has happened can be said to have been in reliance on the contract as opposed to something that would have happened in any event or was done in reliance on some other factor.

(3) The party seeking to escape from the agreement or obligation must have known that the other party was so acting or refraining from acting, and acquiesced in it. This is part of the purpose of the rule in achieving fair play. It is not necessary that the party has encouraged or incited the action or restraint—it is enough that he knew of it and acquiesced in it. Therefore once the party has knowledge of what the other party is doing or intending to do, if he wishes to avoid being bound by the unwritten contract, he must immediately notify the other party that he does not consider the contract to be valid.

(4) The position of the person seeking to uphold the contract or obligation must have been affected to a material extent by having acted or refrained from acting. This imposes a threshold for the application of these rules and means that they will not apply where the actings in question are minor. For instance, the fact that a party who intended to purchase a house has bought three pots of paint to decorate a bedroom would be unlikely to justify application of the rules. He would not suffer to a material extent if the seller refused to sell.

(5) The effect of allowing one party to withdraw must be that the position of the party seeking to uphold the contract would be adversely affected to a material extent. This follows from the last rule. It provides a threshold for the rules to apply. In imposing a requirement that the party seeking to uphold the contract would be adversely affected the rule is limited to those situations in which the notion of fair play requires the contract to be maintained. The Inner House has held that the materiality of adverse effects is "one of degree to be determined in the particular circumstances on an individual case."[51]

The effect of s.1(3) and (4) is to bar the party who wishes to walk away from doing so. The 1995 Act states that the contract shall not be regarded as invalid on the ground that it is not properly constituted.[52] However, the effect of the personal bar is that it only applies to the parties to the original transaction: it does not extend to third parties, such as singular successors to the original parties.[53]

---

[50] *Advice Centre for Mortgages v McNicoll* [2006] CSOH 58 at [18].
[51] *Caterleisure Ltd v Glasgow Prestwick International Airport* [2005] CSIH 53 at [16].
[52] 1995 Act s.1(3)(b).
[53] *Advice Centre for Mortgages v McNicoll* [2006] CSOH 58 at [17].

CHAPTER 6

GROUNDS OF INVALIDITY

6–01 Even where a contract complies with the rules relating to formation and to formalities, it may still be invalid. Invalidity arises where there is some fundamental defect in its constitution. The bases on which such a challenge may be made have one thing in common—the allegation that one party did not truly consent to the contract. However, as noted in Ch.2, the law also recognises that bargains are made by what people say or do and not by what they think. Therefore a balance must be struck between, on the one hand, recognising where there is no true consent and the contract should not be enforced and, on the other hand, upholding an objectively valid contract. To reconcile these two factors the law has developed grounds on which the validity of a contract may be challenged.

The Effect of a Successful Challenge

6–02 What is the effect of a successful challenge? The traditional view is that a successful challenge renders a contract either void or voidable. A contract which is **void** is a complete nullity. It is treated as if it had never existed. There are two important consequences which flow from a contract being declared void. First, there is in theory no need to have a court decree that it is void. It is enough to notify the other party that the contract is no longer regarded as binding. If, however, that is disputed, the issue will have to be determined by a court. Secondly, no one can acquire rights under a void contract. Accordingly, a third party who has obtained property which was transferred under a void contract is obliged to restore it to its original owner. The court may however impose an equitable solution on the parties. For example, if goods are delivered under a void contract, the courts may stipulate that the buyer must pay the appropriate market price for the goods.[1] In contrast, a contract which is **voidable** is valid and effective until it is set aside by the courts. Unlike void contracts, a contract which is voidable can confer rights until it is set aside. Accordingly, third parties who acquire rights before the contract has been set aside are protected. There are certain requirements which must be satisfied before a voidable contract can be set aside:

---

[1] This could be by way of the doctrine of unjustified enrichment, see Ch.1.

(a) Restoration to the original position (*restitutio in integrum*) must
    be possible. Where a car has been sold under a voidable contract
    and is then written off in an accident, it will not be possible to
    return the parties to their original position. It will therefore not
    be possible to have the contract set aside;
(b) There must have been no unnecessary delay in taking action to
    annul the contract;
(c) The rights of third parties must not be affected; and
(d) The contract must not have been affirmed under the Age of
    Legal Capacity (Scotland) Act 1991, nor through the operation
    of personal bar under the Requirements of Writing (Scotland)
    Act 1995.

The crucial difference between void and voidable contracts concerns the **6–03**
rights of third parties. This is demonstrated by contrasting two well-
known cases: *Morrisson v Robertson*[2] and *Macleod v Kerr*[3]:

> In *Morrisson*, a man claiming to be the son of Wilson of Bonnyrigg
> approached Morrisson and offered to buy two cows from him.
> Although Morrisson did not know the man, he knew of Wilson, who
> was a neighbouring farmer of good financial standing. Accordingly,
> he let the man have the two cows on credit. In fact, the man was not
> the son of Wilson but a rogue called Telford. Telford sold the two
> cows to Robertson. When Morrisson found this out, he sought to
> recover the cows from Robertson. The action was successful. It was
> held that there had been no contract between Morrisson and Tel-
> ford. The purported transaction was a complete nullity. Accord-
> ingly, Telford had no rights which he could pass on to Robertson, so
> Morrisson was entitled to recover his cows.

Macleod v Kerr provides a more modern setting for the same problem:

> A rogue paid for a Vauxhall car with a stolen cheque. As soon as the
> seller discovered that the cheque had been dishonoured, he notified
> the police. Shortly afterwards, the car was sold by the rogue to an
> innocent third party. It was held that the contract between the seller
> and the rogue was voidable rather than void. As it had not been
> reduced before the rogue had sold the car, title to the car had passed
> to the purchaser. It followed that the third party purchaser could
> acquire good title. The original owner could not get his car back.

The distinction between the two cases is a narrow one. In *Morrisson*, it
was held that the seller had never intended to contract with the person
before him, Telford, but rather with Wilson. As Wilson knew nothing of
the transaction there could be no contract. The seller in *Macleod*, on the
other hand, was prepared to contract with the person in front of him. He

[2] *Morrisson v Robertson*, 1908 S.C. 332.
[3] *Macleod v Kerr*, 1965 S.L.T. 358.

did not know the identity of the person with whom he was dealing. The House of Lords adopted the same reasoning in *Morrisson* in a recent English case, *Shogun Finance Ltd v Hudson*.[4] They concluded that the initial hire purchase contract for a new Shogun car was therefore void. Accordingly, the bona fide third party purchaser, Hudson, lost the car and his money.

What is important to notice is the varying results between a finding of void or voidable. In *Morrisson*, the owner was the protected party; in *Macleod* it was the third party purchaser. It can be argued that it boils down to a question of policy. Should the law protect the seller or the innocent third party? As the seller is normally in a better position to take precautions to prevent the fraud, it is arguable that he should take the risk:

> "As between two innocent persons the loss is more appropriately borne by the person who takes the risks inherent in parting with his goods without receiving payment."[5]

THE GROUNDS OF CHALLENGE

Force and fear

6–04   The clearest case of invalidity is where coercion or unfair pressure is applied to secure consent to the contract. This renders the contract void. A person who is threatened with a gun to make him sign a contract cannot be regarded as acting freely. Were the law to hold such bargains binding, this would legitimise terrorism and extortion. In Scotland, this ground of challenge is known as force and fear (*vis ac metus*). It is the subversion of consent by fear, rather than the force, which is important:

> "Although ... we couple together force and fear as one ground of reduction, the act of force is truly ... only one means of inducing fear, the true ground of reduction being extortion, through the influence of fear, induced in the various ways".[6]

An early and colourful example of force and fear is provided by the case of *Earl of Orkney v Vinfra*[7]:

The Earl sued Vinfra for payment of 1,000 merks that he said were owed to him under a deed which Vinfra had signed. Vinfra claimed that he had initially refused to sign but then "the said Earl was so offended that with terrible countenance and words and laying his hand upon his whinger [short sword], he threatened with execrable oaths to bereave this

---

[4] *Shogun Finance Ltd v Hudson* [2003] UKHL 62.
[5] This was the view expressed by one of the dissenting judges in *Shogun Finance Ltd v Hudson* [2003] UKHL 62, per Lord Nicholls at [35].
[6] *Priestnell v Hutcheson* (1857) 19 D. 495, per Lord Deas at 499.
[7] *Earl of Orkney v Vinfra* (1606) Mor. 16481.

Vinfra of his life and stick him presently through the head with his whinger, if he subscribed not."

The Earl maintained that he had only used boisterous words. The court preferred Vinfra's account of events and held the contract invalid.

Threat to do an unlawful act

Sometimes lawyers speak in this connection of the "overborne will." **6–05** However, we should be clear that the person threatened has a choice—he chooses the lesser of two evils. He consents to enter into the contract to avoid the threat being carried out. Indeed, the greater the threat, the more likely it is that the person will do the act in question. It is not therefore strictly correct to say that one person's will is actually overborne. More accurately, the person threatened is influenced or pressured in such a way as to choose one course of action instead of the one he would have adopted had he not been subject to such pressure. So it is the illegitimacy of the threats which is the crucial factor. Some forms of pressure will not ground an action for force and fear. It is legitimate, for example, for one party to tell the other that he will resort to litigation. A creditor can tell his debtor that he will raise an action for payment unless the debtor agrees to pay off the debt. This is a proper course of action for: "If the only threat is a threat to do a lawful act then the plea of force and fear must fail."[8] In *Hunter v Bradford Property Trust Ltd*[9]:

> Two sisters were in financial difficulties. They signed an agreement with a property company. The terms of the agreement were that the sisters would be paid certain sums of money when the company sold properties belonging to them. On the night before the sale was due to take place, one of the company's directors found that the written contract did not accurately record the agreement that he thought had been reached. He told the sisters that unless they signed a second contract, he would cancel the sale. After discussions long into the night, the sisters signed. They sought to reduce this second contract on the ground that it had been signed through force and fear. They claimed that they were anxious about their financial position should the sale not go ahead the following day. It was decided that the sisters had not made out a case of force and fear. The threat to cancel the sale could not be regarded as unlawful and could not therefore be a ground for setting the contract aside.

---

[8] *Hunter v Bradford Property Trust Ltd*, 1977 S.L.T. (Notes) 33, per Lord Migdale at 34.
[9] *Hunter v Bradford Property Trust Ltd*, 1977 S.L.T. (Notes) 33.

Severity of threats

6–06 The threats employed to induce the contract must not have resulted in "vain or foolish fear".[10] Rather, they must have been such as would have overcome the fortitude of a person of reasonable constancy. Where a weapon is used, or actual violence is threatened, then the issue is clear cut. Usually, however, some more insidious pressure is brought to bear.

Then it is a question of evidence as to whether the plea of force and fear is made out. Was consent subverted or not? A good illustration is provided by *Hislop v Dickson Motors (Forres) Ltd*[11]:

> The cashier of a garage in Forres was confronted by her employer. He shouted at her and accused her of embezzling sums from the garage accounts. She admitted the allegation and agreed to try to repay the sums. The next morning the employer arrived at her home with another director of the company. She handed over her car registration documents and keys together with a blank deposit-account withdrawal form which she signed. The directors drove her car away and withdrew all the money from her deposit account (£385). At the bank, they found out that the cashier also had a current account. They returned to her house and after further argument obtained a signed blank cheque from her which they used to withdraw the total credit balance (£195) from her current account. Subsequently the cashier was prosecuted in respect of the sums that had disappeared from the garage accounts. A not proven verdict was returned. She raised an action for reduction of the two transactions with her employer on the ground of force and fear. It was held that the transaction involving the car and deposit account was valid, but that the transaction involving the current account was invalid through force and fear.

It is not easy to draw a clear distinction between the two transactions. On both occasions, the pursuer was prepared to trade off her assets against the threat of a criminal prosecution. Although her optimism on that point proved unfounded, that was not a relevant factor in the decision reached. The line drawn by Lord Maxwell was to say that in giving over the documents relating to the car and the deposit account the cashier was acting voluntarily: she was handing them over in return for not being prosecuted. On the second occasion, however, she was not acting voluntarily. Instead, she was coerced by her two employers into handing over the blank cheque in respect of an account about which she thought they knew nothing. By disclosing certain of her assets, she was indicating the extent to which she was prepared to go to avoid prosecution. But when she was confronted by the two men returning with information which she had not volunteered, no true consent on her part was discernible. Accordingly the second arrangement was struck down. This is

---

[10] Stair, I, 10, 14.
[11] *Hislop v Dickson Motors (Forres) Ltd*, 1978 S.L.T. (Notes) 73.

probably the correct analysis of a fact situation where, superficially at least, it is difficult to measure the consent given and the degree to which it was undermined.

Economic threats

Some English cases have given colour to the notion that there can be **6–07** economic duress, as opposed to physical duress or pressure to the person. Thus, where a creditor accepted a lesser sum from the debtor than that due, solely because he himself was in difficult financial circumstances and the debtor took advantage of his position, the bargain was declared invalid.[12] The threat by the debtor not to pay at all unless the lesser sum was accepted amounted to unfair pressure. It followed that the balance of the debt was recoverable. As yet there has been no detailed discussion of such types of pressure in Scots law. In the case of *Hunter v Bradford Property Trust Ltd*,[13] although the pressure brought to bear was economic, the court held that the defenders had been entitled to cancel the sale that was scheduled to take place and the issue of the nature of the threat did not therefore arise. The essence of force and fear, however, is that agreement is extorted from one party by the other's use of illegitimate pressure. Today economic pressure can be as effective as physical violence was of old.

In all the cases referred to above, the pressure to induce the contract has come from one of the parties to the contract. For some time the law appeared to be that this was necessary if a challenge was to succeed on this ground. For example, in *Stewart Bros v Kiddie*,[14] Mrs Kiddie sought to challenge an agreement whereby she agreed to accept a sum of money in full settlement of a claim for damages on the basis that her paramour had pressured her to sign. The court said that because the other party to the contract did not know of the improper pressure, they were not affected by it and the challenge on that basis failed. In *Trustee Savings Bank v Balloch*,[15] the court stated that if the effect of the force and fear is that there is no consent the result is that the contract is void and it does not matter who it was that exerted the force. This has been approved by the House of Lords.[16]

Facility and circumvention

Facility and circumvention involves one party taking unfair advantage of **6–08** another who, for some reason, is in a vulnerable state. A contract is voidable for facility and circumvention when a weak-minded (facile) party has been imposed upon unfairly and their will has been circumvented.

---

[12] *D&C Builders Ltd v Rees* [1966] 2 Q.B. 617.
[13] *Hunter v Bradford Property Trust Ltd*, 1977 S.L.T. (Notes) 33.
[14] *Stewart Bros v Kiddie* (1899) 7 S.L.T. 92.
[15] *Trustee Savings Bank v Balloch*, 1983 S.L.T. 240.
[16] *Smith v Bank of Scotland*, 1997 S.C. (HL) 111 at 117D; 1997 S.L.T. 1061 at 1065H.

Example: A motorist, Colin, is in a state of shock after a car accident: Ross takes advantage of Colin's condition to purchase Colin's
car from him at 25 per cent of its market value.

Three elements must be present before such a challenge will be successful.
The person attempting to set aside the contract must prove:

(1) weakness and facility[17];
(2) circumvention; and
(3) loss (lesion).

6–09 The greater the facility and loss, the less circumvention required. In each
case it is a question of degree. The court will examine whether the person
seeking to be released from the obligation was easily influenced or preyed
upon because of his or her vulnerable mental state at the time. A person
who is ill and in hospital is not on that account alone "of facile disposition"[18] but a recently bereaved widow may be in such a condition.[19]

For a challenge to succeed on this ground, the acts of circumvention
must have been carried out by or on behalf of the other party to the
contract.[20]

Undue influence

6–10 Where a person is in a position of trust or authority, and abuses that
position in order to persuade someone to enter into a contract, then the
resulting contract may be voidable through undue influence. The law
recognises that where parties are not at arm's length, any transactions
between the parties must be closely scrutinised to make sure that one
party does not abuse his position. As Lord President Inglis put it in the
leading case of *Gray v Binny*[21]:

> "If ... the relation of the parties is such as to beget mutual trust and
> confidence, each owes to the other a duty which has no place
> between strangers ... the party trusted and confided in is bound, by
> the most obvious principles of fair dealing and honesty, not to abuse
> the power thus put in his hands."

There, a 24-year-old man, on the advice of his mother and the family
solicitor, sold his inheritance rights for an inadequate amount, to the
benefit of his mother. It was decided that if he could show that he had
only entered the contract because of the advice he had received from his
mother and her solicitor, it could be set aside.

6–11 At one time, it was thought that the classes of relationship which could

---

[17] If the person lacks capacity entirely, rather than merely being weak-minded, then he is
incapable of giving consent.
[18] *Mackay v Campbell*, 1967 S.C. (HL) 53; 1967 S.L.T. 337.
[19] *MacGilvary v Gilmartin*, 1986 S.L.T. 89. See also *Edgar v Edgar* [2014] CSOH 60.
[20] See *Smith v Bank of Scotland*, 1997 S.C. (HL) 111 at 117C; 1997 S.L.T. 1061 at 1065F.
[21] *Gray v Binny* (1879) 7 R. 332 at 343.

ground an action of undue influence were closed. It is now accepted that it is always a question of fact whether such a relationship is present and it can exist as much between client and art dealer as between doctor and patient, or parent and child.[22] The issue is whether one person actually did repose trust and confidence in another; and whether that confidence was abused. However, to succeed in an action for undue influence, the courts are clear that the pursuer must show *undue* influence and not merely influence.[23]

The difficulty with challenge on this ground is that the influence may be exercised in such a way that there is no independent evidence of the abuse. To counter this problem, the courts are willing to infer that there has been undue influence where there is a relationship of the type referred to in *Gray* and the following two conditions are met:

(1) the party with the influence has received a material and gratuitous benefit to the prejudice of the party trusting him/her; and
(2) the party disadvantaged did not have independent advice.

Here too, for a challenge to be successful it is necessary that the undue influence be exerted by or on behalf of the other party to the contract.

Inequality of bargaining power

So far we have been considering grounds of challenge where it is alleged **6–12** that something improper has occurred in the course of the bargaining process, such that one party's consent has not truly been given. However, it may be that without being able to point to anything specific at the time of negotiating, one party claims that the contract should not be enforced because its terms are grossly unfair. In common parlance, someone has made a "bad bargain" and seeks relief. This can occur where there is a gross inequality between the relative bargaining strengths of the parties. Take, for example, a contract between a small business and a large multinational company. Because of the company's superior bargaining strength, it may be able to ensure that the contract terms are weighted heavily in its favour.

There is some early authority in Scots law to the effect that such **6–13** bargains may be reducible:

"All bargains which from their very appearance discover oppression, as an intention in any of the contractors to catch some undue advantage from his neighbour's necessities, lie open to reduction on the head of dole or extortion, without the necessity of proving any special circumstances of fraud or circumvention on the part of that contractor."[24]

---

[22] *Honeyman's Executors v Sharp*, 1978 S.C. 223.
[23] *Clydesdale Bank Plc v Black*, 2002 S.C. 555, per Lord Coulsfield at [13].
[24] Erskine, IV, 1, 27.

Despite this statement, at common law no such general ground of challenge on the basis of extortion of inequality of bargaining power now exists in Scotland. The general principle is that such contracts must stand. The courts have been unwilling to intervene directly to decide whether a bargain is or is not unfair. To do so would arguably be to usurp the function of the parties in making their own contract. It is not for the court to determine whether or not a person has made a good or bad bargain. A flood of claims would occur, it is argued, if the courts had power to set aside a bargain on the ground of "fairness" alone. Reduction can probably only be granted where a contract is so inequitable in its terms as to raise an overwhelming presumption that it has been involuntarily granted.

6–14   In certain areas, however, most notably concerning consumers, legislation has intervened.[25] For example, there are detailed provisions in relation to unfair terms in consumer contracts.[26] There are also specific protections, such as a statutory "cooling-off" period for those entering distance contracts, consumer credit agreements, and timeshare agreements.[27] This gives individuals an opportunity to pause and reflect before committing themselves to such major financial relationships. In addition, the courts have power to consider the fairness of non-negotiated terms in consumer contracts.[28] It is now highly unlikely that there will be a move toward a general principle of inequality of bargaining power. In *National Westminster Bank Plc v Morgan*, Lord Scarman stated:

> "I question whether there is any need in the modern law to erect a general principle of relief against inequality of bargaining power. Parliament has undertaken the task (and it is essentially a legislative task) of enacting such restrictions on freedom of contract as are in its judgment necessary to relieve against the mischief ... I doubt whether the courts should assume the burden of formulating further restrictions."[29]

Error and misrepresentation

6–15   Suppose the parties enter into a contract as a result of an error. Once the mistake is notified, one party may want to proceed, while the other party may seek to walk away from the contract. In adjudicating the dispute, the court will take into account several factors. Was the error unilateral, or were both parties in error? How serious was the error? Did one party induce the other party to enter into the contract as a result of a

---

[25] Some contracts are considered in Ch.9.

[26] Unfair Terms in Consumer Contracts Regulations (SI 1999/2083); see Ch.9.

[27] Consumer Contracts (Information, Cancellation and Additional Charges) Regulations 2013 (SI 2013/3134) reg.29; Consumer Credit Act 1974 ss.67–73 (as amended); Timeshare Act 1992.

[28] Unfair Terms in Consumer Contracts Regulations 1999 (SI 1999/2083).

[29] *National Westminster Bank Plc v Morgan* [1985] 1 All E.R. 821 at 830.

misleading statement? This is a complex area of law. One judge has recently stated that: "The effect of error on the validity of a contract is one of the most uncertain areas in our private law."[30]

The nub of the problem is the conflict between two different approaches to contract law. A *subjective* approach suggests that where error is present there can be no true consent and therefore no contract. An *objective* approach, on the other hand, takes the view that parties are bound by what they say, not what they think. This conflict can be seen as far back as Stair. In an early passage in the *Institutions* he takes a subjective approach: "These who err in the substantials of what is done, contract not."[31] But later on, he narrows the compass of this passage to a significant degree: "But the exception upon error is seldom relevant, because it depends upon the knowledge of the person erring, which he can hardly prove."[32] In modern terms, "So long as a clear and enforceable bargain emerges, the subjective intention, or lack of consent of one party, is defeated by an objective interpretation of what was said or done."[33]

The analysis of error through the centuries has led to considerable **6–16** confusion as to its exact scope and application.[34] It is, however, possible to identify five questions that can help determine whether a contract resulting from error is enforceable or not:

(1) Is the error so serious that it prevents *consensus in idem*, and there is therefore no contract at all?
(2) Is the error "in the substantials"?
(3) Is the error unilateral or bilateral?
(4) Is there an additional factor which would justify the contract not being enforced, ie in the words of Professor McBryde is there "error plus"?
(5) Has the error been induced by the other party to the contract?

Each of these elements will be looked at in turn. The final question concerns error which has been induced by misrepresentation. This is arguably the most significant type of error today, and it will be considered in detail at paragraphs 6–27—6–38.

---

[30] *Wills v Strategic Procurement (UK) Limited* [2013] CSOH 26, per Lord Malcolm at [1].
[31] Stair, I, 10, 13.
[32] Stair, IV, 40, 24.
[33] *Wills v Strategic Procurement (UK) Limited* [2013] CSOH 26, per Lord Malcolm at [1].
[34] For a review of the historical development of error, see William W. McBryde, "Error", in Kenneth Reid and Reinhard Zimmermann (eds), *A History of Private Law in Scotland* (Oxford: Oxford University Press, 2000), Vol.II, "Obligations"; Dot Reid and Hector MacQueen, "Fraud or error: a thought experiment?" (2013) 17 Edin. L.R. 343; John MacLeod, "Before Bell: The Roots of Error in the Scots Law of Contract" (2010) 14 Edin. L.R. 385; William W. McBryde, *The Law of Contract in Scotland*, 3rd edn (Edinburgh: SULI/W. Green, 2007), paras.15–04—15–22.

Question 1: Does the error prevent consensus?

6–17 As noted at the outset of this Chapter, the grounds of invalidity are based on the principle that one party did not truly consent and there was therefore no *consensus in idem*. Where there is an error which is so serious that it prevents consensus, then the contract will be void. Although in theory a unilateral error which is so serious could result in a lack of consensus,[35] in practice cases in this category involve both parties being mistaken. Typically, they are at cross purposes.

> *Example*: David believes that he is selling the 1628 "Madonna and Child", Scott that he is buying the 1630 version, which David also owns.

This is known as mutual error results and results in dissensus, rather than consensus. Often there is an element of ambiguity. The most famous case concerned the sale of a cargo of grain which was to be transported on a ship called the *Peerless* from Bombay to England.[36] Unknown to the parties at the time they made the contract, there were two ships of that name, one sailing in October, the other in December. The buyer thought that he was contracting in respect of the October *Peerless*. The seller meant the December *Peerless*. It was held that there was no contract. At no stage were the parties at one regarding the contract both thought they had entered into. An equivalent Scottish case is *Stuart & Co v Kennedy*.[37] There, a quantity of stone-coping was sold at so much per foot. One party thought that the measure was the lineal foot, the other that it was the superficial foot. The charge if made by the superficial foot would be more than double what it would be if made by the lineal foot. It was held that there was no contract.

In the case of mutual error, a finding that the parties have not truly reached agreement will result in the contract being void. There are relatively few error cases of this type and two factors account for this. First, the court will normally prefer one party's version of the contract to that of the other. For example, they will declare that, on an objective analysis, it is a contract of credit sale rather than hire-purchase.[38] This means that the error is unilateral rather than mutual, and the contract will usually be enforceable. Secondly, where the court does find that there is no consensus, it is more likely to classify the situation as falling under the heading of offer and acceptance than of error. There was no consensus and therefore no contract. An example is provided by *Mathieson Gee (Ayrshire) Ltd v Quigley*, where the parties' mistaken view that they had achieved agreement was held to have arisen because the offer did not meet the acceptance. There was an offer of plant for hire, and an

---

[35] William W. McBryde, *The Law of Contract in Scotland*, 3rd edn (Edinburgh: SULI/W. Green, 2007), para.15–41.

[36] *Raffles v Wichelhaus* (1864) 2 H. & C. 906.

[37] *Stuart & Co v Kennedy* (1885) 13 R. 221.

[38] *Muirhead and Turnbull v Dickson* (1905) 7 F. 686; (1905) 13 S.L.T. 151. See Ch.2 for discussion of this case.

acceptance of plant and services.[39] The mutual error prevented *consensus in idem*, and there was therefore no valid contract.

Thus, if the error is so serious that it prevents consensus, there will be no contract. In all other cases, it is necessary to consider the remaining four questions.

Question 2: Is the error in the "substantials"?

Error in the substantials.[40] Clearly there is little justification for holding **6–18** that the consent to the contract is invalid where the error relates to a peripheral matter. It is sometimes said that the mistake must go to the root of the contract. What constitutes such a mistake?

Stair's view was that error in the substantials would render a contract void, that is, which constituted essential error. It remained to lay down with precision what constituted error in the substantials. The formulation of another institutional writer, Bell, was adopted by Lord Watson[41]:

> "I concur ... as to the accuracy of the general doctrine laid down by Professor Bell [*Principles*, s.11] to the effect that error in substantials such as will invalidate consent given to a contract or obligation must be in relation to either (1) its subject-matter; (2) the persons undertaking or to whom it is undertaken; (3) the price or consideration; (4) the quality of the thing engaged for; if expressly or tacitly essential; or (5) the nature of the contract or engagement supposed to be entered into. I believe that these five categories will be found to embrace all the forms of essential error which, either per se or when induced by the other party to the contract, give the person labouring under such error a right to rescind it."

We can illustrate the five categories as follows: **6–19**

   (1) Subject matter: A thinks he is buying wheat from B, B thinks he is selling barley to A.
   (2) Identity: A thinks he is contracting with B, whereas he is contracting with C.
   (3) Price: A thinks the price is £1,000, B thinks it is $1,000.
   (4) Quality: A thinks he is buying a stallion, when in fact the beast is a gelding.
   (5) Nature of the contract: A thinks he is signing a lease, whereas in fact the document is a guarantee.

---

[39] *Mathieson Gee (Ayrshire) Ltd v Quigley*, 1952 S.C. (HL) 38.
[40] This is sometimes referred to as "essential error". However, the word "essential" can be confusing, for reasons given by Professor McBryde, and so the terminology used here will be "error in the substantials". See William W. McBryde, *The Law of Contract in Scotland*, 3rd edn (Edinburgh: SULI/W. Green, 2007), para.15–04. See also *Wills v Strategic Procurement (UK) Limited* [2013] CSOH 26, per Lord Malcolm at [22].
[41] *Stewart v Kennedy* (1890) 17 R. (HL) 25 at 28.

However, Lord Watson went on to note that this list was not exhaustive: there could possibly be exceptions, or other categories of error which were in the substantials.[42]

If the error is not in the substantials, the contract stands. For example, A's belief that he will make a profit from his contract affords no ground of relief should he prove mistaken. His error is one of motive, which does not affect the contract.

However, even if there is an error in the substantials, which goes to the root of the contract, the current legal approach is that it will only invalidate the contract if there is some additional factor relating to the error which would justify the contract being set aside. In Professor McBryde's terminology, this is "error plus". This will be examined below, at para.6–23.

Question 3: Is the error unilateral or bilateral?

6–20 **Unilateral error.** In unilateral error only one party is mistaken as to a feature of the contract.

> *Example*: Eric believes the painting he is buying is an original by Max Ernst. The seller George knows it is a copy.

A unilateral error is usually irrelevant. There must be an additional factor to justify the reduction of the contract. In Professor McBryde's terminology, this is "error plus". In cases where there has been no additional factor, then such an error is not sufficient to reduce the contract. The courts will not interfere to relieve the party from its mistake. In one case, parties were negotiating an out of court settlement. A number of communications took place between the parties' solicitors. For most of the negotiations, the date from which interest was to run on the settlement sum remained constant. Finally, one party's solicitor accepted an offer to settle the action, failing to notice that the other side's solicitor had altered the date on which interest was to run.[43] The mistake could not be relied upon in order to avoid the transaction. The solicitor ought to have read the offer more carefully, as it clearly stated the new date from which interest was to run. Similarly, if a company erroneously believes that a property being sold by it is subject to a lease of 990 years, rather than 99 years, it will not be relieved of that mistake unless it was induced by the other party.[44] Even a lay person is expected to understand that a document signed by him gives rise to obligations. In *Royal Bank of Scotland Plc v Purvis*[45]:

---

[42] *Stewart v Kennedy* (1890) 17 R. (HL) 25 at 28.
[43] *Steel v Bradley Homes (Scotland) Ltd*, 1974 S.L.T. 133.
[44] *Spook Erection (Northern) Ltd v Kaye*, 1990 S.L.T. 676.
[45] *Royal Bank of Scotland Plc v Purvis*, 1990 S.L.T. 262.

A wife signed a guarantee to the bank in respect of a loan to a company of which she and her husband were directors. Subsequently, the bank sued both the husband and wife under the guarantee for payment of a sum of £21,635.17. The wife contended that she was in essential error at the time of signature because: (a) she signed the document at the request of her husband; (b) she had not read it, nor was it explained to her; (c) she was not formally educated and was unfamiliar with commercial documents; and (d) she did not realise that the document was a guarantee and would not have signed it if she had.

Lord McCluskey repelled this defence and stated:

"The whole point of committing such obligations to writing is to avoid any inquiry into antecedent states of mind unless the whole picture is one of a signature induced by misrepresentation. I find it virtually impossible to envisage a situation in real life in which a person could repudiate a document signed by him when he was innocently, unilaterally and not negligently in ignorance of the character of the document which he was signing at the time. I think one would need to wait and see what circumstances were averred that could give rise to such a special exception to a rule upon which so much commerce depends."[46]

Two points can be made about this case. First, the error was not induced. Secondly, the wife in this case derived a benefit from the guarantee: the bank released funds to the company of which she was one of the directors. This situation can therefore be distinguished from cases where the person who signed the document did not derive any benefit from it, i.e. it was a gratuitous contract.[47]

Bilateral error. Where both parties are in error, they might share the same **6–21** mistaken belief, or they may be at cross purposes. A bilateral error may be "common" or "mutual".[48] In cases where the parties share the same mistaken belief, this is known as common error. Mutual error is where the parties were at cross purposes. In some cases where the parties are in mutual error, there will be no *consensus in idem* and no contract. In other cases, the mutual error may be relevant for "error plus".

---

[46] *Royal Bank of Scotland Plc v Purvis*, 1990 S.L.T. 262 at 266; see also *McCallum v Soudan*, 1989 S.L.T. 522, per Lord Morison at 523.
[47] See the sections below regarding gratuitous contracts (para.6–25) and the bank's duty of good faith (para.6–42).
[48] However, some judges and commentators use the terms "mutual" and "common" interchangeably. See Professor McBryde's discussion of the problems of terminology here: *The Law of Contract in Scotland*, 3rd edn (Edinburgh: SULI/W. Green, 2007), para.15–36.

6–22 **Common error.** Here, both parties hold the same mistaken belief.[49] They share an assumption about the state of affairs upon which the contract is based, which turns out to be erroneous.

> *Example*: In a contract for the sale of a painting, both parties think the painting is in existence, whereas it was destroyed the day before the contract was made.

In principle, common error as to some essential feature renders a contract invalid. In practice few cases of common error arise. That is mainly because rules exist regarding risk allocation and rectification. Where a house is sold, for example, risk passes on completion of the missives. This means that if both parties believe that a house is in existence at the time the contract is made, whereas in reality it has been destroyed by fire, the risk is with the seller. But once the missives are completed, any damage to the house which occurs subsequently is the risk of the buyer. This means that each party knows the exact moment at which they should ensure that they have insurance cover in place. Where the common error was in the expression of a term in the contract, a party can have the contract rectified.[50] That situation might arise if the parties agreed a price of £10,000, but the contract mistakenly shows it as $10,000. Rectification is discussed in Chapter 8.

Question 4: Is there "error plus"?

6–23 **"Error plus".** From his analysis of case law, Professor McBryde has advanced a theory of "error plus". Error will only be relevant if (a) the error is in the substantials and (b) there is some additional factor which makes it necessary for the courts to correct the error. Although Professor McBryde does not set out explicitly what additional factor(s) might be relevant, he goes on to identify four situations where the courts have set aside contracts founded on error.[51] In each of these situations, there is an additional factor which justifies the intervention. Judicial approval has been given to this analysis:

> "If a rule of thumb were required it would be difficult to improve on Professor McBryde's suggestion that for error to be relevant there must be some other factor in addition."[52]

---

[49] In one recent case involving common error, the sheriff principal described the error as "mutual". Nonetheless, he was clear that both parties had made the same mistake and he therefore held the contract was void: *McLaughlin v Thenew Housing Association Ltd, 2008 S.L.T. (Sh Ct) 137.*

[50] Law Reform (Miscellaneous Provisions) (Scotland) Act 1985.

[51] William W. McBryde, *The Law of Contract in Scotland*, 3rd edn (Edinburgh: SULI/W. Green, 2007), paras 15–23—15–39.

[52] *Parvaiz v Thresher Wines Acquisitions Ltd* [2008] CSOH 160, per Lord Brodie at [11].

The four situations that Professor McBryde identifies are: where the error is mutual; where the error was induced; where the party took advantage of the error; or where the contract was gratuitous. These four situations can therefore be classed as "error plus".

Mutual error has already been considered, and induced error is discussed in more detail below. What about situations where advantage was taken of the other party's error, or the contract was gratuitous?

Taking advantage of the other party's error. A person is not allowed 6–24 unfairly to "snatch at a bargain".[53] In *Steuart's Trustees v Hart*, a seller sold some land believing it to be burdened with a feu duty (annual land charge) of £9 15s.[54] The purchaser knew that the feu duty was only three shillings and also knew of the seller's mistake. The seller was held entitled to reduce the contract since the mistake was essential and his error had been taken advantage of by the purchaser. This decision is a controversial one. Some commentators point to its equity in emphasising the good faith of the bargaining process. Others note its far reaching consequences: a person who picked up a book or an antique "for a song" might find that the seller would seek to have the sale set aside on the basis of his own error.[55]

The ratio in *Steuart's Trustees* was considered and affirmed in two more recent cases: *Angus v Bryden*[56] and *Wills v Strategic Procurement (UK) Ltd.*[57] In *Angus v Bryden*:

> Annbank Angling Club were the tenants of certain river fishings in the River Ayr. The river fishings were owned by Angus, who also owned sea fishings at the mouth of the river. In 1986, the club offered Angus £30,000 to purchase the fishings. This was accepted and subsequently a disposition was granted transferring the whole fishings. Angus claimed that on a true construction, all that was agreed to be transferred was the river fishings and the disposition should be corrected. As an alternative argument, he contended that if the sea fishings had been disponed, this was an error on his part known to and taken advantage of by the club. Lord Cameron of Lochbroom disposed of the action by upholding Angus' position on the principal argument. However, he went on to consider the alternative argument and stated: "I consider that *Steuart's Trs. v Hart* is still good law and is therefore binding upon me."[58]

---

[53] The idea of "snapping up" a bargain was also discussed in the case of *Chwee Kin Keong v Digilandmall.com Pte Ltd* [2004] 2 S.L.R. 594 at [115]–[120], concerning goods for sale online at the wrong price: here there was a unilateral error of which the other party took advantage.

[54] *Steuart's Trustees v Hart* (1875) 3 R. 192.

[55] See William M. Gloag, *The Law of Contract: a Treatise on the Principles of Contract in the Law of Scotland*, 2nd edn (Edinburgh: W. Green, 1929), p.438.

[56] *Angus v Bryden*, 1992 S.L.T. 884.

[57] *Wills v Strategic Procurement (UK) Limited* [2013] CSOH 26.

[58] *Angus v Bryden*, 1992 S.L.T. 884 at 887.

In *Wills v Strategic Procurement (UK) Limited*[59] the pursuer raised an action alleging that the defender had failed to provide him with shares worth £3.5m. The parties agreed to end the Scottish proceedings and litigate in England instead. Accordingly, they entered into an agreement that a decree of absolvitor should be granted in respect of the Scottish proceedings. This was to allow the pursuer to continue the action in England. However, he (and his solicitors) were unaware that a decree of absolvitor would prevent the claim in England. The correct order should have been a decree of dismissal, which would have allowed the claim to proceed in England. Mr Wills alleged that the defender knew of this error and took advantage of it.

Here the question was "what is the position if it is proved that the person seeking to enforce a contract was aware that there was no true agreement on a key element?"[60] While there was no suggestion that the error was induced by the defenders, the fact that they knew about the pursuer's mistake as to the effect of the agreement—a key element— meant that the objective approach to contract formation was suspended.[61] The pursuer was therefore able to plead his own unilateral, uninduced error, as relevant. The defender's knowledge of the mistake constituted "error plus". Importantly, the decision in *Wills* clearly affirms that *Steuart's Trustees* is good law. Moreover, Lord Malcolm also addressed the concern that this approach would lead to untoward consequences in cases where an antique was purchased "for a song":

> "The expert who spots a rare first edition for sale in a bookshop at a low price is an often quoted example. In such a case the seller's error has no impact on the validity of the contract. It relates to a collateral matter, namely the value of the item, not the subject-matter, meaning or effect of the bargain. If both were ignorant as to the true value of the book, again that shared error has no effect."[62]

6–25 Gratuitous contracts. Unilateral error in the substantials is also relevant to gratuitous transactions. The rationale is straightforward. As the recipient is receiving something for nothing, it is inequitable to enforce the obligation if it has been made by mistake. Suppose that Robert makes a written promise to give £500 to Jane, believing her to be his long lost cousin. If Robert subsequently discovers that Jane is not related to him, he should be discharged from his obligation. In the case of *Hunter v Bradford Property Trust Ltd*, which was discussed above with regard to force and fear, the sisters successfully set aside the contract on the basis that it had been entered gratuitously under essential error as to its effect.[63]

---

[59] *Wills v Strategic Procurement (UK) Limited* [2013] CSOH 26.
[60] *Wills v Strategic Procurement (UK) Limited* [2013] CSOH 26, per Lord Malcolm at [10].
[61] *Wills v Strategic Procurement (UK) Limited* [2013] CSOH 26, per Lord Malcolm at [17].
[62] *Wills v Strategic Procurement (UK) Limited* [2013] CSOH 26, per Lord Malcolm at [12].
[63] *Hunter v Bradford Property Trust Ltd*, 1970 S.L.T. 173. This principle has been applied more recently in *Edgar v Edgar* [2014] CSOH 60, in which Lord Burns cited and applied *Hunter v Bradford Property Trust*.

Summary

As we have seen, the courts are reluctant to relieve people of their con- **6–26** tractual obligations simply because they allege that they made a mistake on entering into them. The courts are likely to grant relief only where the error is so serious that it prevents consensus (as in *Mathieson Gee (Ayrshire) Ltd v Quigley*) OR where there is error in the substantials, plus some additional factor which justifies intervention. Such factors include (i) the error being mutual; (ii) one party attempting to snatch at a bargain; or (iii) the contract being gratuitous. In other cases, error will usually only be relevant if has been induced through misrepresentation.

Question 5: Was the error induced?

Induced error or misrepresentation. Misrepresentation is now "probably **6–27** the largest sub-category of the modern law of error".[64] In Scots law, the shift from uninduced to induced error can be traced to two House of Lords' decisions in the late nineteenth century. In *Stewart v Kennedy*[65]:

> A contract for the sale of an entailed estate was made "subject to the ratification of the court." The seller, Sir Archibald Stewart, mistakenly thought that the phrase meant that the court would determine if the price was fair and reasonable. In fact, it was a simple statutory requirement which had to be followed in the case of entailed estates. He sought to reduce the missives of sale, claiming amongst other things that he had entered the contract under essential error. In the Court of Session it was held that there was no essential error, as the person, the price and the subject-matter of the contract were clearly established.[66] The House of Lords took an entirely different line. It decided that there had been an error, but that of itself was not enough to set aside the contract. Error would only be relevant if it were induced.

That decision marked a sea change in the law. The focal point became the *cause* rather than the *nature* of the error. If the pursuer's mistake was attributable to the other party then the contract could be challenged. But if the mistake arose simply through his own uninduced error, then it would not be operative and he would be unlikely to be able to set aside the contract.

In the second case, *Menzies v Menzies*,[67] Lord Watson confirmed this approach. He stated that:

---

[64] Dot Reid and Hector MacQueen, "Fraud or error: a thought experiment?" (2013) Edin. L.R. 343.

[65] *Stewart v Kennedy* (1890) 17 R. (HL) 25.

[66] That is, the three essential elements of the contract had been established, and therefore there could not be error in the essentials.

[67] *Menzies v Menzies* (1893) 20 R. (HL) 108.

"Error becomes essential whenever it is shown that but for it one of the parties would have declined to contract. He cannot rescind unless his error was induced by the representations of the other contracting party, or of his agent, made in the course of negotiation, and with reference to the subject matter of the contract. If his error is proved to have been so induced, the fact that the misleading representations were made in good faith affords no defence."[68]

6–28 It follows that a person who is induced to enter a contract as a result of a misleading statement by the other party has the right to be relieved of his obligations under the contract.

Examples:

(1) Alasdair buys Amy's car on the faith of an assurance that the car possesses an MOT certificate. Amy's statement in this regard turns out to be false. Alasdair is entitled to return the car and receive back the purchase price.

(2) Cameron arranges for Donald to install new wiring in his house. Cameron chose Donald because Donald told him that he was a qualified electrician and that he could arrange finance for Cameron. Both statements are false. Cameron can withdraw from the contract.

The statement that constitutes the misrepresentation

6–29 To be relevant, a misrepresentation must be material and made in the course of negotiations. A trivial statement, for example, cannot be relied upon. Moreover, the misrepresentation must be an inaccurate statement of fact and not simply an expression of future intent or opinion. In one case, a seller stated that a farm would carry so many head of sheep.[69] The purchaser knew that the farm had never been used for sheep before. The statement was held not to amount to a misrepresentation. It was merely an expression of the seller's opinion which a reasonable buyer would not have relied upon. But a deliberately false statement of opinion is a representation of fact. "Trade puffs" are allowed a degree of latitude. Reasonable people are not expected to place too much reliance on the material to be found in advertisements. No one should really expect a new brand of shampoo to improve their social life. Accordingly, literature which might fairly be termed "misleading" does not allow a consumer to set aside the contract. The Consumer Protection from Unfair Trading Regulations 2008 (SI 2008/1277) (as amended) and independent advertising watchdogs such as the Advertising Standards Authority provide certain sanctions in the event of serious misdescriptions.

---

[68] *Menzies v Menzies* (1893) 20 R. (HL) 108 at 142, 143.
[69] *Bisset v Wilkinson* [1927] A.C. 177.

Reliance

The misrepresentation must be relied upon by the innocent party. If a **6–30** purchaser carries out his own inspection and valuation of an antique table, he cannot set aside the contract for misrepresentation based upon the seller's brief description if the table turns out to be a reproduction.[70]

Normally there is no duty of disclosure in contract, so silence cannot constitute a misrepresentation. But silence may amount to mis-representation in a number of situations, of which the most important class is contracts uberrimae fidei (of utmost good faith), such as insurance contracts. Here, there is a duty to disclose all material facts. An illus-tration is provided by *The Spathari*[71]:

A vessel was registered and insured in the name of a British subject. It sank in calm waters and a claim was made under the insurance policy. The insurance company then discovered that the true owner was a Greek subject. The company refused to pay out on the policy. It was held that the company were entitled to do so. At the time, Greek ships were vir-tually uninsurable because they had bad risk records. Accordingly, the nationality of the owner was material. As it had not been disclosed, there had been a misrepresentation which rendered the contract voidable.

Other situations where silence may amount to misrepresentation occur where: (a) the parties are in a fiduciary relationship, for example parent and child, trustee and beneficiary, solicitor and client; (b) where a statement, true when made, is falsified by circumstances; and (c) where there is a half-truth that has not been completed. Half-truths can include actions. For example, where an antique furniture showroom places a reproduction piece amongst originals, this will create a misleading impression. The furniture showroom is obliged to make it clear which pieces of furniture are reproductions.[72]

By whom the misrepresentation is made

A contract cannot be challenged by the innocent party unless the mis- **6–31** representation in question was made by or on behalf of the other con-tracting party.[73]

The degree of misapprehension produced

How serious must the misapprehension be? Lord Carmont has provided **6–32** probably the most accurate statement of the present law:

"It appears clear that Scots law recognises ... that when mis-representation by a party is alleged inducing error in the other in regard to some matter, that matter need not be an essential of the contract, *but it must be material and of such a nature that not only the*

---

[70] *Lyon & Turnbull v Sabine* [2012] CSOH 178.
[71] *Demetriades & Co v Northern Assurance Co Ltd (The Spathari)*, 1925 S.C. (HL) 6.
[72] For a similar case, see *Patterson v Landsberg* (1905) 7 F. 675.
[73] *Universal Import Export GmbH v Bank of Scotland*, 1995 S.C. 73; 1995 S.L.T. 1318.

contracting party but any reasonable man might be moved to enter into the contract; or put the other way, if the misrepresentation had not been made, would have refrained from entering into the contract."[74]

In other words, the court is directed to look at the reasons why the person was induced to enter the contract. If they are material and pass the 'reasonable man' test then the contract can be set aside.

Remedies for misrepresentation

6–33 The remedies open to a person depend upon whether the misrepresentation is fraudulent, negligent or innocent.[75] If the misrepresentation is innocent, the only remedy is to set aside the contract. But if negligence or fraud is present, damages may also be recovered.

6–34 **(a) Fraudulent misrepresentation.** Fraud is a "machination or contrivance to deceive."[76] Since the end of the nineteenth century, a statement has been regarded as fraudulent if (a) the maker of the statement was aware that his representations were untrue; or (b) he made them recklessly, without knowing or caring whether they were true or not. The second proposition was established in the case of *Derry v Peek*[77]:

> The directors of the Plymouth Devonport and District Tramways company issued a prospectus which stated that the company had the right to use steam power in its trams. The plaintiff bought shares in the company on the strength of this statement. In fact the company was only entitled to use steam power if it was issued with an appropriate certificate by the Board of Trade. The certificate was refused. It was held that the plaintiff could not succeed in his action of damages for fraud. The directors had made the statement in the honest belief that it was true.

This decision changed the law. Until that point, almost any statement which turned out to be untrue and induced a person to enter a contract grounded an action for fraud. In effect the decision in *Derry* raised the standard for civil fraud to that of criminal fraud. Damages became much more difficult to recover. It has been suggested that the judges were swayed in arriving at their decision by the argument that to call a man "fraudulent" was tantamount to expelling him from polite society. As the judges looked at the directors, all proper Victorian gentlemen, they had a marked reluctance to place such a stain on their reputations.

The actual effect of the decision in relation to directors' liability was

---

[74] *Ritchie v Glass*, 1936 S.L.T. 591 at 593, 594 (emphasis added).
[75] For a discussion on the anomaly caused by having both intentional and unintentional misrepresentation covered by this doctrine, and the relationship between intentional misrepresentation and fraud, see Dot Reid and Hector MacQueen, "Fraud or error: a thought experiment?" (2013) Edin. L.R. 343.
[76] Erskine, III, 1, 16.
[77] *Derry v Peek* (1889) 44 App.Cas. 337.

overturned by statute. But its general importance as a test of fraud remains undiminished. In the Scottish case of *Boyd & Forrest v Glasgow & South Western Railway Co*,[78] which occurred shortly after *Derry*, it was held that contractors who had built a railway line could not recover damages against the railway company in respect of wrong information which the latter had given. This was because the employee who had furnished the information had altered it honestly but mistakenly, so he could not be guilty of fraud.

(b) Negligent misrepresentation. A misrepresentation is negligent if the **6–35** person failed to take reasonable care in making the representation and was in the circumstances under a duty to do so. This category originated in a dissenting judgment of Lord Denning MR in a case from 1951.[79] The House of Lords adopted his view in *Hedley Byrne & Co Ltd v Heller & Partners Ltd*, where a bank gave information regarding the creditworthiness of one of its customers.[80] When it was found that the information was incorrect and the bank had not exercised sufficient care in assessing the situation, it was held they could be liable to the person who had requested the information. These cases were concerned with non-contractual situations. The law has continued to develop in that field and is not considered here.

Originally negligent misrepresentation did not apply to contracts. The theory was that during negotiations, each party must rely on his own means of information. Being at arm's length meant that neither owed the other a duty of care. A false statement would allow one party to withdraw from the contract, but it would not afford a ground an action for damages unless there was fraud. However, the concept of negligent misrepresentation was extended to pre-contractual negotiations in England in *Esso Petroleum Co Ltd v Mardon*.[81] There an oil company was held liable in respect of statements made to a prospective tenant of a petrol filling station. An employee of the company with many years' experience had misled the tenant regarding the volume of petrol that the station could expect to sell. The effect of that decision was to extend the right to recover damages to a situation where one party had special skill or knowledge and the other party was reasonably entitled to rely on that knowledge, which turned out to be false.[82]

There are two recent Scottish decisions on negligent misrepresentation: **6–36** *Hamilton v Allied Domecq Plc*[83] and *Cramaso LLP v Ogilvie-Grant, Earl of Seafield*.[84]

In the first case, the parties entered into an agreement with for the distribution of bottled mineral water under the name "Gleneagles". The

---

[78] *Boyd & Forrest (A Firm) v Glasgow & South Western Railway Co*, 1912 S.C. (HL) 93.
[79] *Candler v Crane Christmas & Co* [1951] 2 K.B. 164.
[80] *Hedley Byrne & Co Ltd v Heller & Partners Ltd* [1964] A.C. 465.
[81] *Esso Petroleum Co Ltd v Mardon* [1976] Q.B. 801.
[82] Recently applied by the Supreme Court in the Scottish case of *Cramaso LLP v Ogilvie-Grant, Earl of Seafield* [2014] UKSC 9.
[83] *Hamilton v Allied Domecq Plc* [2007] UKHL 33.
[84] *Cramaso LLP v Ogilvie-Grant, Earl of Seafield* [2014] UKSC 9.

venture was not a success and the business was put into administration. Hamilton's shareholding was virtually worthless. He alleged that the business failed because Allied Domecq did not market the water through the on-trade (in hotels and restaurants). Instead, it initially distributed the water only through the off-trade (in supermarkets and off-licences). He claimed that Allied Domecq's representatives had told him that they would distribute the water to both markets simultaneously.

The House of Lords decided that this was a commercial agreement at arm's length and that there was no duty of disclosure. The misrepresentation would have to be created through an active misstatement of fact, rather than through silence. On the evidence, there was nothing which Allied Domecq had said which would amount to a misrepresentation.

In contrast, negligent misrepresentation was established in *Cramaso LLP v Ogilvie-Grant, Earl of Seafield*. Here, agents for the Earl of Seafield sent an email to Mr Erskine, estimating the grouse population of a moor. This information was relevant to Mr Erskine when deciding whether he wished to lease the moor for commercial purposes. On the basis of the figures given in the email, Mr Erskine decided to proceed. He then incorporated a limited liability partnership, Cramaso, which entered into the lease. Only after the lease was concluded did Mr Erskine discover that these grouse population figures were inaccurate, and the lease would therefore be less profitable than expected. Mr Erskine alleged that the agents of the Earl of Seafield had deliberately misled him.

One question was whether the misrepresentation could be operative when it was addressed in an email to Mr Erskine, yet the lease was concluded by Cramaso LLP—a legal entity which was not even in existence at the date the misleading email was sent. The Supreme Court held that a negligent misrepresentation is capable of having a continuing effect from when it is made until the contract is concluded.[85] In this case, the change in the identity of the contracting party did not affect the continuing responsibility of the agents' for its accuracy. When Mr Erskine incorporated Cramaso LLP as the vehicle to enter the lease, neither party drew a line under the previous discussions or disclaimed previous statements. Cramaso was therefore entitled to rely on the negligent misrepresentation made to Mr Erskine.

Where negligent misrepresentation is established, damages are recoverable under Scots law.[86]

6–37 **(c) Innocent misrepresentation.** Here the representation, although inaccurate, is made with the honest belief that it is true. The only remedy is to reduce the contract. There is no additional right to damages.

---

[85] *Cramaso LLP v Ogilvie-Grant, Earl of Seafield* [2014] UKSC 9, per Lord Reed at 23.
[86] Law Reform (Miscellaneous Provisions) (Scotland) Act 1985 s.10.

Misrepresentation or a term of the contract?

A statement which is made during the course of negotiations leading up **6–38** to the contract may: (1) have no legal effect; (2) amount to a misrepresentation; or (3) be a term of the contract. Whether a pre-contractual statement has legal force or not is largely a question of intention and reliance. Was it sought to induce the other party to enter the contract by means of the statement? Was it intended and understood that it should become a term of the contract?

Statements in advertisements usually have no legal effect because reasonable persons know they are exaggerated to "puff up" the product. By contrast, in many contracts for the sale of goods, statute decrees that there is a term in the contract that the goods are of satisfactory quality. Difficulties arise in cases which fall between these positions. Usually the buyer will wish to argue that the statement on which he founds his claim is a term of the contract. This is because it is easier to prove breach of contract than misrepresentation. Moreover in a breach of contract case, damages can be recovered even though fraud or negligence is not proved.

The flowchart on p.88 provides a short summary of the key questions to be addressed when considering questions of error.

Alternative analyses of error

As error is a complex area, there are alternative ways of analysing the **6–39** situation where a contract is challenged as a result of a mistake. Three different analyses are set out below.

Implied terms and personal bar. Because the doctrine of error is so com- **6–40** plex, the courts sometimes prefer to apply various other principles in order to resolve error-type situations. As well as the two already mentioned—of offer and acceptance and passing of risk—there are two other important techniques: implied terms and personal bar. The use of implied terms converts a problem of error into a breach of contract question.

> *Example*: A person buys a pair of shoes which fall apart after two weeks' light wear. Clearly it would be possible to say that the person seeks redress because he bought the shoes under mistake—he thought they would be hard-wearing. However, such cases are invariably treated as a question of breach of the implied term of satisfactory quality under the Sale of Goods Act 1979.

The second technique is personal bar. Where performance follows on from an agreement alleged to be defective, the subsequent actions of the parties may prove decisive in determining whether the parties are bound or not. In *Morrison-Low v Paterson*, both parties believed that the defenders had inherited the tenancy of an agricultural lease.[87] This belief

---

[87] *Morrison-Low v Paterson*, 1985 S.L.T. 255.

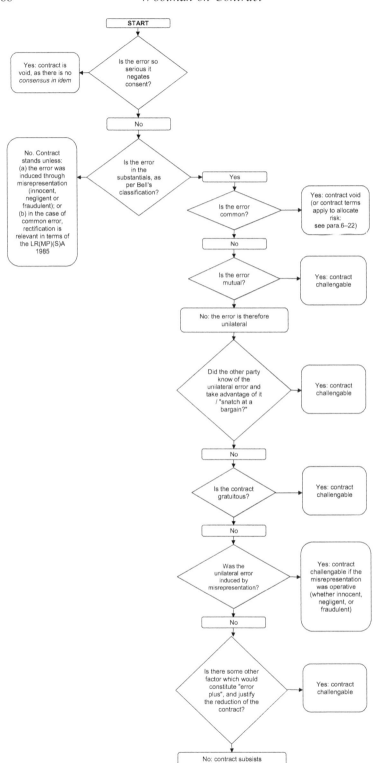

arose because the solicitor, who had acted for both parties, told them that this was the position. The House of Lords accepted that the tenancy had not been validly transferred. Both parties were therefore mistaken as to their legal position. Nevertheless the subsequent actions of the parties, which involved inter alia the defenders remaining in occupation and paying rent for six years, were only explicable on the footing that a new agreement had been entered into. Accordingly, the House of Lords held that despite the error there was a contract of lease and the landlord's action of removing must fail. He was personally barred from founding on the error.[88]

Error in motive and error in transaction. A further doctrine of error dis- **6–41** tinguishes between error in motive and error in transaction.[89] An uninduced error in *motive* (such as the mistaken belief that the party would make a profit) would be irrelevant. An error in *transaction* (such as the mistaken belief that the price is £1,000 rather than $1,000) would be relevant, but only if it relates to the substantials. Although this analysis was discussed by the Scottish Law Commission in 1978, it has not found its way into widespread use. It is arguably flawed since:

"... there may be an error in motive in many cases of error in transaction and it is very doubtful if the distinction is useful. The problem remains of the meaning and effect of error in transaction."[90]

Good faith in contract: failure to give advice

This basis of challenge to a contract arose out of *Smith v Bank of Scot-* **6–42** *land*,[91] which was a "conscious extension"[92] of Scots law in relation to good faith:

The pursuer, Mrs Smith, sought to challenge a contract she had entered into in favour of the bank. In particular, she sought to reduce a standard security she had granted over her half share of the matrimonial home. She had granted the security to the bank in respect of sums borrowed by a firm in which her husband was a partner. She argued that the security was invalid because she had been induced to sign it as a result of misrepresentations made by her husband.[93]

---

[88] The operation of personal bar to prevent the pursuer from walking away from the contract was recently discussed in *Wills v Strategic Procurement (UK) Limited* [2013] CSOH 26, per Lord Malcolm at [1] and [17].
[89] See Scottish Law Commission, *Defective Consent and Consequential Matters* (HMSO, 1978), Scot. Law Com. Memo. No.42, Vol.II, paras 3.45–3.47.
[90] William W. McBryde, *The Law of Contract in Scotland*, 3rd edn (Edinburgh: SULI/W. Green, 2007), para.15–21.
[91] *Smith v Bank of Scotland*, 1997 S.C. (HL) 111; 1997 S.L.T. 1061.
[92] *Clydesdale Bank Plc v Black*, 2002 S.C. 555, per Lord Coulsfield at [32].
[93] In this case, she had actually signed the document: if her signature had been forged, however, then different remedies would apply: *Cooper v Bank of Scotland* [2014] CSOH 16, per Lord Tyre at [29].

The House of Lords held that the security was invalid but not on the basis argued by Mrs Smith. Any misrepresentations had been made by Mrs Smith's husband and could not be said to have been made on behalf of the bank. The House of Lords then considered an English case in which a guarantee obligation given in similar circumstances had been declared to be invalid.[94] The basis for that decision was that, in the circumstances, the bank were deemed to have notice of the wrongful acts committed by the husband in order to obtain his wife's consent to the obligation.

Mrs Smith's challenge did not succeed on that basis either. Instead it was held that there was a duty on the bank to advise Mrs Smith as to the consequences of her actions and recommend that she take independent legal advice. This duty arose because the circumstances were such that the bank might reasonably have suspected that, as a result of the relationship between Mrs Smith and Mr Smith, her consent was not properly given. In the circumstances, the bank should have warned Mrs Smith of the possible consequences of the transaction and told her to get independent advice. That warning was necessary to ensure that the bank remained in good faith.

The duty referred to in *Smith* arose because of the element of good faith required of the creditor in a transaction where one party undertakes to pay the debts of another in the event that the other party defaults.[95] It was noted that there was a broad principle in the law of contract of dealing in good faith. Although this principle of good faith is of general application, it is likely that a duty to warn a party to take independent advice will be found to exist only in circumstances similar to those in *Smith*. In particular, the pursuer must show that the obligation to be set aside was undertaken gratuitously.[96] Where the pursuer derives some personal benefit from the obligation, such as being joint recipient of the loan granted by the bank, then this challenge is not available.

Following *Smith*, the House of Lords considered the obligation on the lender in another English case, *Royal Bank of Scotland Plc v Etridge (No.2)*.[97] This provided clearer guidance to banks in England as to what was required to comply with the duty to give advice. The lender has to be able to show that the risks were "brought home" to the guarantor. However, the Inner House has rejected this test and the more precise requirements set out in *O'Brien* and *Etridge*.[98] Instead, the test in Scotland remains that as set out in *Smith*, which requires the lender to warn the guarantor of the potential consequences of entering the agreement and advise him to take independent legal advice. The warning must be expressly done: a letter "in bland terms" which "conveys an impression

---

[94] *Barclays Bank Plc v O'Brien* [1994] 1 A.C. 180.
[95] The obligation where one party guarantees the debts of another is known in Scotland as caution.
[96] *Royal Bank of Scotland v Wilson*, 2004 S.C. 153; *Cooper v Bank of Scotland* [2014] CSOH 16, per Lord Tyre at [22].
[97] *Royal Bank of Scotland Plc v Etridge (No.2)* [2001] UKHL 44.
[98] *Clydesdale Bank Plc v Black*, 2002 S.C. 555, per Lord Coulsfield at [31], with reference to the House of Lords decisions in *Etridge* and *Smith*.

that the execution of the security is something of a formality" will not be sufficient to discharge the bank's obligation.[99]

CHAPTER 7

TERMS OF THE CONTRACT

7–01 The previous chapters examined the legal principles which are used to decide whether a valid and enforceable contract exists. Once a contract exists the next requirement is to determine the rights and obligations that the parties have. Clearly, these depend on the terms of the contract.

7–02 The terms of the contract may be express or implied. Express terms are those that the parties are deemed to have agreed upon and made part of their contract. Other terms may be incorporated by reference, notice or a course of dealing. There are flexible rules that provide guidance on these matters. Even with flexibility, however, it would be unrealistic to assume that in every contract all the terms will be fully agreed by the parties. Where an important term is missing, it can be implied into the contract by the courts. Further rules are needed to determine how terms may be implied into contracts.

Once the contract terms are identified, the parties may be in dispute as to what they mean or how they should be applied to the situation that confronts them. Yet more rules are required to interpret the agreed terms to translate them into practical rights and obligations. Finally, when the contract is interpreted there may be an argument that there has been a mistake in the wording of the contract so that it does not reflect what the parties had agreed. Courts have a limited power to rectify contracts when this situation occurs and it is necessary to consider whether that is justified. Chapter 8 will consider issues of interpretation and rectification.

7–03 The purpose of this chapter is to consider the rules that determine the terms of the contract. The overriding principle is the intention of the parties. Again, this is subject to the qualification that the intention is to be determined objectively, by asking:

> "... what the reasonable person (who sometimes appears, in this context, in the dubious guise of the officious bystander), would understand the parties to have intended to be the terms of their contract."[1]

---

[1] *Credential Bath Street Ltd v Venture Investment Placement Ltd* [2007] CSOH 208, per Lord Reed at [55].

EXPRESS TERMS

As had already been noted, the range of situations in which a contract **7–04** may be concluded is huge. At one end of the spectrum the parties may negotiate the terms of a written agreement for months prior to signing it. At the other end, there are everyday contracts which may be concluded with little or no exchange of words. In any situation it is necessary to determine what terms form part of the contract.

Written contracts

Where the contract is contained in a formal written agreement or in other **7–05** written communications passing between the parties, the starting point is those documents. However, they may not tell the whole story. It may be that other agreements were made between the parties at the same time and these have a bearing on the express terms.

> *Example*: Contractors building an office development enter into a written contract with a supplier for delivery of 50 tonnes of cement. The contract contains a standard clause that all terms of the contract are to be found within the written document. At the completion meeting, where the written contract is signed, both parties agree that, if it turns out that the development requires only 45 tonnes, the contractors will not be required to take the full 50 tonnes.

The issue that arises here is whether it is possible to rely on the agreement made orally to override the apparently clear terms of the written agreement. The Contract (Scotland) Act 1997 ("the 1997 Act") provides that if there is a term in the contract documents to the effect that they comprise all the express terms of the contract then such a term shall be conclusive of the matter.[2] In our example, the oral agreement could not contradict the written agreement. If there is no such clause, the rule is that where the contract documents *appear* to comprise all the express terms of a contract, then it shall be presumed that this is so.[3] The presumption can be rebutted. The existence of additional express terms may be proved by either further documents or oral evidence given by the parties.[4] The additional terms may be either written or oral.

Verbal contracts

Where there is no formal (i.e. signed) written agreement, the starting **7–06** point will be to consider the words exchanged between the parties prior to the contract being concluded. These may be contained in written communications such as letters and emails, or may have been spoken by the parties in meetings and telephone calls. The rules as to offer and

---

[2] 1997 Act s.1(3). This section does not prevent terms from being implied. Implied terms are considered in more detail below.
[3] 1997 Act s.1(1).
[4] 1997 Act s.1(2).

acceptance may be used to identify which written and oral communications form the contract and therefore contribute to its terms. Where there has been an ongoing dialogue between the parties, it is particularly important to identify the point when the contract was concluded. Once the contract is concluded its terms are fixed.[5] The terms will remain as they were when the contract was concluded, unless the parties agree to vary them or to make a new contract. A party to a concluded contract may not unilaterally alter or add to its terms. An illustration is provided by *Thornton v Shoe Lane Parking Ltd*[6]:

> The owners of a carpark attempted to exclude liability not only for damage to property but also for personal injury to those parking their cars on the premises. The clause to that effect appeared on a ticket issued by an automatic machine at the entrance to the carpark and on a notice inside the carpark. The court considered that the term was not part of the contract. Once the customer took his ticket from the machine as he entered the car park the contract was formed. Thereafter it was too late to introduce additional terms.

Incorporation of terms

7–07 Irrespective of the means by which the contract was concluded, terms may be incorporated either directly or by reference, rather than being spelled out in the contract. For example, when sending out a quotation for work to be done to repair a car, a garage will often indicate that their standard terms and conditions will apply if the offer is accepted. Similarly, tickets for travel will often indicate on their face that they are issued subject to the terms and conditions of the carrier. Where this is done, questions may arise as to whether the terms have validly been incorporated into a contract. One general rule is that the more unusual the term is, the more must be done to draw it to the other party's attention:

> "If there is some condition which is of particular importance, in the sense of departing in a material way from the terms usually incorporated into that type of contract, then, by a parity of reasoning, the recipient of the document should not only be made aware that the document contains contractual terms but should have his attention drawn to that condition. This has been described in the cases as applying to unusual, onerous, exorbitant or draconian conditions, but I do not think that anything turns on the epithet. The important characteristic is that the condition departs in a material way from the terms which would reasonably be expected to apply to that type of contract."[7]

[5] See for example *Baillie Estates Ltd v Du Pont (UK) Ltd* [2009] CSIH 95.
[6] *Thornton v Shoe Lane Parking Ltd* [1971] 2 Q.B. 163.
[7] *Langstane Housing Association Ltd v Riverside Construction (Aberdeen) Ltd* [2009] CSOH 52, per Lord Glennie at [41].

This has been applied in a wide range of situations, although there is some doubt as to whether it applies at all (or at any rate with equal force) where written terms and conditions have been signed by the parties.[8]

There are a number of ways in which terms can be incorporated into a contract: by signature; by express assent; by notice; and by a course of dealing. These rules are summarised below and are shown in the diagram on p.96.

Incorporation by signature

Where a document has been signed and it contains either terms or a clear **7–08** reference to terms in another document, those terms will form part of the contract. By signing a document a person is deemed to have assented to its terms and consequently to be bound by it.

> "[W]here an action is brought on a written agreement which is signed by the defendant, the agreement is proved by proving his signature and, in the absence of fraud, it is wholly immaterial that he has not read the agreement and does not know its contents."[9]

This principle is capable of covering situations in which an agreement (either negotiated by the parties or pre-printed) is signed by the parties or where there has been an exchange of correspondence. In the latter situation the letter of acceptance which is signed will incorporate all the terms of the contract. The principle holds even where the clause in question is in "legible, but regrettably small print".[10] It does not apply where the writing is illegible, or where the effect of the clause has been misrepresented. This rule may operate particularly harshly where one party is required to sign a pre-printed contract prepared by the other party.[11] Dissatisfaction with this rule has frequently been expressed:

> "If it were possible for your Lordships to escape from the world of make-believe which the law has created into the real world in which transactions of this sort are actually done, the answer would be short and simple. It [signature] should make no difference whatsoever. This document is not meant to be read, still less to be understood. Its signature is in truth about as significant as a handshake that marks the formal conclusion of a bargain."[12]

There is force in this observation. Even contract lawyers are unlikely to **7–09** pore over the fine print of every holiday booking terms and conditions, car hire document and receipt which they sign (or click to accept online). Like Homer, their heads may nod. Perhaps in recognition of that fact, it

---

[8] *Langstane Housing Association Ltd v Riverside Construction (Aberdeen) Ltd* [2009] CSOH 52 at [30], [42], with authorities cited therein.
[9] *Parker v South Eastern Railway Co* (1877) 2 C.P.D. 416, per Mellish L.J. at 421.
[10] *L'Estrange v F Graucob Ltd* [1934] 2 K.B. 394.
[11] Measures to prevent the unfairness that may result are considered in Ch.9.
[12] *McCutcheon v David MacBrayne Ltd*, 1964 S.C. (HL) 28, per Lord Devlin at 39, 40.

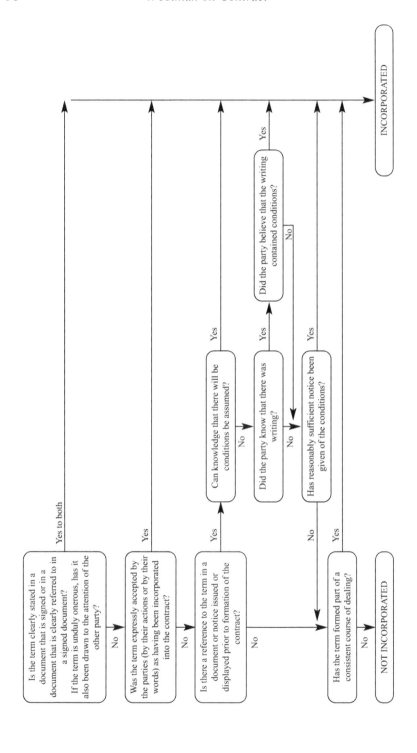

Is the term clearly stated in a document that is signed or in a document that is clearly referred to in a signed document? If the term is unduly onerous, has it also been drawn to the attention of the other party? — **Yes to both** → INCORPORATED

No ↓

Was the term expressly accepted by the parties (by their actions or by their words) as having been incorporated into the contract? — **Yes** → INCORPORATED

No ↓

Is there a reference to the term in a document or notice issued or displayed prior to formation of the contract? — **Yes** → Can knowledge that there will be conditions be assumed? — **Yes** → INCORPORATED

No ↓   No ↓

                                                        Did the party know that there was writing? — **Yes** → Did the party believe that the writing contained conditions? — **Yes** → INCORPORATED

                                                        No ↓   No ↓

                                                        Has reasonably sufficient notice been given of the conditions? — **Yes** → INCORPORATED

                                                        No ↓

Has the term formed part of a consistent course of dealing? — **Yes** → INCORPORATED

No ↓

NOT INCORPORATED

has been held that a signature may not suffice where a clause is so unusual and onerous that the party offering the term ought to have drawn it to the attention of the other party. In *Montgomery Litho Ltd v Maxwell*[13]:

> Maxwell was a director of a company. He signed an agreement for the supply of printing services to that company, and the contract was clearly between the printers and Maxwell's company. Nevertheless, when his company went into liquidation the printers sought to recover sums owing to them from Maxwell personally. They relied on the fact that Maxwell had signed a credit application on behalf of his company which said that he had read the printers' standard terms and conditions. There was a clause in those conditions to the effect that the director of a company was liable along with the company for any amount owing to the printers.

The Inner House considered Maxwell was not liable, since the clause purportedly imposing liability had not been properly drawn to his attention. In particular, he had not been given "fair notice" that the contract imposed liability on him personally, rather than solely on his company. They considered the English case of *Interfoto Picture Library Ltd v Stiletto Visual Programmes Ltd*[14] and concluded:

> "... we see no reason to doubt that the general principle on which they ... proceeded, viz that the failure by a *proferens* fairly to draw attention to a particularly onerous and unusual provision may disable him from effectually founding on it, represents also the law of Scotland."[15]

The clause was both onerous and unusual, and the pursuers were therefore not entitled to rely upon it, since it had not been brought to Maxwell's notice.

This is arguably a bold innovation in applying the test of reasonable notice even where a contract has been signed. The decision in *Interfoto* was concerned with the quite different situation in which the term was contained in a document that had not been signed. That decision and the tests of reasonable notice in such a situation are considered below. Nonetheless, in the decade since *Montgomery Litho*, it has not been expressly overturned and has been cited in a number of other decisions.[16] One Inner House case has, however, distinguished *Montgomery Litho* and emphasised the importance of construing that case within its facts. In *Brandon Hire plc v Russell*,[17] the pursuers sought to recover sums due

---

[13] *Montgomery Litho Ltd v Maxwell*, 1999 S.L.T. 1431.
[14] *Interfoto Picture Library Ltd v Stiletto Visual Programmes Ltd* [1989] Q.B. 433; [1988] 2 W.L.R. 615; [1988] 1 All E.R. 348.
[15] *Montgomery Litho Ltd v Maxwell*, 1999 S.L.T. 1431.
[16] Including *Crimin v Cairnbay Ltd* [2004] CSOH 157; *Langstane Housing Association Ltd v Riverside Construction (Aberdeen) Ltd* [2009] CSOH 52.
[17] *Brandon Hire plc v Russell* [2010] CSIH 76.

from the director of a defaulting company. The director, Mr Russell, contested his liability. However, the Inner House upheld the terms of the contract. Even though Mr Russell was not a party to the contract, he had signed directly below the wording which made him personally liable, and this wording was clear.

Incorporation by express assent

7–10 Where no document is actually signed, one party may, at the time of contracting, point out an exemption clause and say: "I am contracting on the basis of this term being part of our contract, do you agree?" Following the signature principle, the term will be held to be part of the contract if the other party does expressly agree. If the agreement to be bound by the term is not clear, it may be necessary to consider whether the term has been incorporated by notice.

Incorporation by express consent may prove to be particularly useful in relation to online contracts. Where a notice on a website is brought to the attention of the customer and he clicks on an "I agree" box, this would appear to amount to an express assent to that term being part of the contract.

Incorporation by notice

7–11 A party seeking to incorporate a term may rely upon a notice. Many terms incorporated in this way have the intention of restricting the liability of the contracting party providing goods or services. The notice may itself contain the term, such as those one sees on dry cleaners' counters. Alternatively it may refer to another document which actually contains the term. Bus tickets often refer to terms and conditions of carriage which are printed elsewhere. These notices may be used in situations where there is no writing to constitute the contract and little if any oral exchange. Over the years the courts have had to consider the question of incorporation in relation to such notices many times. In answering the question whether such a reference is effective the courts have had regard to the nature of the document in which the reference is made. The issue is whether the document containing the reference is a core element of the contract and might therefore reasonably have been expected to contain contract terms. For example, in *Thompson v London Midland & Scottish Railway Co*[18]:

> Mrs Thompson had sustained injuries as a result of the railway company's negligence. It was held that the railway company had incorporated an exemption clause into the contract. This was despite the following: Mrs Thompson could not read; the ticket had been bought for her by her niece; and the relevant exemption clause referred to in the ticket was contained on p.552 of a separate timetable which itself cost 6d. Lord Hamworth M.R. based his decision

---

[18] *Thompson v London Midland & Scottish Railway Co* [1930] 1 K.B. 41.

on the fact that the contract in question was a contract of carriage in which the ticket was required to get on to the platform and thence the train. The issue of a railway ticket accordingly ought to indicate to a reasonable person that there were conditions to be found upon it. This could be distinguished from a contract of deposit where no written document was required where the customer would treat the ticket as a mere voucher.

A similar distinction between reference in a mere voucher and reference **7–12** in a document fundamental to the contract was made in *Taylor v Glasgow Corp*[19]:

> Mrs Taylor went weekly for a hot bath to her local public baths in Glasgow. On one such occasion she fell down a stair and suffered serious injury. The corporation sought to rely on an exemption clause. This clause appeared on the ticket with which all bathers were issued when they entered the building and paid the price for the facility they sought. On the front of the ticket it said, "For conditions see other side" and on the reverse were words to the effect that the corporation accepted no liability for an injury which was caused to anyone using the establishment.

Lord Justice-Clerk Thomson said that the ticket performed the following functions: (a) it was a domestic check on the running of the establishment; (b) it was a receipt for the price; and (c) it was a voucher, indicating what facility had been paid for. He regarded the voucher aspect as the significant one. A person would not regard a voucher as containing contractual conditions, unlike a railway ticket where it was accepted that the ticket was a contractual document. Glasgow Corporation were therefore liable to Mrs Taylor, since they had failed to incorporate their exclusion clause into the contract.

Where the reference is in a document which would *not* be expected to **7–13** contain terms of the contract, the court will examine whether the party knew there was writing that contained conditions or, if they did not, whether enough had been done to bring the reference to the term to their attention. In the English case of *Parker v South Eastern Railway Co*[20]:

> Mr Parker deposited a bag worth £24 10s. in a railway cloakroom. He was charged 2d. and received in return for his money a ticket which bore on its face the opening hours of the cloakroom and the words "see back." On the reverse it stated that the company would not be responsible for any bag worth more than £10. A notice to the same effect hung in the cloakroom. Although Mr Parker admitted that he knew there was writing on the ticket he denied that he had read either it or the notice. He said that he imagined that the ticket was a receipt for the bag.

---

[19] *Taylor v Glasgow Corp*, 1952 S.C. 440.
[20] *Parker v South Eastern Railway Co* (1877) 2 C.P.D. 416.

By a majority, the court held that if the plaintiff knew that there was writing and also knew that it was the other party's intention that these constituted terms of the contract he would be bound. But if he had not read the term, nor knew that the intention was to constitute contractual terms, then the correct question to ask was, "whether the railway company did what was reasonably sufficient to give the plaintiff notice of the condition."[21] The point is illustrated by *Taylor v Glasgow Corp.*[22] Mrs Taylor said that she knew there was writing on the ticket but not that it referred to contractual terms. It was held that the corporation had not sufficiently brought the clause to Mrs Taylor's notice. The term was therefore not incorporated into the contract.

7–14   What is meant by reasonable notice? In deciding this, a court will consider the nature of the term that is to be incorporated. In *Thornton v Shoe Lane Parking Ltd,*[23] the term in dispute excluded liability of car park owners for damage to property and personal injury. As noted above, the attempt to have a notice on the ticket issued by the car parking machine came too late. In relation to the notice on a board inside the car park the Court of Appeal held that no reasonable notice of the clause had been given. To see the notice the customer would have to leave his car at the entrance and enter the carpark. No one was likely to follow this course of action. Lord Denning M.R. suggested that to exempt liability for personal injury as well as damage to property the notice would have to be "in red ink with a red hand pointing to it—or something equally startling".[24] Because the term was so onerous, and so destructive of the rights of the other party, the party seeking to rely upon it would have had to have taken significant steps to draw it to the other party's attention. The approach which underlies Lord Denning's view has been accepted by other judges in the Court of Appeal. In the case of *Interfoto Picture Library Ltd v Stiletto Visual Programmes Ltd*[25] referred to above in relation to incorporation by signature:

> The defendants asked the plaintiffs whether they had photographs that would be of use to them in preparing a presentation. The plaintiffs sent negatives to the defendants together with a set of terms that provided for a very high charge to be levied if the negatives were retained for more than 14 days. The defendants telephoned the plaintiffs acknowledging receipt of the negatives but not referring to the terms. The defendants said that they might be interested in using some of the images. The negatives were returned late. The plaintiffs sought to rely on the terms for payment of the late return sum. The terms were not contained in a signed document.

---

[21] *Parker v South Eastern Railway Co* (1877) 2 C.P.D. 416, per Mellish L.J. at 424.
[22] *Taylor v Glasgow Corp*, 1952 S.C. 440.
[23] *Thornton v Shoe Lane Parking Ltd* [1971] 2 Q.B. 163.
[24] *Thornton v Shoe Lane Parking Ltd* [1971] 2 Q.B. 163 at 170.
[25] *Interfoto Picture Library Ltd v Stiletto Visual Programmes Ltd* [1989] Q.B. 433; [1988] 2 W.L.R. 615; [1988] 1 All E.R. 348.

The court held that the claim failed as the term relating to payment for late return was not part of the contract. This was because the plaintiffs had not done enough to bring the term to the defendants' attention. The judges referred to the term as "very onerous" and "unreasonable and extortionate". Dillon L.J. concluded:

> "It is in my judgment a logical development of the common law into modern conditions that it should be held, as it was in *Thornton v Shoe Lane Parking Ltd*, that, if one condition in a set of printed conditions is particularly onerous or unusual, the party seeking to enforce it must show that that particular condition was fairly brought to the attention of the other party."[26]

In short the position appears to be that a term will only be incorporated by notice where the other party has had fair notice of that term.

These cases typically deal with the incorporation of exclusion or limitation clauses, by which the party providing goods or services attempts to limit its liability in the event of its default. This leads to potentially unfair results for the customer who has been harmed or suffered financial loss. In the absence of statutory protection, the courts attempted to protect the weaker parties by holding that the clause in question had not been incorporated into the contract. Many of these cases therefore have a strong policy element underlying the judicial reasoning. The majority of these cases were decided in the period prior to the enactment of the Unfair Contract Terms Act 1977. This legislation, which will be discussed in Ch.9, can be seen as a parliamentary response to the problem. Whereas the courts aimed to protect consumers by deeming terms not to have been incorporated, the 1977 Act renders unfair exclusion or limitation clauses unenforceable.

A final, and rather salutary, lesson about incorporation of terms and technology can be drawn from *CR Smith Glaziers (Dunfermline) Ltd v Toolcom Supplies Ltd*.[27] The front of the pursuer's order sheet contained a reference that the terms and conditions were printed on the back. However, the pursuers faxed through the order sheets without faxing the reverse side. Lady Clark had little trouble in concluding that the terms had not been incorporated and could not be relied upon.

Incorporation by a consistent course of dealing

Even though no notice is given, a person may nevertheless be bound by a **7–15** contractual clause because he knows of it as a result of a consistent course of dealing. In each case the question to be asked is whether or not the

---

[26] *Interfoto Picture Library Ltd v Stiletto Visual Programmes Ltd* [1988] 1 All E.R. 348 at 352.
[27] *CR Smith Glaziers (Dunfermline) Ltd v Toolcom Supplies Ltd* [2010] CSOH 7.

circumstances yield the inference that both parties proceeded on the basis that the exemption clause was a term of the contract.[28] The most famous case on this topic is *McCutcheon v David MacBrayne Ltd*[29]:

> The pursuer sought damages in respect of his car which had been lost when the defenders' ferry sank on a trip from Islay to Tarbert. His brother-in-law had arranged the shipment of the car and both men had transferred items on the ferry in the past. In principle the defenders required shippers to sign a risk note exempting them from liability, and the pursuer and his brother-in-law had sometimes, but not always, signed such a note. Inadvertently no such note had been signed on this occasion. Notices containing the exemption clause were also displayed in the defenders' office and on the pier but the pursuer had never read them.

The House of Lords first distinguished *Parker v South Eastern Railway Co* on the ground that there was no contractual document such as a ticket or receipt seeking to import conditions. Further as the notices had not been read they could not bind the pursuer. On the question of the prior dealings of the parties, the House held that while a consistent course of dealing could in principle bind the parties, there had been no consistent course here. The risk note had sometimes been signed, sometimes not. Since there was no consistency, the defenders had also failed to establish that the clause had been inserted on the basis of notice by means of consistent course of dealing. Mr McCutcheon was accordingly entitled to full compensation in respect of his car.

In *Tekdata Interconnections Ltd v Amphenol Ltd*, the Court of Appeal held that there must be a very clear course of dealings to incorporate a term into an otherwise complete contract. It will not be sufficient to point to a long-term relationship of itself, without further evidence.[30]

7–16   One Scottish case which discusses these principles is *WS Karoulias SA v Drambuie Liqueur Co Ltd*[31]:

> Here, the pursuer had acted as distributor for Drambuie products in Greece since at least 1977. The parties entered into written distributorship agreements to regulate their relationship, and the fourth of these agreements was due to expire in June 2003. Prior to its expiry, the parties negotiated and concluded a written agreement, but neither party signed it. When Karoulias attempted to enforce the written but unsigned agreement, Drambuie argued that the agreement was not binding. One reason they advanced for this was that

---

[28] *Continental Tyre & Rubber Co Ltd v Trunk Trailer Co Ltd*, 1987 S.L.T. 58; *William Teacher & Sons Ltd v Bell Lines Ltd*, 1991 S.L.T. 876.

[29] *McCutcheon v David MacBrayne Ltd*, 1964 S.C. (HL) 28.

[30] *Tekdata Interconnections Ltd v Amphenol Ltd* [2009] EWCA Civ 1209 at [21].

[31] *WS Karoulias SA v Drambuie Liqueur Co Ltd* [2005] CSOH 112.

there was a consistent course of dealings between the parties, which required their contracts to be in writing and signed. An unsigned agreement was therefore not binding.

Lord Clarke accepted this argument, stating:

"It is, therefore, clear to me that since 1990, at least, these parties chose to regulate their contractual arrangements with a significant degree of formality and did so on a consistent basis ... There was certainly nothing in the way that the parties had dealt with each other, in the past, to lead him to believe [on this occasion] that they would consider themselves bound before formal execution of the relevant agreement."[32]

On the basis of their prior dealings, there was no contract because there was no signature on the written document. The curious point about the case is that the consistent course of dealing was used to incorporate a term which effectively precluded contractual effect. That is in marked contrast to the usual type of case, such as *McCutcheon*, where the course of dealings incorporated a term into an already existing contract.

Another variation on this principle was successfully invoked in an **7–17** English case from 1975 where a crane was hired under an oral contract made by telephone.[33] Both the companies concerned were engaged in the business of hiring cranes and both used the standard industry conditions of contract when hiring out cranes. The standard conditions contained an exemption clause. Although there was not strictly a course of dealing between the parties, both ought to have reasonably assumed that the term in question would be part of the contract. Long usage of the term by both parties indicated that it was to be incorporated. A contrasting case is *Grayston Plant Ltd v Plean Precast Ltd.*[34] Over a period of four years there were 12 instances in which the pursuers followed up an oral contract by sending an "acknowledgement of order form" which referred to the general conditions upon which they traded. It was held that the general conditions were not incorporated into the contract because it could not be proved that the defenders were aware of the conditions.

IMPLIED TERMS

The parties can never provide for every contingency that may arise under **7–18** the contract. Accordingly, they will leave some terms to be implied. If it is a typical contract in a familiar context, few difficulties will arise. Over the years the incidents of these contracts have been fully worked out. Originally the courts were most willing to imply terms in contracts of

---

[32] *WS Karoulias SA v Drambuie Liqueur Co Ltd* [2005] CSOH 112 at [50].

[33] *British Crane Hire Corp Ltd v Ipswich Plant Hire Ltd* [1975] Q.B. 303; [1974] 1 All E.R. 1059.

[34] *Grayston Plant Ltd v Plean Precast Ltd*, 1976 S.C. 206.

everyday occurrence, such as sale, hire and lease. Implication would usually be based upon the custom which had grown up regarding such transactions. Many of these individual instances of implication of terms eventually found their way into statute. The contract of sale of goods provides the classic example of this process. By the end of the nineteenth century the implied terms of this contract had been so well worked out by judicial decisions that it was possible to codify the law. This was done by the Sale of Goods Act 1893. Over the years various amendments were made to the 1893 Act and the law was consolidated in the Sale of Goods Act 1979.

> *Example*: Fred paid £600 for a chair which was described on the seller's website as "a reclining chair". Shortly after taking delivery Fred discovers that the chair can only remain in a fixed position and cannot recline. In a sale by description there is an implied term that the goods correspond with that description.[35] Fred is entitled to return the chair to the seller and to recover his money.

In other instances implied terms have originated directly with Parliament rather than having been developed by the courts. Statutes may imply certain terms to give effect to some economic or social policy. For instance, the Consumer Contracts (Information, Cancellation and Additional Charges) Regulations 2013 (SI 2013/3134) require that each contract concluded at a distance carries a right of cancellation for the consumer.

7–19   In contracts of less common occurrence two general principles may be stated regarding implication of terms by the courts. First, no term will be implied which is directly contradictory to an express term.[36] Secondly, a term will more easily be implied in a oral than in a written and formal contract,[37] especially where the written contract has been the subject of lengthy negotiations, or both parties have been represented by lawyers in the negotiation and drafting of the contract.[38] Beyond those two principles it becomes more difficult to state the law with precision. The classic statement on this branch of contract law was made by Lord McLaren:

> "The conception of an implied condition is one with which we are familiar in relation to contracts of every description, and if we seek to trace any such implied conditions to their source it will be found in almost every instance that they are founded either on universal custom or in the nature of the contract itself. If the condition is such that every reasonable man on the one part would desire for his own protection to stipulate for the condition, and that no reasonable man

---

[35] Sale of Goods Act 1979 s.13.
[36] *Crawford v Bruce*, 1992 S.L.T. 524. Recently re-confirmed in *Morrish v NTL Group* [2007] CSIH 56.
[37] Gloag, *Contract*, 2nd edn, 1929, pp.288, 289. Approved in *Crawford v Bruce*, 1992 S.L.T. 524, per Lord President Hope at 531G.
[38] *Dear and Griffith v Jackson* [2013] EWCA Civ 89 at [30].

on the other would refuse to accede to it, then it is not unnatural that the condition should be taken for granted in all contracts of this class without the necessity of giving it formal expression."[39]

It is worth noting that in this passage, Lord McLaren flirts with two different bases for the implication of terms. The first basis is that of "universal custom or the nature of the contract itself". We have already seen that this applies perfectly to everyday contracts such as sale, hire or lease. It is assumed in such cases that the parties simply did not trouble to express the term. The passage goes on to discuss terms being implied by reference to the test of the "reasonable man". However, it should be noted that it is not suggested that the fact that a reasonable man would imply such a term is enough. The second part of Lord McLaren's dictum is still referring to terms that might be implied into certain *classes* of contract. It adds an additional test that no reasonable person on either side would refuse the term sought.[40]

7–20 Lord McLaren's approach has been approved and adopted in the Inner House.[41] In *Crawford v Bruce*, shop premises were leased for an initial period of 10 years.[42] It was provided that the rent should be reviewed every three years, but no mechanism was provided to determine how that rent should be assessed. The landlord contended that a term fell to be implied into the lease that the rent should be market rent at each three year review. The Inner House rejected this contention. Delivering the opinion of the court, Lord President Hope stated that:

> "The hypothesis on which we are asked to say the rent should be fixed is that the rent should be a market rent, and that the duration on the expiry of each three year period is to be the same as the initial duration of the lease. But both points could be said to be likely to operate to the disadvantage of the tenant, and it is far from clear that the hypothesis is one which satisfies the test which Lord McLaren described in *Morton & Co. v Muir Bros.*, namely that the implied condition is such that no reasonable man in the tenant's position would have refused to accede to it."[43]

By considering the matter from the position of the tenant, the court was able to reject the idea that a term fell to be implied. The second part of Lord McLaren's dictum was used to define a situation in which a term should not be implied.

7–21 Lord Hope (in the House of Lords) has recently applied Lord

---

[39] *William Morton & Co v Muir Bros & Co*, 1907 S.C. 1211 at 1224.
[40] This is comparable to the "officious bystander" test, from the English case of *Southern Foundries (1926) Ltd v Shirlaw* [1939] K.B. 206. This test asks if the parties would have without doubt agreed to the term if it has been suggested by an "officious bystander".
[41] *GM Shepherd Ltd v North West Securities Ltd*, 1991 S.L.T. 499; *Crawford v Bruce*, 1992 S.L.T. 524.
[42] *Crawford v Bruce*, 1992 S.L.T. 524.
[43] *Crawford v Bruce*, 1992 S.L.T. 524 at 532I.

McLaren's dictum in order to imply a term into a contract for sale of goods. In *J&H Ritchie v Lloyd Ltd*[44]:

> A farmer bought a combination seed drill and a power harrow. After using the harrow for two days, the farmer grew concerned at the rattling noise and reported the problem to the seller. The seller agreed to take the harrow away to investigate the problem. Some weeks later, the seller told the farmer the harrow was now repaired and ready for use, but refused to tell the farmer what the problem had been. The farmer was concerned at the long-term damage to the harrow that may have been caused, and purported to reject the goods in accordance with his rights under the Sale of Goods Act 1979. The seller claimed that the farmer was too late to reject the goods, and that they were now of satisfactory quality.

In his judgment, Lord Hope considered the question of whether there was an implied term in a contract for sale of goods that the buyer would be given the details of any repair carried out to his goods. In wording which echoes Lord McLaren's, he said:

> "A condition that the seller would provide this information [about the defect and repair], if it was asked for, was one which every buyer would seek for his own protection in such circumstances. It was one which no reasonable seller, who was already in breach of contract, could refuse as a condition of being given the opportunity to cure the defect and preserve the contract."[45]

Accordingly, the seller's failure to provide the necessary information was a breach of contract which entitled the purchaser to reject the goods.

7-22   The courts have also considered whether the implied term in question is *necessary* for the contract. Reasonableness alone will not be sufficient. This is especially relevant where there is no established usage which indicates that a term would be implied without question.[46] Thus, the question that can be asked is whether the term sought to be implied is necessary to make the contract work.[47] This is sometimes known as the "business efficacy" test, and was originally developed in an English case, *The Moorcock*.[48] There, the court approached the question from the angle of "efficacy".

---

[44] *J&H Ritchie v Lloyd Ltd* [2007] UKHL 9.
[45] *J&H Ritchie v Lloyd Ltd* [2007] UKHL 9 per Lord Hope at [18]. The other Scottish Law Lord, Lord Rodger, reached the same conclusion but by a different route. He held that the contract to repair the goods was a separate contract from that of the sale, and that the seller had breached an implied term in this ancillary contract of repair (see [32]–[38]).
[46] *Credential Bath Street Ltd v Venture Investment Placement Ltd* [2007] CSOH 208, per Lord Reed at [57].
[47] The courts sometimes use the term "workable".
[48] *The Moorcock*, (1889) L.R. 14 P.D. 64.

A vessel had arranged to discharge its cargo at a pier on the River Thames. At low tide the keel of the vessel was damaged when it grounded on the bed of the river. There was held to be an implied term in the contract between the owner of the vessel and the wharfingers that the latter had taken reasonable steps to ensure that it was safe anchorage. In awarding damages against the wharfingers, Bowen L.J. framed the test for implying terms as follows: "I believe if one were to take all the cases, and they are many, it will be found that in all of them the law is raising an implication from the presumed intention of the parties with the object of giving to the transaction such efficacy as both parties must have intended that in all events it should have."[49]

This indicates that terms are implied on this basis not because they themselves were intended by the parties but because they are necessary to reach a result that the court is satisfied was intended by the parties. Lord Rodger has applied the concept of business efficacy in a Scottish case before the House of Lords, in order to imply a term into an ancillary contract for repair, in *J&H Ritchie v Lloyd Ltd*.[50]

As Lord Reed has noted, the test of necessity means that "a term cannot be implied where there are a number of different terms to which the parties might have agreed."[51]

The test of business efficacy, or necessity, has been used together with the "officious bystander" test, which asks whether an objective bystander would think the parties intended the implied term in question to be part of their contract.[52] Was the implied term so obvious that the parties would have unhesitatingly agreed to it? In *Aberdeen City Council v Stewart Milne Group Ltd*, the Supreme Court implied a term into the contract on the basis of these tests:

> "If the officious bystander had been asked whether such a term should be implied, he or she would have said "of course". Put another way, such a term is necessary to make the contract work or to give it business efficacy. I would prefer to resolve this appeal by holding that such a term should be implied rather than by a process of interpretation."[53]

In a recent Scottish case, *Henderson v Royal Bank of Scotland Plc*[54]:   **7–23**

---

[49] *The Moorcock* (1889) L.R. 14 P.D. 64 at 68.

[50] *J&H Ritchie v Lloyd Ltd* [2007] UKHL 9.

[51] *Credential Bath Street Ltd v Venture Investment Placement Ltd* [2007] CSOH 208, per Lord Reed at [58].

[52] *Shirlaw v Southern Foundries (1926) Ltd* [1939] 2 K.B. 206. Recently referred to in *Credential Bath Street Ltd v Venture Investment Placement Ltd* [2007] CSOH 208, per Lord Reed at [55].

[53] *Aberdeen City Council v Stewart Milne Group Ltd* [2011] UKSC 56, per Lord Clarke at [33].

[54] *Henderson v Royal Bank of Scotland Plc* [2008] CSOH 146.

In 1997, Mr and Mrs Henderson each took out a loan from the Royal Bank of Scotland for their hotel, the Portree Hotel in Skye. In 1998, the Hendersons sought advice from RBS as to the cost of repaying their loans. They were advised that the early repayment charge would be £120,000 on each loan. They decided not to make the early repayment. It later transpired that this figure was wrong: in fact, the early repayment charge would have only been £12,000 per loan. Following 1999, the hotel business declined, and the Hendersons were sequestrated in 2002 at the instance of RBS. The Hendersons argued that if RBS had provided an accurate early repayment charge in 1998, they would have repaid the loans at that time and the solvency of their business would not thereafter have been compromised by the loans or the high interest rates they were paying to RBS. The Hendersons claimed that RBS was in breach of an implied term in the loan agreement that they would provide an accurate early repayment charge.

Lord Woolman held that there was an implied term in the contract that RBS would take reasonable care in providing these figures. Such a clause was necessary in order to allow the Hendersons to exercise their contractual right to repay the loan early: it therefore was required to make the contract workable. However, it was not necessary that the implied term should amount to a warranty, whereby RBS warranted the accuracy of the figure. Thus, although the court implied the appropriate term into the contract, RBS was not in breach of it.

Thus, for a pursuer to succeed in implying a term in a contract, he must show that the term is objectively reasonable, and that it is necessary for the contract.

It can be difficult to decide whether a term falls to be implied in a particular case. It has been observed that "there is a close affinity between the interpretation of express terms of a contract and the implication of terms which have not been expressed."[55] Interpretation of contract terms will be considered in Ch.8. However, where the courts are called upon to determine if a term should be implied, they will be seeking to ensure any implication is consistent with the purpose of the contract. The rules outlined above all tend to this end. Our final example is a case where the Supreme Court declined to interpret the contract to reach a certain result, but instead implied in a term. In *Aberdeen City Council v Stewart Milne Group Ltd*:

> Aberdeen City Council sold land to Stewart Milne for development. Under the missives, Stewart Milne were to pay a further amount to the Council if they sold the land on. The sum was to be calculated as a percentage of the sale value. This is known as a profit share arrangement. However, Stewart Milne sold the land to another

[55] *Credential Bath Street Ltd v Venture Investment Placement Ltd* [2007] CSOH 208, per Lord Reed at [54] with reference to the words of Lord Hoffmann in *South Australia Asset Management Corp v York Montague Ltd* [1997] A.C. 191.

company within the Stewart Milne group, for £483,020. This was far below the open market value of the land, which was £5,670,000. This meant that the profit share was a fraction of the amount it would have been if the land had been sold on the open market. The Council argued that the profit share should still be calculated by the open market value. Although the clause did not specify that, the Supreme Court nevertheless had no difficulty in implying a term to the contract "to the effect that, in the event of a sale which was not at arms' length in the open market, an open market valuation should be used ... for the calculation of the profit share."[56] The Supreme Court reached this decision by looking at the contract as a whole and giving effect to the parties' "unspoken intention".[57]

English law

Various tests have been adopted by the English judiciary to determine **7–24** whether or not a term should be implied into a particular contract, including the test of business efficacy.[58] In *Liverpool City Council v Irwin*[59] Lord Wilberforce identified four different bases on which a term might be implied: (i) established usage; (ii) necessity; (iii) reasonableness; and (iv) spelling out the contract the parties have made. However, in the 2009 case of *Attorney General of Belize v British Telecom*,[60] Lord Hoffman sought to redefine the test for implying terms. He stated:

> "... in every case in which it is said that some provision ought to be implied in an instrument, the question for the court is whether such a provision would spell out in express words what the instrument, read against the relevant background, would reasonably be understood to mean. It will be noticed from Lord Pearson's speech that this question can be reformulated in various ways which a court may find helpful in providing an answer—the implied term must 'go without saying', it must be 'necessary to give business efficacy to the contract' and so on—but these are not in the Board's opinion to be treated as different or additional tests. There is only one question: is that what the instrument, read as a whole against the relevant background, would reasonably be understood to mean?"[61]

This reformulation is in keeping with Lord Hoffmann's approach to interpreting contracts (considered in Ch.8), and places the emphasis on reasonableness. Is it necessary to imply a term in order to give effect to the reasonable expectations of the parties? However, the English courts

---

[56] *Aberdeen City Council v Stewart Milne Group Ltd* [2011] UKSC 56, per Lord Hope at [20].

[57] *Aberdeen City Council v Stewart Milne Group Ltd* [2011] UKSC 56, per Lord Hope at [22] and Lord Clarke at [32] and [33].

[58] *The Moorcock* (1889) L.R. 14 P.D. 64.

[59] *Liverpool City Council v Irwin* [1977] A.C. 239; [1976] 2 All E.R. 39.

[60] *Attorney General of Belize v British Telecom* [2009] UKPC 10.

[61] *Attorney General of Belize v British Telecom* [2009] UKPC 10, per Lord Hoffmann at 21.

have not entirely embraced this approach,[62] and therefore concepts such as "business efficacy" and the "officious bystander" may still be relevant.[63]

A recent English case has indicated that the parties may exclude the possibility of any implied terms through their use of an entire agreement clause.[64] This is a clause which specifically states that the written document constitutes the entire agreement between the parties. This point has not yet been tested in Scots law.

---

[62] *Stena Line v Merchant Navy Ratings Pension Fund Trustees Ltd* [2011] EWCA Civ 543. The Scottish courts have not considered or applied Lord Hoffmann's approach in any detail at all.
[63] *Dear and Griffith v Jackson* [2013] EWCA Civ 89.
[64] *Axa Sun Life Services plc v Campbell Martin Ltd* [2011] EWCA Civ 133.

CHAPTER 8

CONSTRUCTION OF THE CONTRACT

Having determined what the terms of the contract are, it is necessary to **8–01** determine what effect they have. To do this requires both that the terms of the contract are interpreted and that they are applied to the facts in question. These two matters together may be referred to as construction of the contract. When interpreting a contract, the court is seeking to determine the intention of the parties at the time the contract was made. The relevant question is what the parties intended when the matter is examined objectively: it is not a question of what the parties subjectively though. What rules should the courts apply when attempting to understand the wording of the contract? In the last decade there have been numerous decisions in Scotland and England concerning construction of the contract, and it is possible to speak of the "modern approach" to construction.[1] Unfortunately, the modern approach is not always uniform and, especially in Scots law, there appears to be a divergence of judicial opinion over how to interpret contracts, as we shall see. Nevertheless, the rules on interpretation are of increasing importance in contract law.

Two approaches to construction

The leading case in English law is *Investors Compensation Scheme Ltd v* **8–02** *West Bromwich Building Society*.[2] The leading speech was given by Lord Hoffmann, who stated:

> "Interpretation is the ascertainment of the meaning which the document would convey to a reasonable person having all the background knowledge which would reasonably have been available to the parties in the situation in which they were at the time of the contract."[3]

This is an objective approach, but one which takes account of the specific context in which the parties were placed. The court is thus entitled to consider the surrounding circumstances of the contract, sometimes

---

[1] *Credential Bath Street Ltd v Venture Investment Placement Ltd* [2007] CSOH 208, per Lord Reed at [38].

[2] *Investors Compensation Scheme Ltd v West Bromwich Building Society* [1998] 1 W.L.R. 896.

[3] *Investors Compensation Scheme Ltd v West Bromwich Building Society* [1998] 1 W.L.R. 896 at 912.

referred to as the "factual matrix". However, this approach has not been adopted without question in Scots law and there is an apparent division between the approaches taken by the Scottish courts. This can be illustrated by the case of *Bank of Scotland v Dunedin Property Investment Co Ltd*.[4]

Dunedin converted a number of bank loans into one consolidated loan of £10 million. The interest of the loan was a fixed rate. The borrowing was intended to last for 10 years. There was a term in the loan agreement which gave the company a right to terminate the borrowing prior to the 10 years. That was subject to the bank "being reimbursed for all costs, charges and expenses incurred by it in connection with the stock". In order to lend to the company, the bank in turn borrowed £10 million from another institution. The money that the bank borrowed was at a fluctuating rate of interest. To protect itself against the possibility that the fluctuating interest that it was paying would rise above the fixed interest it was receiving, the bank entered into an interest rate swap contract. Dunedin terminated the borrowing from the bank prior to the 10-year term. The bank also terminated its borrowing and the interest swap agreement and thereby became liable to pay termination charges. The dispute between Dunedin and the bank was whether these termination charges for which the bank had become liable were costs "in connection with" the loan stock.

It was established that Dunedin were aware that, in order for the bank to lend to them, it would require to borrow money and to take steps to protect itself from interest rate fluctuations. They were also aware that if the loan was terminated prior to the 10-year period, the bank would incur costs in terminating the agreements that it would enter into. Against that background the court considered that the expression "costs ... in connection with the stock" was wide enough to include the costs of terminating those arrangements.

While all three of the Inner House judges reached the same conclusion as to the meaning of the contract, they took different routes. Lord President Rodger adopted the approach taken in another English case,[5] namely that the starting point should be to consider the ordinary meaning of the words but that the court was entitled to examine the circumstances in which the words were used. Lord Kirkwood and Lord Caplan both referred to Lord Hoffmann's dictum quoted above. They took the view it was necessary to consider the knowledge that the parties would have had at the time that they made the contract and the result that they must have intended. These two doctrines can be thought of as focusing on the surrounding circumstances (Lord Hoffmann) and the literal approach, focusing on the wording of the contract (Lord President Rodger).

8–03   There is scope for both approaches, however. In *Credential Bath Street Ltd v Venture Investment Placement Ltd*, a dispute arose over the correct meaning of a clause in a guarantee:

---

[4] *Bank of Scotland v Dunedin Property Investment Co Ltd*, 1998 S.C. 657; 1999 S.L.T. 470.
[5] *Charter Reinsurance Co Ltd (In Liquidation) v Fagan* [1997] A.C. 313.

When the tenants defaulted under a lease, the landlord raised an action to enforce the guarantee, to recover from the guarantors. The court was required to construe the clause in the guarantee which transferred liability to the guarantor and concluded that the landlord had failed to demand performance from the guarantor before the deadline passed. Thus, the guarantor was not liable to the landlord.[6]

In reaching this conclusion, Lord Reed drew on both approaches. He started by emphasising that the meaning of a document is not the same as the meaning of its words. When reading the words in a contract or other document, it is necessary to read them in the context in which they were written. Nevertheless, he interpreted the disputed clause by asking whether the commercial background led away from the starting point:

"... that one would ordinarily expect the parties to a formal document to have chosen their words with care, and to have intended to convey the meaning which the words they chose would convey to a reasonable person."[7]

Thus, words should be given their ordinary meaning, unless the surrounding circumstances make it clear that an alternative reading was intended by both parties. Lord Reed also referred to Lord Hoffmann, to emphasise that where the ordinary meaning of the words makes sense in the context of the document and the factual background, then "the court will give effect to that language, even though the consequences may appear hard for one side or the other."[8]

Given that there is authority in Scots law for both approaches, it is helpful to examine them in more detail.

The literal approach

This has been the traditional approach of the Scottish courts. Here, **8–04** consideration must be given to the words that are actually used in the contract: the inquiry "will start, and usually finish, by asking what is the ordinary meaning of the words used".[9]

Considering the meaning of words involves examining not only the words that are directly in dispute but also the remainder of contract.

---

[6] This case neatly illustrates the perils of drafting which fails to achieve what the clients want: after the action against Venture Investment Placement Ltd failed, Credential Bath Street Ltd raised an action for damages against their former legal advisors who drafted the lease: *Credential Bath Street Ltd v DLA Piper Scotland LLP* [2010] CSOH 26.

[7] *Credential Bath Street Ltd v Venture Investment Placement Ltd* [2007] CSOH 208, per Lord Reed at [37].

[8] *Credential Bath Street Ltd v Venture Investment Placement Ltd* [2007] CSOH 208, per Lord Reed at [36], quoting from Lord Hoffmann in *Jumbo King Ltd v Faithful Properties Ltd* (1999) 2 HKCFAR 279.

[9] *Bank of Scotland v Dunedin Property Investment Co Ltd*, 1998 S.C. 657; 1999 S.L.T. 470.

Example: In a contract for repairs to be carried out to a house there might be a clause whereby the builder is liable for any water damage arising while he is working on the house. The builder works for a week in January, stops for a fortnight and then resumes work at the start of February. When he restarts he discovers that a pipe has frozen and burst during the fortnight causing damage. The issue would be whether the expression "while he is working" includes the period when the builder was off site. If the contract provided that, from the start of the works until they were completely finished, the householders were to leave the house solely in his possession, that he would be responsible for heating the house and that he was to insure the house against damage caused by water the conclusion might be that he was liable. However, if the contract said that the house-holders would continue to live in the house and that the "work" could be carried out only between the hours of 09.30 and 16.30, the outcome might be different, leaving the householders liable for the damage.

Sometimes the words will be ones used in everyday conversation and will need no explanation. In other cases it may not be so straightforward. In *Multi-Link Leisure Developments Ltd v North Lanarkshire Council*, the wording of the clause in question was impossible to reconcile with the rest of the contract. Lord Hope noted that the poor quality of the drafting must be taken into account when interpreting the contract, and that the court must try to give a sensible meaning to the clause in light of the factual background.[10] Lord Rodger also adopted a literal approach and focused on the meaning of the words and the contract as a whole:

"When translating a document written in a foreign language, it often makes sense to begin with the parts whose meaning is clear and then to use those parts to unravel the meaning of the parts which are more difficult to understand. The same applies to interpreting con-tracts or statutes."[11]

Surrounding circumstances

8–05   In some situations the meaning of the words may be affected by the context in which the words were used. In *Reardon Smith Line Ltd v Hangsen-Tangen (The Diana Prosperity)*,[12] Lord Wilberforce stated:

"No contracts are made in a vacuum; there is always a setting in which they have to be placed. The nature of what is legitimate to have   regard   to   is   usually   described   as   'the   surrounding

---

[10] *Multi-Link Leisure Developments Ltd v North Lanarkshire Council* [2010] UKSC 47, per Lord Hope at 19.
[11] *Multi-Link Leisure Developments Ltd v North Lanarkshire Council* [2010] UKSC 47, per Lord Rodger at 28.
[12] *Reardon Smith Line Ltd v Hangsen-Tangen (The Diana Prosperity)* [1976] 1 W.L.R. 989; [1976] 3 All E.R. 570.

circumstances' but the phrase is imprecise: it can be illustrated but hardly defined. In a commercial contract it is certainly right that the court should know the commercial purpose of the contract and this in turn presupposes knowledge of the genesis of the transaction, the background, the context, the market in which the parties are operating."[13]

Courts are therefore willing to consider these surrounding circumstances—often referred to as the "factual matrix"[14]—for the purpose of deciding what the parties meant when they used certain words or forms of words for their agreement. This may involve inquiry as to the aim or purpose of the contract. However, this is done for a limited purpose. The courts do not determine the aim and then attempt to make the wording meet that aim. They determine what the aim was and consider it as something that the parties had in mind when they used the words in question. It is therefore only a means to a proper understanding of the words that have been used. This can be illustrated by the English case of *Prenn v Simmonds*[15]:

Simmonds was employed by a subsidiary of RTT as its managing director. He was entitled to purchase part of the share capital of RTT provided that "the aggregate profits of RTT earned during the four years ending 19 August 1963 ... shall have amounted to £300,000". The parties were in dispute as to whether the reference to the aggregate profits of RTT meant that company alone or the group of companies consisting of RTT and its subsidiary.

After examining the background, the House of Lords took the view that Simmonds was engaged to generate profits at the subsidiary and was to receive an incentive for that purpose. On that basis they concluded that the reference to profits of RTT only made commercial sense if it was construed to mean the aggregate profits of both RTT and its subsidiary.

In addition to the purpose of the contract, the courts will also consider **8–06** all the facts that are known to the parties at the time that the agreement was concluded, and those facts of which they ought reasonably to have been aware. Again, this is not with the intention of deciding what the agreement *ought* to have been. It is simply that the circumstances may indicate what the parties *actually* meant when they used the particular words in the contract.

However, there is debate as to whether the courts may consider the surrounding circumstances only if the wording is ambiguous. The Supreme Court has confirmed that where the parties have used unambiguous language, the court must apply it.[16] In contrast, in the Scottish

---

[13] *The Diana Prosperity* [1976] 1 W.L.R. 989 at 995H; [1976] 3 All E.R. 570 at 574.
[14] *The Diana Prosperity* [1976] 1 W.L.R. 989 at 997C; [1976] 3 All E.R. 570 at 575, per Lord Wilberforce.
[15] *Prenn v Simmonds* [1971] 3 All E.R. 237.
[16] *Rainy Sky SA v Kookmin Bank* [2011] UKSC 50, per Lord Clarke at 23, with reference to *Cooperative Wholesale Society Ltd v National Westminster Bank Plc* [1995] 1 E.G.L.R. 97.

case of *Luminar Lava Ignite Ltd v Mama Group Plc*, the Inner House held that:

> "It is not part of our law of contract that the court can have regard to relevant background circumstances only if there is ambiguity in the words of an agreement."[17]

This makes sense, since:

> "Contracts do not exist in isolation from the rest of the world and it would be foolish for a court to ignore the circumstances in which the contract was created."[18]

8–07 As was noted by Lord Wilberforce in his dictum from *Reardon Smith Line* the expression "surrounding circumstances" is imprecise and there can be considerable difficulty in deciding where a court should draw the line in relation to what it will consider and what it will not consider. The following principles may be drawn from the cases:

(1) For the courts to refer to any facts that existed at the time that the contract was concluded in order to interpret it, those facts must have been known to all the contracting parties.[19] This may be justified by the rationale that the contract is the product of agreement between two (or more) parties and what the court is doing is attempting to discover the presumed common intention of those parties. If the facts were known to only one of the parties they could not have a bearing on the common intention.

(2) The details of and terms of prior negotiations of the parties may be looked at only for the purpose of determining what facts were known to the parties at the time they concluded their agreement.[20] It is not permissible to examine the terms of the prior negotiations and argue that the words used at that stage provide any guidance to the words in the final agreement. This is referred to as the prior communings rule.[21] The justification for the rule is easily apparent. When the parties are negotiating their intentions are not fixed. There may be considerable change between their intention at that time and their intention when agreement is concluded.

(3) It is not possible to have regard to the subjective intent of the parties. This is justified on the basis that the exercise of

---

[17] *Luminar Lava Ignite Ltd v Mama Group Plc* [2010] CSIH 01, per Lord Hodge at [38].

[18] McBryde, *The Law of Contract in Scotland*, 3rd edn (Edinburgh: SULI/W. Green, 2007), para.8–22.

[19] *Scottish Power Plc v Britoil (Exploration) Ltd* [1997] T.L.R. 616, referred to in *Bank of Scotland v Dunedin Property Investment Co Ltd*, 1998 S.C. 657.

[20] *Bank of Scotland v Dunedin Property Investment Co Ltd*, 1998 S.C. 657, per Lord President Rodger at 665F.

[21] See *Chartbrook Ltd v Persimmon Homes Ltd* [2009] UKHL 38; [2009] 1 A.C. 1101; *Luminar Lava Ignite Ltd v Mama Group Plc* [2010] CSIH 01.

interpretation is to determine the objective intention of the parties. The issue is not what parties think they have undertaken, but what they said and did and how that would look from the perspective of a reasonable businessperson.

Commercially sensible construction

The courts interpret commercial agreements, as far as possible, to pro- **8–08** duce commercially sensible results. In *R&J Dempster Ltd v Motherwell Bridge & Engineering Co Ltd*, Lord Guthrie stated:

> "The object of our law of contract is to facilitate the transactions of commercial men and not to create obstacles in the way of solving practical problems arising out of circumstances confronting them, or to expose them to unnecessary pitfalls."[22]

The rationale behind this policy has been stated to be that the "commercial construction is more likely to give effect to the intention of the parties."[23] Thus presumed intention is once more at play. Although the test of commercial good sense has been described as a "makeweight",[24] it can play a useful role in relation to the literal construction. Where a literal construction is not consistent with a commercially sensible result, the court can depart from the literal approach.[25] Where there are two possible constructions of the contract, the court is entitled to apply the one which is commercially sensible.[26]

Lord Reed has, however, recognised that judges are not businessmen and should therefore be wary of substituting their interpretation of what a commercial deal means:

> "It is also necessary to heed the warnings which have been given, not least by judges with commercial experience ... against excessive confidence that a judge's view as to what might be commercially sensible necessarily coincides with the views of those actually involved in commercial contracts".[27]

Some final guidance

Interpretation may not always be the appropriate solution. In the case of **8–09** *Aberdeen City Council v Stewart Milne Group Ltd*, the parties put forward conflicting interpretations of a particular clause. The Supreme Court

---

[22] *R&J Dempster Ltd v Motherwell Bridge & Engineering Co Ltd*, 1964 S.C. 308.
[23] *Mannai Investment Co Ltd v Eagle Star Life Assurance Co Ltd* [1997] 3 All E.R. 352, per Lord Steyn at 372. See also the opinion of the Lord President in *Bank of Scotland v Dunedin Property Investment Co Ltd*, 1998 S.C. 657; 1989 S.L.T. 470.
[24] *Aberdeen City Council v Stewart Milne Group Ltd* [2011] UKSC 56, per Lord Hope at [22]. A "makeweight" is an unimportant person (or item) that is simply included to make up numbers.
[25] *Multi-Link Leisure Developments Ltd v North Lanarkshire Council* [2010] UKSC 47.
[26] *Rainy Sky SA v Kookmin Bank* [2011] UKSC 50.
[27] *Credential Bath Street Ltd v Venture Investment Placement Ltd* [2007] CSOH 208 at [24].

declined to interpret the clause in order to resolve the dispute. Instead, the judges agreed that the correct solution was to imply an additional term into the contract—albeit that the end result was the same.[28]

8-10   It is also helpful to bear in mind the words of warning issued by Lord Reed. In construing contracts, he stated:

> "The court will not, of course, interpolate words or substitute one word for another merely because the result might appear to be fairer or more commercially sensible. One of the parties may simply have made a bad bargain; and the court is not entitled to impose on the parties some other bargain, under the guise of construction, on the basis that it might be thought to be fairer or more sensible."[29]

Thus, regardless of which rule of construction the court applies, it is not the court's job to re-make or improve the terms of the original bargain: in the words of McBryde, their task is construction not reconstruction.[30]

Legal principles

8-11   There are some other legal principles that have previously been used to help interpret a contested term. While they have not been overruled, some caution is needed in applying them in light of Lord Reed's opinion that:

> "Canons of that kind require in my opinion to be reconsidered, and in some cases reformulated or discarded, in the light of the modern approach to the construction of contracts."[31]

Contra proferentem

8-12   Where a clause is ambiguous, it is construed against the interest of the party who seeks to rely upon it. This is known as interpretation *contra proferentem*. It applies only when there is an ambiguity—it may not be used to create any ambiguity. It is also applied more readily in contracts with standard terms. Where the parties have negotiated and drafted a complete contract, it has not been applied.[32] In many circumstances both parties to the dispute will be relying on the same clause, so there is no obvious party against whom it may be construed.

Application of the principle may be illustrated by a case in which an insurance company stipulated in a contract of life insurance that the contract would be void should any of the statements made by the proposer turn out to be untrue.[33] A lady made statements on the proposal

---

[28]   *Aberdeen City Council v Stewart Milne Group Ltd* [2011] UKHL 56, per Lord Clarke at [33]. For further discussion of this case, see Ch.7.

[29]   *Credential Bath Street Ltd v Venture Investment Placement Ltd* [2007] CSOH 208 at [24], and approved by the Inner House in *Forbo-Nairn Ltd v Murrayfield Properties Lt*d [2009] CSIH 94 at [8].

[30]   McBryde, *The Law of Contract in Scotland*, 3rd edn (Edinburgh: SULI/W. Green, 2007), para.8-07.

[31]   *Credential Bath Street Ltd v Venture Investment Placement Ltd* [2007] CSOH 208 at [38].

[32]   *Credential Bath Street Ltd v Venture Investment Placement Ltd* [2007] CSOH 208 at [38].

[33]   *Life Association of Scotland v Foster* (1873) 11 M. 351.

form indicating that she was not suffering from any malady. Unknown to her, at the time of filling out the form, she was already suffering from the disease which was to cause her death some months later. The company initially refused to pay out on the policy. The court held that the company was bound to do so. Construing the clause *contra proferentem* it meant that the proposer required to disclose any illness known to her; it did not apply where she did not know of her true medical condition.

A particular manifestation of the *contra proferentem* rule exists in **8–13** relation to exemption clauses. These are clauses whereby a party seeks to exclude or restrict his legal liability to the other party. They may seek to exclude, either totally or partially, liability on the part of one party. Where they seek merely to impose a cap on the maximum liability of a part they are often referred to as limitation clauses. Some familiar examples of exemption and limitation clauses are: "The management accepts no liability for any article lost on the premises"; "In the event of any damage occurring to this item when in the control of the company, the company shall not be liable for any loss in excess of £100"; and "Persons enter these premises at their own risk".

Statutory regulation of these clauses is considered in the next chapter. **8–14** However, apart from such statutory regulation the courts have traditionally been hostile to such terms. As we saw in Ch.7, the courts developed rules in relation to the incorporation of such clauses into a contract. In particular, the strong presumption of the law is that one party will not agree to release the other from liability for his own negligence. Such a course is regarded as "inherently improbable."[34] So in a series of cases it has been established that unless the draftsman is particularly precise, actually uses the term "negligence" or some synonym and exempts from all other forms of liability, the defender might still be liable. An example illustrates the rigour with which the courts follow this approach[35]:

> A clause in a contract for the carriage of household goods from Aberdeen to Glasgow stated: "The contractors shall not be responsible for loss and damage to furniture and effects caused by or incidental to fire or aircraft but will endeavour to effect insurance on behalf of the customer on receipt of instructions." The goods were destroyed by fire and the owners sought compensation from the transport company. It was held that the clause did not exempt the carriers from liability.

This apparently surprising result was reached because the clause could be construed to refer both to the carrier's liability under contract and also to its liability under statute. The Mercantile Law Amendment Act (Scotland) 1856 makes carriers of goods liable for loss caused by fire while the

---

[34] *Gillespie Bros & Co Ltd v Roy Bowles Transport Ltd* [1973] Q.B. 400, per Buckley L.J. at 419.

[35] *Graham v Shore Porter's Society*, 1979 S.L.T. 119; see also *Golden Sea Produce Ltd v Scottish Nuclear Plc*, 1992 S.L.T. 942.

goods are in their possession.[36] Construing the clause strictly, the court decided that it only exempted the carriers from their statutory liability.[37] What the decision shows is the willingness of the courts to prevent a contracting party from relying on an exemption clause by adopting a strict construction of the contract. Thus, it was interpreted *contra proferentem*: against the interest of the party seeking to rely upon it. However, this judicial willingness was most apparent in situations where the courts considered it necessary to "protect" one party to the contract, typically consumer contracts. Statutory controls now exist for that purpose.

The *contra proferentem* rule has a further incarnation in the Unfair Terms in Consumer Contracts Regulations 1999 (SI 1999/2083). These regulations are considered in the following chapter.

Legality

8–15   "[A] ... presumption of legality ... exists where a contract is reasonably susceptible of two meanings."[38]

Thus if the possible means of interpretation throw up two alternatives and one of them would be unlawful and therefore unenforceable, the courts will prefer the interpretation that gives the contract lawful effect.

Change in circumstances: equitable adjustment

8–16   It was noted at the outset of this chapter that the courts are using interpretation in a wide range of disputes. One such example is *Lloyds TSB Foundation for Scotland v Lloyds Banking Group*.[39] Between the date of contract formation and the date of performance, there was a change in the accounting method for calculating "pre-tax profits". Using the old accounting method, the sum due to be paid under the contract was £38,920. Applying the new accounting standards, which included "negative goodwill", the sum due was £3,543,433. The change in legislation meant that the contract would be performed in a radically different way. The bank argued that there is a doctrine of "equitable adjustment" in Scots law. This would enable the court to adjust the contract where there had been an unexpected change in circumstances which had arisen after the contract had been concluded[40] and "as a result of supervening events, performance of a contract no longer bears any realistic resemblance to that which was originally contemplated."[41] This equitable

---

[36] Mercantile Law Amendment Act (Scotland) 1856 s.17.

[37] The same strict approach applies in relation to limitation clauses but not with the same rigour. See *Bovis Construction (Scotland) Ltd v Whatlings Construction Ltd*, 1995 S.C. (HL) 19; 1995 S.L.T. 1339.

[38] *Neilson v Stewart*, 1991 S.L.T. 523, per Lord Jauncey at 525.

[39] *Lloyds TSB Foundation for Scotland v Lloyds Banking Group* [2013] UKSC 3.

[40] Importantly, the change was not sufficient to frustrate the contract. For more detail on the doctrine of frustration, see Ch.13.

[41] *Lloyds TSB Foundation for Scotland v Lloyds Banking Group* [2013] UKSC 3, per Lord Hope at 39.

adjustment would mean that the contract would reflect the parties' intentions at the time when they entered into it. However, the Supreme Court rejected this argument, and held that there was no doctrine of equitable adjustment in Scots law.[42] Instead, they used the rules of interpretation to say that the contract should be viewed in the legal and accounting context in which it was made.[43] This meant that the original calculation applied, and the bank only had to pay £38,920.

RECTIFICATION OF THE CONTRACT

On occasions the parties may have reached agreement but the terms of **8–17** that agreement are then incorrectly recorded. This is sometimes referred to as an "error in expression". But error is not the appropriate term to use since the error is not as to the parties' intention. Rather, it is a defect in its expression. There is a discrepancy between what A and B have agreed and the terms of the document expressing the agreement. At common law in Scotland there was an equitable power to deal with such situations. This can be seen from the case of *Krupp v John Menzies Ltd*.[44] There, a clerk had been instructed to record an agreement whereby a hotel manageress was to receive one twentieth of the annual profits of the hotel. By mixing up percentages and fractions,[45] the clerk recorded that the manageress was entitled to one fifth of the profits. The court rectified the error. Likewise the court intervened where there was a discrepancy between the missives of sale and the disposition as to the ambit of the subjects to be sold.[46]

The courts have now been granted a wide power under statute to **8–18** rectify documents that are defectively expressed.[47] This power is discretionary, and there is no obligation on the court to exercise it. Where the need for rectification occurs, parties generally rely on this power rather than the common law rules. The power applies where:

"... a document intended to express or give effect to an agreement fails to express accurately the common intention of the parties to the agreement at the date when it was made".

---

[42] *Lloyds TSB Foundation for Scotland v Lloyds Banking Group* [2013] UKSC 3, per Lord Hope at 47.
[43] *Lloyds TSB Foundation for Scotland v Lloyds Banking Group* [2013] UKSC 3, per Lord Mance at 30 and 31. The Supreme Court rejected the literal approach to interpretation applied by the Inner House in this case: [2011] CSOH 87.
[44] *Krupp v John Menzies Ltd*, 1907 S.C. 903.
[45] When one twentieth is written as a percentage it should be 5 per cent: by erroneously writing it as 20 per cent, the fraction becomes one fifth instead of one twentieth.
[46] *Anderson v Lambie*, 1954 S.C. (HL) 43.
[47] Law Reform (Miscellaneous Provisions) (Scotland) Act 1985 ss.8, 9.

It does not matter whether the defect in expression was due to a common mistake, shared by the parties, or to a unilateral mistake.[48] Further, the agreement of the parties need not be an enforceable contract: "... rectification can be ordered so as to give effect to an agreement by which neither party was bound."[49]

The court may rectify the document to give effect to the parties' common intention. Where a third party has relied upon the defective contract and would therefore be adversely affected to a material extent by the proposed rectification, then the court may only order rectification if:

(i) the party concerned consents to it; or
(ii) if the party concerned was aware of the defect when they relied on the contract or they ought reasonably to have been aware of it.[50]

It is of note that the document in question must fail to give effect to a common intention of the parties. The party seeking rectification must prove that there was an underlying agreement and establish the common intention that lay behind it.[51] For example, they may be able to produce an email exchange in which both parties agreed that the price was to be in US dollars, rather than in pounds. If the contract states the price in pounds but there is no evidence of a subsequent agreement to set the price in pounds, this could be used to show that their agreement had been recorded incorrectly. Where a party seeks rectification, it must specify the correct drafting for the court to apply.

8–19   There is a critical difference in the evidence that can be used when seeking to rectify a contract: the "prior communings" rule does not apply. Unlike interpretation, the court can therefore take account of pre-contractual negotiations when determining the common intention of the parties for rectification. Similarly, the post-formation conduct of the parties may be relevant to establish what they thought they had agreed on. One case which illustrates this, and highlights how important rectification can be, is *Patersons of Greenoakhill Ltd v Biffa Waste Services Ltd*.[52] Here, Lord Hodge held that a literal interpretation of the contract wording did not reflect the common intention of the parties.[53] When the pre-contractual negotiations and the post-formation conduct of the parties were considered, it was clear that they both thought the clause had

---

[48] *MacDonald Estates Plc v Regensis (2005) Dunfermline Ltd* [2007] CSOH 123, per Lord Reed at [172].
[49] *MacDonald Estates Plc v Regensis (2005) Dunfermline Ltd* [2007] CSOH 123, per Lord Reed at [159].
[50] Law Reform (Miscellaneous Provisions) (Scotland) Act 1985 s.9.
[51] It is not necessary for the pursuer to specify the date on which this agreement was reached: *Patersons of Greenoakhill Ltd v Biffa Waste Services Ltd* [2013] CSOH 18, per Lord Hodge at [79].
[52] *Patersons of Greenoakhill Ltd v Biffa Waste Services Ltd* [2013] CSOH 18.
[53] *Patersons of Greenoakhill Ltd v Biffa Waste Services Ltd* [2013] CSOH 18, per Lord Hodge at [89].

a particular effect.[54] A literal interpretation did not do justice to what the parties had originally agreed. Accordingly, he rectified the contract to reflect this original agreement.

Where the contract contained an "entire agreement clause", it might be thought that the party seeking rectification would be prevented from bringing this additional evidence to prove the mistake. However, this has been held to be an unpersuasive argument, which would not preclude the rectification of a defect in expression.[55] The statutory power of rectification is most commonly used to amend defects in a disposition, so that it accurately reflects the prior missives.

The agreement and common intention must be proved by objective means in the same way as *consensus in idem* would be established for proving any contract.[56]

---

[54] *Patersons of Greenoakhill Ltd v Biffa Waste Services Ltd* [2013] CSOH 18, per Lord Hodge at [84]–[87].

[55] *MacDonald Estates Plc v Regensis (2005) Dunfermline Ltd* [2007] CSOH 123, per Lord Reed at [178].

[56] *Rehman v Ahmad*, 1993 S.L.T. 741. Lord Reed provided a review of the arguments for subjective intention and objective intention and concluded, in an obiter comment, that he was inclined to favour an objective approach: *MacDonald Estates Plc v Regensis (2005) Dunfermline Ltd* [2007] CSOH 123 at [176]. See also *Patersons of Greenoakhill Ltd v Biffa Waste Services Ltd* [2013] CSOH 18, per Lord Hodge at [42].

CHAPTER 9

STATUTORY CONTROL OF CONTRACT TERMS

9–01 Suppose all contracts were the product of negotiations between two well-informed parties of equal bargaining strength. In such a world, there would be a greater likelihood that each party would have secured the best arrangement available, having regard to its own interests. In the real world, however, the majority of contracts are not freely negotiated between parties. In many situations one party is in a position to impose the terms that he wants on the relationship between himself and the other party. He will often have his own standard terms which are non-negotiable. For example, an individual who wishes to hire a car cannot discuss and revise all the terms of the hire agreement, and a person taking clothes to a dry cleaner cannot haggle about the cleaner's liability in the event that the clothes are damaged. Often this is a good thing. If it was necessary to negotiate and agree all the terms every time one sought to hire a car it would be quicker to take the bus—and then one might have to negotiate conditions of carriage with the bus company. Another advantage of a standardised contract is that the party offering the product or service is in a position to know exactly where they stand in concluding agreements that make up their business. This degree of certainty is necessary to permit businesses to set their prices—if each customer hiring a car demanded different contract terms, it would be necessary to charge different rates. With the advantages of standardised contract terms there also come disadvantages. The freedom to determine the conditions under which a person is willing to enter into a contract may be quite illusory where they are used. This problem has been recognised by the courts.[1] As noted previously, the intention of the parties underlies many aspects of the law of contract. Where standard form contracts are concerned, any approach based on intention is, at best, artificial, since the contract terms are likely to represent only the drafting party's intention.

9–02 The problems that can arise were considered by the Law Commissions in relation to exemption clauses.[2] The legislation that followed is the Unfair Contract Terms Act 1977 ("the 1977 Act"). There have also been harmonisation measures across the European Union. This resulted in

---

[1] *McCutcheon v David MacBrayne Ltd*, 1964 S.C. (HL) 28 referred to in Ch.7.

[2] Law Commission and Scottish Law Commission, *Exemption Clauses in Contracts First Report: Amendments to the Sale of Goods Act 1893* (HMSO, 1969), Law Com. No.24; Scot. Law Com. No.12; Law Commission and Scottish Law Commission, *Exemption Clauses Second Report* (HMSO, 1975), Law Com. No.69; Scot. Law Com. No.39.

controls which are now contained in the Unfair Terms in Consumer Contracts Regulations 1999.[3] These are the two principal sources of legislative control of contract terms. Other legislation applies controls in certain areas. The Sale of Goods Act 1979 implies specific terms to protect purchasers of goods. The Consumer Contracts (Information, Cancellation and Additional Charges) Regulations 2013[4] came into force in June 2014 and implements various consumer protection measures originating in European Directives. Our discussion will focus on the general scheme of control provided by the 1977 Act and the Unfair Terms in Consumer Contracts Regulations 1999.

However, further change is imminent. At the date of writing, a new piece of legislation is being debated: the Consumer Rights Bill. As and when this Bill is passed by the UK Parliament and the resulting Act comes into force, it will sweep away the consumer protection elements of the 1977 Act and revoke the Unfair Terms in Consumer Contracts Regulations 1999. The new Act will replace the existing statutory protections with a consolidated set of consumer protection measures.[5] The legal protection for consumers discussed in this chapter is therefore likely to be subject to extensive change in the near future.

THE UNFAIR CONTRACT TERMS ACT 1977

The title of the 1977 Act is a misnomer. It does not cover all unfair **9-03** contract terms, only clauses which exclude or restrict liability. The 1977 Act does not define these terms, but generally they are clauses which attempt to remove or limit the liability of one party. Identifying such clauses in a contract is a question of fact rather than law. It will depend on the substance of the clause, rather than its label. Examples of exclusion clauses include a term which states that a window cleaner will not be liable for failure to perform, or alternatively for any damage caused by performance. A provision which states that he will only be liable for damage caused up to the value of £100 is a limitation or restriction clause. These clauses may also operate by limiting the circumstances in which one party will be liable. For example, a seller of goods could stipulate that he will only be liable for any defects in the goods supplied if the purchaser notifies him within 24 hours and provides the original receipt in triplicate. Such a clause would limit the seller's liability by hampering the purchaser's exercise of rights. Under the 1977 Act, some exclusion and restriction clauses are declared void; others are subject to a "fair and reasonable" test before they can be given effect. The 1977 Act does not prohibit such clauses being inserted into contracts. It simply provides that they cannot be relied upon in the event of a claim for damages arising.

---

[3] Unfair Terms in Consumer Contracts Regulations 1999 (SI 1999/2083).
[4] Consumer Contracts (Information, Cancellation and Additional Charges) Regulations 2013 (SI 2013/3134).
[5] It will also replace sections of the Sale of Goods Act 1979.

The scope of the Act

9–04   The provisions of the 1977 Act apply to a variety of contracts: contracts for the sale and supply of goods, contracts to enter upon land, employment contracts and contracts for services.[6] These contracts are the most common ones in which exemption clauses appear. To take some examples, the 1977 Act covers contracts to (i) park a car; (ii) attend a sporting venue; (iii) have an item repaired; and (iv) deposit luggage. But the 1977 Act does not apply to contracts of insurance, nor to contracts relating to the formation or dissolution of a company or partnership.

The 1977 Act not only covers clauses which actually appear in a written document, but also to notices.[7] Such notices are commonly found on walls and counters in restaurants, hotels and drycleaners. Non-contractual notices are also within the ambit of the 1977 Act.[8] Such notices may accompany information or professional advice. For example, a surveyor providing a house report to a building society has no contract with the prospective purchaser. However, the purchaser may learn of the contents of the report and rely upon it in determining whether or not to buy the house.[9] Although the surveyor in this situation does not have a contract with the purchaser, he may seek to exclude liability to the purchaser by way of a non-contractual notice. If so, an attempt by the surveyor to exclude liability to the house purchaser is capable of being struck down under the 1977 Act, unless it satisfies the requirement of reasonableness.[10]

9–05   The most common exemption clauses are those which expressly seek to exclude or restrict liability. To ensure that other devices are not used to circumvent the 1977 Act, its scope is widened to include other attempts to hinder or prevent one party's right to pursue his normal legal remedies[11]:

(1) "Refunds must be accompanied by a receipt."
(2) "The purchaser's claim shall be restricted to damages and he shall not be entitled to sue for delivery."
(3) "Any claim relating to this contract must be made within fourteen days of the date hereof."

The 1977 Act only applies to the attempted exclusion of liability by businesses. For the purpose of the Act, "business" covers most forms of enterprise: companies, firms, professionals, sole traders as well as

---

[6] 1977 Act s.15.
[7] 1977 Act s.25(3)(d), (4). This is another example of the title being misleading, since it applies to unfair terms in non-contractual documents, as well as in contracts.
[8] Law Reform (Miscellaneous Provisions) (Scotland) Act 1990 s.68.
[9] The purchaser may be content to rely upon one carried out for valuation purposes for his lender, or he may decide to instruct his own survey, in which case he would have a contract with the surveyor.
[10] *Smith v Eric S Bush (A Firm)* [1990] 1 A.C. 831; [1989] 2 W.L.R. 790; cf. *Robbie v Graham & Sibbald*, 1989 S.L.T. 870; 1989 S.C.L.R. 578 (decided prior to the amendment to the Act).
[11] 1977 Act s.25(3)(a), (b), (c).

government and local authority departments.[12] The only clear exception is an individual acting in a personal capacity, who is not subject to the controls of the 1977 Act, although he will benefit from its protections.

Control (1)—liability for "negligence"

The 1977 Act talks about "breach of duty". That term is designed to refer **9–06** to one party's liability for breach of a contractual term and for delictual liability. What does this mean? Let us take an example. An architect may be commissioned to prepare plans for a loft extension. The planned extension turns out to be dangerous. The architect could be sued for "breach of duty". This encompasses breach of contract and delict. The expression used is, however, rather unwieldy and in most instances simply means "negligence". We shall use "negligence" in preference to "breach of duty" in our discussion of the 1977 Act's provisions. The extent of the control applied depends on whether the clause seeks to exclude liability for death or personal injury, or for economic loss.

Death or personal injury

Parliament took the view that there was no justification for allowing **9–07** businesses to avoid liability where their negligence had occasioned death or personal injury. Such terms are void and of no effect.[13] Any attempt by a business to avoid liability for death or personal injury caused by their negligence will therefore be void.

It is a complete defence to a delictual action if the injured person voluntarily assumed the risk of the harm that occurred.[14] To take an extreme example, suppose that Dean asks his friend to drive him to work but insists on travelling on the roof of his car. The risk is obvious and Dean will be taken to have accepted the risk. If he is injured in the course of his journey, his friend would probably have a complete defence to any action of negligence that Dean might bring. An argument might be made that the negligence provisions of the 1977 Act would not apply where a person had his attention specifically drawn to the exemption clause at the time of contracting and consented to assume a particular risk. In order to guard against such an argument, the 1977 Act specifically provides that the fact that a person agreed to, or was aware of, the term would not of itself be sufficient evidence of voluntary assumption of risk.[15] Something more is required. In the decades since the 1977 Act was passed, this provision has not been the subject of judicial scrutiny.

---

[12] 1977 Act s.25(1).
[13] 1977 Act s.16.
[14] This defence is called volenti non fit injuria (to he who consents no wrong is done).
[15] 1977 Act s.16(3).

Economic loss

9–08 Negligence on the part of one party will often give rise to financial loss rather than to death or personal injury. This is particularly true of contracts for services. If drycleaners negligently clean your garment it is more likely that you will suffer financial loss because your garment is ruined, rather than that you will be injured by getting a skin inflammation. Similarly, if a solicitor or architect does not take reasonable care, the loss sustained by a client will normally be financial rather than physical. Under the 1977 Act, clauses which attempt to evade liability for financial loss are not automatically void. Rather they are subject to a "fair and reasonable" test. If the court thinks they are justified in the circumstances, such clauses will be upheld. Otherwise they will be denied effect. It has, for example, been held that it is not reasonable for a photographic developing company to exclude liability in respect of films deposited with it for processing which are lost or damaged as a result of its negligence.[16]

Control (2)—liability for breach of contract not involving negligence

9–09 Many breaches of contract are not concerned with "negligence". A builder does not complete a house extension on time; a coach tour goes to a different destination from that advertised; a wedding photographer fails to turn up at the church; a plumber uses different fittings from those specified in his estimate. In each of these cases one party has failed to fulfil his contractual obligations, but the breach has not necessarily occurred as a result of negligence. The controls in the 1977 Act here apply to exemption clauses in two types of contract: consumer contracts and standard form contracts.[17] In both cases the test of fairness and reasonableness is used to determine if the clause should be upheld. In the case of consumer and standard form contracts, the fair and reasonable test applies not only to exclusion and restriction clauses but also to clauses which attempt to allow a party (a) to render no performance, or (b) to render a performance substantially different from that which the other party reasonably expected from the contract.[18]

Consumer contracts

9–10 The term "consumer contract" is defined in the 1977 Act.[19] There are three elements: a consumer contract will arise where (a) one party deals in the course of a business; and (b) the other does not; and (c) in contracts involving the transfer of ownership or possession of goods, the goods are of a type ordinarily supplied for private use or consumption. If a law firm buys a kettle from a high street retailer for use in the staff kitchen, it will fall within this definition. The firm is not in the business of buying or selling kettles, whereas the retailer is. Further, the item in question is one

---

[16] *Woodman v Photo Trade Processing Ltd* (1981) *Scolag* 281.
[17] 1977 Act s.17.
[18] 1977 Act s.17(1)(b).
[19] 1977 Act s.25(1).

which is of a type ordinarily supplied for private use. Where the law firm buys an industrial-scale photocopier, however, then it will not fall within this definition, since the goods do not meet the final criterion. However, where the consumer is a natural individual, and is not dealing in the course of a business, then it will be a consumer contract even where the goods are not of a type ordinarily supplied for private use or consumption.[20] Thus, whether buying a kettle or an industrial-scale photocopier, a private individual will be a consumer when acting in a personal capacity.[21] This is sometimes referred to as a "pure" consumer contract.

Section 25(1B)[22] provides that the definition of consumer contract does not extend to contracts where an individual consumer buys second hand goods at a public auction where there is the opportunity to attend in person, or where goods are sold at auction and the buyer is not an individual.

Exemption and limitation clauses are subject to the fair and reasonable **9–11** test when they are used in consumer contracts. So are clauses which attempt to entitle one party to render no performance or a substantially different one from that contracted for.

> *Example*: When Oswald moves into his new flat he hires a washing machine from a shop nearby. Two weeks after it is delivered, a pipe in it bursts and his flat is flooded. When Oswald complains, the shop assistant points out a term of the rental agreement that says the hirer is liable only for damage to the machine itself and not to other property. This clause will be subject to the "fair and reasonable test".

> *Example*: Jessica books tickets to Murrayfield to watch Scotland play the All Blacks. The ticket agent supplies her with tickets to watch the Scottish under 14s team play the New Zealand under 14s, and points to a clause in the contract which states: "In the event of your chosen tickets not being available, we reserve the right to supply tickets to an alternative event." This clause will also be subject to the "fair and reasonable test".

Standard form contracts

Standard form contracts are usually pre-printed, non-negotiable and **9–12** offered to everyone with whom the business deals.[23] Such contracts are not, however, defined in the 1977 Act. It was thought that, however the definition was drawn, there would always be a danger of evasion. Clever draftsmen would draft around the definition. In the debate in Parliament it was suggested that judges recognised such contracts when they saw

---

[20] 1977 Act s.25(1A).

[21] This definition was added to the 1977 Act by the Sale and Supply of Goods to Consumers Regulations 2002 (SI 2002/3045), and brings the definition of a natural consumer into line with the standard European definition.

[22] Also inserted by the Sale and Supply of Goods to Consumers Regulations 2002 (SI 2002/3045).

[23] See *McCrone v Boots Farm Sales Ltd*, 1981 S.L.T. 103.

them. Where a transaction is made using a standard form contract the provisions of the 1977 Act apply. This applies even where the recipient of the standard form is itself a business.

> *Example*: Easiclean Windows arrange to clean the windows of a large office building owned by Bright Ltd. Easiclean makes the contract with Bright on its own standard form in which it seeks to exempt liability for any damage to the windows and the stonework of the building. If damage does occur and Easiclean seeks to rely on the clause, Bright can challenge its validity under the 1977 Act. It will then be subject to the fair and reasonable test.

Control (3)—statutory implied terms

9–13 As noted in Ch.7, in certain common contracts the implied terms have been codified and are contained in statute. In the past it had become common for sellers in contracts for the sale of goods to exempt themselves from the standard terms implied into such contracts by the Sale of Goods legislation. Controls were necessary to prevent this and it was also thought desirable that the law relating to hire-purchase was brought into line with that of sale of goods. A term seeking to exclude an implied term as to title to goods sold or hired is void. A term seeking to exclude implied terms as to conformity of goods with descriptions or samples, quality or fitness for purpose are void in consumer contracts and are of no effect in other contracts if they are not fair and reasonable.[24]

> *Example*: Font Ltd supply bathroom suites to both private and trade customers. Font sells a bath and six bidets to Sid, who is a builder currently involved in converting a large house into flats. The bidets do not actually belong to Font and the bath has a large crack in it. Any attempt by Font Ltd to exempt its liability to Sid will be (a) void in respect of the six bidets, to which it does not have good title; and (b) void in respect of the bath if Sid can show that it was not fair and reasonable for Font Ltd to exclude liability for defective products. If the bidets and bath had been supplied to Sid for his personal use, he would have had additional protection as a consumer buyer. Consequently, Font Ltd would not be able to avoid liability for bad title to the bidets or for the defective bath. The 1977 Act thus interacts closely with the Sale of Goods Act 1979.

The "reasonableness" test

9–14 Clearly the "reasonableness test" in s.24 is of key significance in applying the 1977 Act. It helps determine if a contract clause is fair and reasonable.[25] A number of points can be made about it. The onus is on the party

---

[24] 1977 Act s.20.

[25] See also the judgment of the House of Lords in *George Mitchell (Chesterhall) Ltd v Finney Lock Seeds Ltd* [1983] 2 A.C. 803.

seeking to rely upon the clause to show that it is fair and reasonable.[26] Whether the clause was fair and reasonable is determined at the time the contract was made, not with regard to the subsequent events which have occurred.[27]

In the specific case of limitation clauses restricting liability to a specified sum of money the court must have regard to: (i) the resources open to the party seeking to rely on the term; and (ii) how far he can cover himself by insurance.[28]

So far as exemptions from the implied terms in sale and supply of goods are concerned, the reasonableness test is elaborated even further in Sch.2 to the 1977 Act.[29] In such cases the courts are directed to consider:

(1) the parties' relative bargaining strengths;
(2) whether an inducement was offered to accept the exemption clause or other offending term;
(3) whether the customer knew or ought to have known of the term;
(4) in the case of conditional terms, the likelihood of the condition not being complied with; and
(5) whether in the case of supply of goods, the goods were specially made for the customer.

In addition to these factors, the House of Lords has held that the following four factors should always be considered:

(1) Were the parties of equal bargaining power?
(2) In the case of advice would it have been reasonably practicable to obtain the advice from an alternative source?
(3) How difficult is the task being undertaken for which liability is being excluded? If the task is very difficult or dangerous it may be more reasonable to exclude liability as a condition of doing the work.
(4) What are the practical consequences of the decision on the question of reasonableness? This involves consideration of who will bear the loss and whether insurance for the loss could have been obtained.[30]

Four illustrations of the reasonableness test can be provided. First, a man **9–15** who had deposited a suitcase worth over £300 was held entitled to recover full compensation from British Rail when the suitcase disappeared, despite a limitation clause which attempted to restrict their liability to £7.[31] This clause was held not to be reasonable since the suitcase had disappeared whilst in British Rail's control. Secondly, a clause putting a

---

[26] 1977 Act s.24(4).
[27] 1977 Act s.24(1). Section 24(2A) makes equivalent provision for non-contractual notices, with reference to all the circumstances obtaining when the liability arose.
[28] 1977 Act s.24(3).
[29] 1977 Act s.24(2), Sch.2.
[30] *Smith v Eric S Bush (A Firm)* [1990] 1 A.C. 831 at 858–860.
[31] *Waldron-Kelly v British Railways Board* [1981] C.L.Y. 303.

ceiling on damages that could be claimed where a computer program was at fault was considered not to be fair and reasonable.[32] The court took account of the facts that the defendants were a large company who held insurance for the risk in question and that they were the only company that could meet the plaintiff's requirements. They also considered that all the defendants' competitors dealt in similar terms. The defendants were therefore in a very strong bargaining position. In the third illustration, in contrast, a clause limiting damages to 125 per cent of the contract price was held to be fair and reasonable (and indeed "generous") in a contract between two parties of equal bargaining strength. Other relevant factors included the evidence of ongoing negotiations about the contract terms, the fact that the claimant used similar limitation clauses in its own contracts, and that the claimant had specifically been advised to take out its own insurance against such losses.[33] In the fourth example, the limitation clause was reasonable: even though the parties were not of equal bargaining power, the claimants were still powerful and experienced business people and were not to be regarded as "innocents abroad". The were therefore capable of protecting their own interests.[34]

Further controls

9–16 In order to prevent draftsmen using devices to avoid the application of the 1977 Act controls, the Act itself specifies that it is not possible to evade its provisions by means of a secondary contract. Nor is it possible to attempt to avoid the negligence provisions of the 1977 Act by defining the obligations undertaken rather than exempting liability for breach of duty.[35] Suppose the owner of a sports stadium sought to exempt himself from liability to spectators using the premises. Instead of inserting an exemption clause in respect of negligent acts by himself and his employees, he might state that his sole obligation under the contract was to provide a spectator with a seat with a reasonable view of the event. Under the 1977 Act this would not exempt him from his liabilities. Neither is it possible to use a "choice of law" clause to evade the operation of the 1977 Act.[36] This prevents parties from inserting a clause such as, "this contract shall be subject to the law of Burkina Faso as administered by the courts in Ouagadougou" to circumvent the 1977 Act. Manufacturers' guarantees and indemnity clauses are also regulated.[37]

---

[32] *St Alban's City and DC v International Computers Plc* [1995] F.S.R. 686. This case was appealed on an issue other than the applicability of the clause.
[33] *Regus (UK) Ltd v Epcot Solutions Ltd* [2008] EWCA Civ 361.
[34] *Dennard v PricewaterhouseCoopers LLP* [2010] EWHC 812 (Ch).
[35] 1977 Act s.25(5).
[36] 1977 Act s.27.
[37] 1977 Act ss.18, 19.

THE UNFAIR TERMS IN CONSUMER CONTRACTS REGULATIONS 1999

In one sense, the ambit of the 1977 Act is relatively narrow. The Unfair **9–17**
Terms in Consumer Contract Regulations 1999[38] (the "Regulations")
provide a far more general protection in respect of unfair contract terms
in general. They identify classes of contract terms where the consent of
the weaker party to the contract is not real and then apply a test of
fairness. Their protection is not limited to exclusion or restriction clauses.
On the other hand, the Regulations are more limited in that they only
apply to consumer contracts, whereas the 1977 Act applies to some non-
consumer contracts. Further, the Regulations use the definition of consumer common in European legislation, which requires that the consumer be a natural person.

The Regulations were made in pursuance of a European Union
Council Directive.[39] The Directive seeks to harmonise the rules on unfair
contracts throughout the European Union.

Scope of application

The Regulations apply in relation to unfair terms in contracts concluded **9–18**
between a seller or a supplier and a consumer.[40] What is a "consumer"
under the Regulations? It is defined as "any natural person who ... is
acting for purposes which are outside his trade, business or profession."[41]
This excludes companies and partnerships as well as any individual who
enters into a contract for business purposes. A professional footballer
was not regarded as a consumer in relation to his professional dealings
with his agent.[42] On the other side of the contract, the expression "seller
or supplier" is defined as "any natural or legal person who ... is acting for
purposes relating to his trade, business or profession, whether publicly
owned or privately owned."[43] Accordingly, if a sole trader buys or sells
office equipment or a car for use in his business, he would appear to be
acting for a purpose relating to his business and therefore would not be a
"consumer" in terms of the Regulations.

Terms to which the Regulations apply

What contracts are covered? The Regulations do not spell this out. The **9–19**
use of the expression "seller or supplier" would appear to limit it to
contracts for sale and supply. In contrast to the 1977 Act, this would
exclude a contract of employment but would include a contract of
insurance. There are also references within the Regulations to "goods"

---

[38] SI 1999/2083.
[39] Directive 93/13 on unfair terms in consumer contracts [1993] OJ L95/29. The UK first
implemented this Directive through the Unfair Terms in Consumer Contracts Regulations 1994 (SI 1994/3159), but replaced these with the current regulations from 1999.
[40] See reg.4(1).
[41] See reg.3.
[42] *Prostar Management Ltd v Twaddle*, 2003 S.L.T. (Sh Ct) 11.
[43] See reg.3.

and "services",[44] albeit not in the definition of seller or supplier. However, in the parts of the Regulations which actually set out their scope of application, there is no such limitation. Further, the English Court of Appeal has given the Regulations a wide application, in deciding that they do apply to contracts for land, in this case a lease.[45]

The Regulations do not apply to every contract term. There are two important exclusions: terms that have been individually negotiated and core terms as to price and subject matter will not be subject to the control of the Regulations.

(i) Terms that have been individually negotiated

9–20 The Regulations apply only to terms which have "not been individually negotiated."[46] What is meant by "individually negotiated"? The Regulations provide some guidance:

> "A term shall always be regarded as not having been individually negotiated where it has been drafted in advance and the consumer has therefore not been able to influence the substance of the term."[47]

The onus of showing that a term was individually negotiated rests on the seller or supplier.[48] However, the critical point is not whether the consumer had the opportunity to negotiate, but whether the consumer *did* actually negotiate the term in question. The seller or supplier must therefore prove that the relevant term was in fact individually negotiated.[49]

(ii) Core terms as to price and subject matter

9–21 There is a further limitation on which clauses are subject to the fairness test.[50] Regulation 6(2) states:

> "In so far as it in plain intelligible language, the assessment of fairness of a term shall not relate—
>
> (a) to the definition of the main subject matter of the contract, or
> (b) to the adequacy of the price or remuneration, as against the goods or services supplied in exchange."

9–22 This provision was the subject of extensive judicial consideration in *Office of Fair Trading v Abbey National Plc.*[51]

---

[44] See reg.6(2), Sch.2.
[45] *R. (On the application of Khatun) v Newham LBC* [2004] EWCA Civ 55 at [83].
[46] See reg.5(1).
[47] See reg.5(2). These terms mirror exactly the terms of the Directive on which the Regulations are based.
[48] See reg.5(4).
[49] *UK Housing Alliance (North West) Ltd v Francis* [2010] EWCA Civ 117.
[50] See reg.6(2).
[51] *Office of Fair Trading v Abbey National Plc* [2009] UKSC 6.

The OFT sought a declaration from the courts in relation to certain terms and conditions used by eight high street banks (including the Abbey National) in their agreements with customers of their current accounts. These terms and conditions allowed the banks to charge customers set fees if they went overdrawn on their accounts without consent. By the time the case reached the House of Lords (where it was heard) and the Supreme Court (which gave judgment), the parties had agreed (i) that the terms in question were not individually negotiated between the banks and the customers (therefore the Regulations were relevant) and (ii) that the terms were, in the main, written in plain intelligible English. The only point of dispute between the OFT and the banks was whether or not the terms were covered by reg.6(2). The OFT sought a declaration that the terms were not covered by reg.6(2). The banks countered this. If the banks were successful in arguing that reg.6(2) applied, then the terms in question could not be challenged as unfair simply on the grounds of the adequacy of the price as against the services supplied in exchange. The question for the Supreme Court was therefore whether the terms relating to the charges for unauthorised overdrafts related to the subject matter and the price of the contract.

The trial judge and the Court of Appeal had both concluded that the terms in question were *not* part of the main subject matter. Therefore, the terms could be assessed without the limitation of reg.6(2). However, the Supreme Court reversed the decisions of the lower courts (noting that this outcome may well cause disappointment and dismay to many bank customers). Lord Walker stated:

> "I would declare that the bank charges levied on personal current account customers in respect of unauthorised overdrafts ... constitute part of the price or remuneration for the banking services provided and, in so far as the terms giving rise to the charges are in plain intelligible language, no assessment under the Unfair Terms in Consumer Contracts Regulations 1999 of the fairness of those terms may relate to their adequacy as against the services supplied."[52]

Rather than viewing the unauthorised overdraft charges as a penalty levied on customers, the court concluded that the charges were simply part of the "overall package contract". The charges were clearly set out in the contract and were readily recognisable as part of the price of the banking services. Because the terms were covered by reg.6(2), it was not open to the OFT to challenge the fairness of the terms on the grounds of "adequacy". In the words of the court, reg.6(2) operates to:

> "... preclude an attack on the price or remuneration in question if it is based on the contention that it was excessive by comparison with the services for which it was exchanged."[53]

---

[52] *OFT v Abbey National Plc* [2009] UKSC 6 at [51].
[53] *OFT v Abbey National Plc* [2009] UKSC 6, per Lord Phillips at [78].

9–23 In an earlier case, the House of Lords held that a clause in a banking contract which levied interest on a customer in default was *not* part of the price of the contract. It was not therefore protected by reg.6(2).[54] On first reading, it is difficult to reconcile these two decisions: in one, payments levied for unauthorised overdrafts were part of the contract price; in the other, interest charged for unauthorised default was not part of the contract price. The Supreme Court in *OFT v Abbey National* addressed this issue. The difference lies in the fact that the default interest was charged for a breach of contract, whereas the charges in the *Abbey National* case were part of the overall contract package. Customers did not have to make use of the unauthorised overdraft facility, but if they did, the bank would charge for that service. In some measure, at least, this interpretation was the result of the wording used in the terms and conditions in the later case. The narrowness of this distinction illustrates just how difficult it can be to determine the nature of a contract term under reg.6(2).

Regulation 6(2) makes sense. If it did not exist, consumers would be able to challenge the fairness of the contract price, for example. To strike down these terms at the core of the contract as unfair would amount to making the contract for the parties rather than ensuring that the contract they had made was fair. Of course, if the term defining price or subject matter is not in plain intelligible language, it then becomes subject to the test of unfairness.

The test of unfairness

9–24 "A contractual term ... shall be regarded as unfair if, contrary to the requirement of good faith, it causes a significant imbalance in the parties' rights and obligations arising under the contract, to the detriment of the consumer."[55]

The Regulations provide a lengthy list of the types of terms that may be regarded as unfair.[56] Essentially, the terms "caught" by the Regulations include features which may be summarised as follows:

    (1) Restrictions on the rights that the consumer might have against the supplier. These restrictions may take the form of exclusion of liability, limitation of liability or barriers in the way of taking proceedings to enforce rights. An example would be a term in a contract for sale of a computer printer stating: "The seller will not be liable for any damage caused to other computer equipment caused by the use of this product."

    (2) Granting the supplier a wide discretion as to whether, when or for how long his obligations under the contract should exist. An example would be a clause in the same contract saying:

---

[54] *Director General of Fair Trading v First National Bank Plc* [2001] UKHL 52. Although this case was decided on the earlier version of the Regulations (the 1994 Regulations), the substance was similar and both regulations were derived from the same Directive.

[55] See reg.5(1).

[56] See reg.5(5), Sch.2.

"Delivery of the goods ordered will be made at a time determined by the supplier".

(3) An inability of the consumer to complain if his obligations
under the contract are made more onerous or those of the
supplier are made less onerous. Suppose, for example, that an
insurance contract provided that the policyholder must make a
claim within 14 days of an accident and that the insurer had to
make payment on a valid claim within two months of the
accident. A clause saying, "The insurer reserves the right to vary
the period in which claims must be intimated and/or the period
in which payments will be made", would be unfair.

(4) The imposition of a financial burden on the consumer upon
termination of the contract that is excessive or not matched by
similar burdens on the supplier. Take, for example, a contract
for hire of a television and DVD player in which there is a clause
saying that either party may terminate the contract on 30 days'
notice. If there is another clause that says that if the consumer
exercises his option to terminate he will have to pay a termination charge equivalent to six months' rental it will be caught.

(5) Requirements that the consumer be irrevocably bound to terms
without having given a real opportunity to become acquainted
with them prior to the conclusion of the contract. For example,
a person wishes to hire a car. When he arrives at the garage to
collect it, he is given a contract with a term that states: "Our
standard terms and conditions of hire apply. A copy of these
terms may be obtained by writing to our head office."

In respect of some of the sample unfair terms there are special exceptions
to take account of situations in which they might operate too widely.[57]
For example, terms which have the effect of providing for the price of
goods to be determined at the time of delivery are in the list. Without an
exception this would catch a contract for a broker to buy shares or a
contract in which a bank was to supply foreign currency travellers che-
ques to a customer.

The list in the Regulations is said to be indicative.[58] In other words, **9–25**
inclusion in the list does not automatically mean that the term is unfair.
The fact a term falls within the Schedule would, however, carry a party
most of the way in any argument as to whether it was unfair. Equally it is
not an exhaustive list: other terms may be deemed unfair.

The issue of whether a term was unfair was considered by the House of **9–26**
Lords in *Director General of Fair Trading v First National Bank Plc*[59]:

The bank carried on a consumer credit business. It lent money on the
basis of a standard form of agreement. One of the terms of that

---

[57] See Sch.2(2).
[58] It is sometimes referred to as a grey list. If it had prohibited contract terms, it would have
been a black list: if it had approved contract terms, it would have been a white list.
[59] *Director General of Fair Trading v First National Bank Plc* [2001] UKHL 52.

agreement was to the effect that, where the borrower defaulted in making repayment of an instalment of the loan, the bank could demand repayment of the whole sum of principal and interest then outstanding. By virtue of the County Courts (Interest on Judgment Debts) Order 1991 (SI 1991/1184), the bank could also charge additional interest on this whole sum until it was paid.

The court required to consider whether the term in question was unfair under reg.4(1) of the 1994 Regulations which is in substantially the same terms as reg.5(1) of the 1999 Regulations. In interpreting the Regulations, the court referred to the Directive which they were intended to implement. The court noted that there were three tests for unfairness all of which had to be met: there must be (1) an absence of good faith; (2) a significant imbalance in the parties' rights and obligations; and (3) detriment to the consumer. However, Lord Steyn noted that the "twin requirements of good faith and significant imbalance will in practice be determinative."[60] The third element emphasises that the imbalance in question is against the consumer, rather than the supplier. These elements are to be assessed objectively.

In construing what was meant by the concept of "good faith" the court stated:

> "The requirement of good faith in this context is one of fair and open dealing. Openness requires that the terms should be expressed fully, clearly and legibly, containing no concealed pitfalls or traps. Appropriate prominence should be given to terms which might operate disadvantageously to the customer."[61]

The significant imbalance in the parties' rights will be met if "a term is so weighted in favour of the supplier as to tilt the parties' rights and obligations under the contract significantly in his favour."[62] As noted, a term which tilts the balance in favour of the consumer is not relevant.

The final conclusion of the House of Lords in this case was that the term itself could not be said to be unfair, when the disadvantage to the consumer arose from the interest charged under the County Courts (Interest on Judgment Debts) Order 1991. The remedy lay with Parliament rather than the courts.

9–27   Help in interpreting the test of unfairness is also available from the 1999 Regulations themselves. The list of the features that may be regarded as being unfair may provide guidance as to the considerations that may be taken into account. It is apparent that all these features create an imbalance in the parties' rights and obligations and would be to the detriment of the consumer.

---

[60] *Director General of Fair Trading v First National Bank Plc* [2001] UKHL 52 at [36].
[61] *Director General of Fair Trading v First National Bank Plc* [2001] UKHL 52, per Lord Bingham at [17].
[62] *Director General of Fair Trading v First National Bank Plc* [2001] UKHL 52, per Lord Bingham at [17].

A further complication in the Regulations is the reference to a "pre-formulated standard contract". The Regulations state:

> "Notwithstanding that a specific term or certain aspects of it in a contract has been individually negotiated, these regulations shall apply to the rest of the contract if an overall assessment of it indicates that it is a preformulated standard contract."[63]

As we have seen above, the test of unfairness from the Regulations applies to "[a] contract term which has not been individually negotiated".[64] If a term has not been individually negotiated, it should not matter that other parts of the contract have been negotiated. There appears to be no need for this additional provision as to "a pre-formulated standard contract". Nevertheless, it exists to clarify that consumers will not lose the protection of the Regulations in relation to non-negotiated terms simply because other terms have been individually agreed with the supplier.

The effect of unfairness

If a term is found to be unfair, it shall not be binding on the consumer.[65] **9–28**
The contract shall continue to bind the parties if it is capable of continuing in existence without the unfair term.[66]

One of the types of terms that is indicated in Sch.2 as being unfair is that which binds the consumer to terms which he has had no real chance of considering. This might apply to a term which seeks to incorporate standard terms and conditions contained in another document which the consumer has not had a chance to consider. If this clause is struck at as being unfair, the effect would be that *all* the other standard terms and conditions would cease to bind the consumer irrespective of whether individually they were unfair.

Written contracts

There is a requirement that any written term of a contract be expressed in **9–29**
plain, intelligible language.[67] There is no sanction applied for failure to comply with this requirement.

Where there is a doubt about the meaning of a written term, the interpretation most favourable to the consumer shall prevail.[68] In some situations this would function as a modification of the *contra proferentem* rule referred to in Ch.8.

---

[63] See reg.5(3).
[64] See reg.5(1). See paras 9–19 and 9–20 above.
[65] See reg.8(1).
[66] See reg.8(2).
[67] See reg.7.
[68] See reg.7(2).

Enforcement

9–30 Individual consumers may seek to enforce their rights under the Regulations. In addition, certain public bodies may seek to apply to a court to prevent a seller or supplier from using a term that is considered unfair for consumers as a whole.[69] This is what happened when the Office of Fair Trading took action against First National Bank and Abbey National in the cases discussed above. Where the court is faced with an action on behalf of consumers, it must consider the "hypothetical" typical consumer who might be affected by the clause(s) in question.[70] In contrast, where the action is raised by an individual consumer, there will be specific facts and circumstances to be considered. Part 8 of the Enterprise Act 2002 also makes provision for a general enforcement regime where an act of a trader harms the collective interests of all consumers. The Office of Fair Trading has used this procedure in Scotland to obtain an enforcement order in respect of the Regulations and the Sale of Goods Act 1979, to ensure that certain unfair terms were not used by a company in the sale and supply of double glazing.[71] The Regulations also provide an anti-avoidance measure. As with the 1977 Act, the Regulations prevent a seller or supplier from circumventing the protection to consumers by means of a choice of law clause.[72]

---

[69] See regs 10–15, as amended by the Public Bodies (The Office of Fair Trading Transfer of Consumer Advice Scheme Function and Modification of Enforcement Functions) Order 2013 (SI 2013/783). The Office of Fair Trading closed on April 1, 2014.

[70] *Office of Fair Trading v Foxtons Ltd* [2009] EWHC 1681 (Ch).

[71] *Office of Fair Trading v MB Designs (Scotland) Ltd* [2005] CSOH 85.

[72] See reg.9.

CHAPTER 10

BREACH OF CONTRACT AND REMEDIES

The terms of the contract determine the obligations owed by the parties **10–01** to one another. Breach of contract occurs when a party breaks one or more of those terms, without justification. Breach can occur in a number of ways:

> *Example*: A gas fitter, T, contracts to install a central heating system in B's house.
>
> > (1) T telephones B a week before the work is due to begin and informs B that he will not do the job because he has found more profitable work elsewhere: Anticipatory breach.
> > (2) T fails to turn up on the due date: Failure to perform.
> > (3) T installs the system in such a manner that seriously damages the fabric of B's house. Moreover, the system itself does not work: Defective performance.
> > (4) T takes an unreasonably long time to complete the job: Failure to perform timeously.

In each instance, T fails to fulfil his obligations under the contract. For the sake of convenience, throughout this chapter we shall refer to the party faced by a breach of contract (in the example, B) as the innocent party.

In some cases, T's failure to perform an obligation will not constitute a breach of contract. T may have a legitimate reason for not performing. For example, if B does not allow T access to the house, T will not be in breach of contract when he fails to install the central heating system.

When there is a breach of contract the innocent party will have a **10–02** remedy. Sometimes the remedy is stipulated in the contract itself. Others are provided by the general law of contract, such as damages. Remedies are generally cumulative, which means the innocent party may be able to exercise more than one remedy for the breach of contract.

GENERAL LEGAL REMEDIES FOR BREACH

Some terminology

Scots law uses a number of confusingly similar words in relation to **10–03** breach of contract:

(1) To *resile* from a contract means to withdraw from it lawfully, in the exercise of a right to do so, but not in response to a repudiation or breach.

(2) To *repudiate* a contract means to indicate clearly, by words or acts, that the repudiator will not perform it, having no right to withhold or refuse performance. It does not end the contract but gives the other party an option to rescind.

(3) To *rescind* a contract means to bring it to an end, at least so far as concerns the future performance of primary obligations, in response to a repudiation or material breach by the other party.[1]

Two fundamental principles

Mutuality

10–04 The obligations under the contract are reciprocal in nature. This is known as the principle of mutuality. Either both the parties are bound or neither is bound. This is relevant when considering the remedies that the law grants to the innocent party. Lord Justice-Clerk Moncreiff provided the classic statement on this principle:

> "I understand the law of Scotland in regard to mutual contracts to be quite clear—first, that the stipulations on either side are the counterparts and the consideration given for each other; second, that a failure to perform any material or substantial part of the contract on the part of one will prevent him from suing the other for performance; and, third, that where one party has refused or failed to perform his part of the contract in any material respect the other is entitled either to insist for implement, claiming damages for the breach, or to rescind the contract altogether—except so far as it has been performed."[2]

10–05 The party seeking a contractual remedy should therefore demonstrate that he himself is not in breach of a material part of his obligations. He can only insist on performance by the other party if he himself has fulfilled his side of the bargain. In the case of *Graham & Co v United Turkey Red Co Ltd*[3]:

> Graham entered into an agency contract in 1914, in terms of which he was to sell cotton goods manufactured by the United Turkey Red Co Ltd. Payment for his services was to be made on a commission basis. It was stipulated in the contract that he was not to sell other manufacturers' goods. From 1916 onwards, Graham was in breach

---

[1] Scottish Law Commission, *Discussion Paper on Remedies for Breach of Contract* (The Stationery Office, 1999), Scot. Law Com. D.P. No.109, para.1.14.

[2] *Turnbull v McLean & Co* (1874) 1 R. 730 at 738.

[3] *Graham & Co v United Turkey Red Co Ltd*, 1922 S.C. 533.

of that term. In 1918, after a dispute, Graham terminated the agreement and sued for the balance of his commission for the whole period of the contract.

The court held that he was only entitled to commission up to the time when he was still adhering to the agreement. The moment he began selling goods for other manufacturers, he lost his right to insist on performance by the United Turkey Red Co Ltd. After 1916 he was not fulfilling his side of the bargain so he could not require them to fulfil theirs. The mutuality of their bargain had ceased.

The principle of mutuality is of fundamental importance in Scots contract law: "the remedies that are available to enforce performance and to secure future performance are critically dependent on the concept of mutuality."[4] Thus, mutuality underpins the remedies of retention and rescission.

Until recently, there was some debate as to the operation of mutuality. Does it mean that every obligation in a contract is the counterpart of every other? Or is it the case that certain obligations will be reciprocal with some but not all of the obligations upon the other party?[5] The Supreme Court has affirmed the approach in *Turnbull v McLean & Co*. Lord Hope stated:

> "The guiding principle is that the unity of the overall transaction should be respected. The analysis should start from the position that all the obligations that it embraces are to be regarded as counterparts of each other unless there is a clear indication to the contrary."[6]

Whether each obligation is the counterpart of the others is ultimately a matter of circumstance, but the starting point is to recognise the unity of the contract. The courts have also recognised that in some cases there may be mutuality between obligations contained in different contracts between the same parties, so long as it is clear that these are part of the same transaction.[7]

Materiality

The other factor that influences the remedies available to the innocent **10–06** party is the materiality of the breach. Materiality means the degree of importance or seriousness of the breach.

> "It is familiar law, and quite settled by decision, that in any contract which contains multifarious stipulations there are some which go so to the root of the contract that a breach of those stipulations entitles

---

[4] *McNeill v Aberdeen City Council (No2)* [2013] CSIH 103, per Lord Drummond Young at [20].
[5] *Macari v Celtic Football & Athletic Co Ltd*, 1999 S.C. 628.
[6] *Inveresk Plc v Tullis Russell Papermakers Ltd* [2010] UKSC 19, per Lord Hope at [42].
[7] *Inveresk Plc v Tullis Russell Papermakers Ltd* [2010] UKSC 19, per Lord Hope at [38].

the party pleading the breach to declare that the contract is at an end. There are others which do not go to the root of the contract, but which are part of the contract, and which would give rise, if broken, to an action of damages."[8]

The more serious the breach which has occurred, the greater the range of remedies open to the innocent party. If a customer has ordered a new Porsche, then it is one thing to deliver a Porsche with a scratch on the bonnet[9]; it is quite another to deliver a Ford Focus instead. Where a breach goes to the root or core of the contract it is said that the party in breach has repudiated the contract. What constitutes the core of the contract must be determined by examining the whole contract. Alternatively, the parties may choose to stipulate that a term is material or "of the essence".[10] Breach will then go to the root of the contract.

Rescission

10–07 A person faced by a breach of contract may wish to be released from the contract. Suppose a florist fails to deliver flowers to a hotel on time. The hotel may wish to rescind the agreement and obtain the flowers elsewhere. By rescinding the contract, the innocent party accepts that neither party requires to fulfil the contract.[11] The florist no longer needs to send the flowers; the hotel does not require to pay the price. However, the contract may remain alive for some purposes. For example, certain debts may have accrued or a right to damages, or a liquidated damage clause in respect of the breach may exist, or there may be an arbitration clause to regulate any dispute which has arisen. Accordingly, it is more correct to say that the effect of rescission is to terminate the innocent party's future obligations under the contract. Lord Drummond Young has recently clarified this:

> "It is sometimes said that the effect of rescission is to 'terminate' the contract, or bring it to an end. While this is often a convenient shorthand, it should be noted that the contract is not in fact 'terminated' in its entirety. What happens in the event of rescission is that the parties are relieved of any obligation to make further performance of their primary or substantive obligations under the contract ... the parties' accrued rights are not affected".[12]

---

[8] *Wade v Waldon*, 1909 S.C. 571, per Lord President Dunedin at 576.
[9] Although this may constitute a material breach of contract in consumer contracts, by virtue of statutory regulation: Sale of Goods Act 1979 s.15B(2).
[10] This is common in insurance contracts. See *Dawsons Ltd v Bonnin*, 1922 S.C. (HL) 156. It is also common in contracts for the sale of goods in relation to time, as per s.10 of the Sale of Goods Act 1979.
[11] *GL Group Plc v Ash Gupta Advertising Ltd*, 1987 S.C.L.R. 149.
[12] *McNeill v Aberdeen City Council (No.2)* [2013] CSIH 103, per Lord Drummond Young at [23].

However, where one party does seek to rescind, the fact that it gives the wrong reason, or no reason at all, for that rescission will not usually be significant—provided always that the party did have good grounds for rescinding.[13]

Repudiation

The innocent party may only rescind the contract if faced by a breach **10–08** which is so material as to amount to repudiation of the contract. Courts are slow to hold that there has been repudiation:

"... it is a drastic conclusion which should only be held to arise in clear cases of a refusal, in a matter going to the root of the contract, to perform contractual obligations."[14]

The repudiation may take the form of a breach of contract, or an anticipatory breach of contract. However, where one party seeks to vary the contract terms, the courts have recognised that such a proposal will not necessarily amount to repudiation:

"We consider that a contracting party must always be entitled, especially in altered circumstances, to propose or suggest a future variation of the relevant contractual terms for the other party to consider. Provided that a refusal to perform on existing terms is not simultaneously demonstrated, it does not seem to us that the mere tabling of such a proposal or suggestion will necessarily amount to repudiation of the contract."[15]

It is important to note that repudiation of itself does not terminate the **10–09** contract. It is not open to one party unilaterally to declare the contract terminated. When repudiation occurs, the contract will only be terminated if the innocent party responds by rescinding it. Should the innocent party choose not to rescind, the contract will continue and can be enforced, for example through an action for specific implement.[16] The innocent party will be entitled to seek specific implement unless "circumstances render it impossible, or in exceptional circumstances, wholly unjust."[17] It is therefore not possible for one party to terminate the contract through its own breach and force the innocent party to accept damages.[18] There is, however, a narrow line between rescission and repudiation. In the case of *Wade v Waldon*[19]:

---

[13] *Persimmon Homes Ltd v Bellway Homes Ltd* [2011] CSOH 149, per Lord Drummond Young at [10].

[14] *Woodar Investment Development Ltd v Wimpey Construction UK Ltd* [1980] 1 W.L.R. 277; [1980] 1 All E.R. 571, per Lord Wilberforce at 576.

[15] *Wyman-Gordon Ltd v Proclad International Ltd* [2010] CSIH 99 at [39].

[16] *AMA (New Town) Ltd v Law* [2013] CSIH 61.

[17] *AMA (New Town) Ltd v Law* [2013] CSIH 61, per Lady Dorrian at [48].

[18] *AMA (New Town) Ltd v Law* [2013] CSIH 61, per Lady Dorrian at [46].

[19] *Wade v Waldon*, 1909 S.C. 571.

George Robey, a famous comedian of the time, contracted to appear a year later at two Glasgow theatres, the Palace and the Pavilion, for a one-week engagement. Shortly before his performances were due to take place, Robey looked in vain for advertisements for his show. He contacted the management. They informed him that the booking was cancelled. They referred to cl.6 of his contract which stated: "All artistes engaged ... must give fourteen days' notice prior to such engagements, such notice to be accompanied by bill matter [publicity material]." He had omitted to provide such material. Robey offered to fulfil his engagement but the management refused. He pointed out that he had not given notice or "bill matter" for his last engagement, and sued them for £300. The defenders argued that breach of cl.6 was a serious one which amounted to repudiation and they were therefore entitled to rescind the contract. The court disagreed. It held that the failure to provide bill matter did not go to the root of the contract and found against the management. Since the management were not entitled to rescind the contract, its refusal to allow Robey to appear amounted to repudiation of the contract, thereby giving him a claim for damages.

Some writers have argued that this is a hard decision. Why should the management be forced to accept Robey without proper notice or advertising material? The answer may be that his fame was such that the theatre simply had to put up his name for an audience to appear, so that the failure to provide bill matter was not material. Further, the management had waived the requirement for bill matter in the past. It therefore seems that justice was done.

10–10   Two further cases underline the difficulties of determining who has repudiated the contract. In *Blyth v Scottish Liberal Club* an employee refused to perform certain duties which he believed formed no part of the scope of his employment.[20] Although it was accepted that his belief was an honest one, it was held to be mistaken. Accordingly, his employers were entitled to terminate the employment as a result of his breach. His belief was unjustifiable in the circumstances. In *GL Group Plc v Ash Gupta Advertising Ltd*, an advertising company became concerned about the financial position of their clients.[21] They wrote seeking payment of all their work to date, together with a sum in respect of future work. The letter also stated that if payment was not received within 24 hours they "would have no alternative to resile from the contract." This was held to amount to repudiation.

Retention and lien

10–11   A breach may not be sufficiently material to justify rescission. Alternatively it may be disadvantageous to the innocent party to rescind. Contracts of lease furnish a useful illustration. Where a landlord fails to

---

[20] *Blyth v Scottish Liberal Club*, 1983 S.L.T. 260; see now *Ghaznavi v BP Oil (UK) Ltd*, 1991 S.L.T. 924.
[21] *GL Group Plc v Ash Gupta Advertising Ltd*, 1987 S.C.L.R. 149.

fulfil his obligation to keep the premises in good repair, the tenant will often not wish to terminate the lease. Nonetheless, he will have suffered a breach of contract.

Faced by breach, a person may withhold performance of his own obligations under the contract (retention) or retain possession of the other party's goods (lien). Retention and lien are ways of exerting pressure on the other party to perform his side of the bargain. If a solicitor is carrying out work for a client and is faced by a refusal to pay interim fees that are due, he may refuse to carry out the remainder of the work that he had agreed to do until he is paid. Commonly, retention takes the form of a refusal to make a payment due under the contract because the other party is in breach of their obligations. For payment to be retained in this way it is necessary that the breach existed when the payment fell due.[22]

Retention operates to *suspend* performance. It does not operate to cancel the innocent party's obligation to perform. Once the party in breach has complied with his obligation, the party who has retained performance must then perform too. Accordingly, "the right of retention is of considerable practical importance in Scots law, as it serves to provide security for future performance of the contract."[23] This concept of securing future contractual performance can be seen as the key objective of retention.

Two points are central to the remedy of retention. First, although the **10–12** breach does not have to be so material to justify rescission, it does have to be more than trivial.[24] Secondly, retention relies on the doctrine of mutuality. In order to exercise the remedy of retention, the innocent party has to show that the obligation he is withholding and the obligation which was breached are mutual. Where a contract is regarded as operating in stages, then the right of retention may only be exercised separately at each stage.[25] There is also judicial approval of the notion that "retention cannot generally be invoked in respect of a breach of contract that has occurred in the past and is unlikely to be repeated".[26] This reflects the fundamental function of the right, in providing security for future performance. However, since all breaches (other than anticipatory breaches) will have happened and therefore by definition will be in the past, it is suggested that this should be interpreted to mean breaches which are in the distant past and do not affect the ongoing performance of the contract.

To give an example, a builder is engaged to build six houses and he installs the wrong kitchen in the first house. While this breach is in the past, it could easily be repeated when he builds the subsequent houses. Retention may therefore be appropriate to secure future performance,

---

[22] *Redpath Dorman Long Ltd v Cummings Engine Co Ltd*, 1981 S.C. 370; 1982 S.L.T. 489.

[23] *McNeill v Aberdeen City Council (No.2)* [2013] CSIH 102, per Lord Drummond Young at [27].

[24] *Inveresk Plc v Tullis Russell Papermakers Ltd* [2010] UKSC 19, per Lord Hope at [43].

[25] *Bank of East Asia Ltd v Scottish Enterprise*, 1997 S.L.T. 1213; affirmed *Inveresk Plc v Tullis Russell Papermakers Ltd* [2010] UKSC 19.

[26] *McNeill v Aberdeen City Council (No.2)* [2013] CSIH 102, per Lord Drummond Young at [29].

and to encourage the builder to fit the correct kitchen. In contrast, say only the first house is to have a conservatory, and the builder uses the wrong glass in the conservatory. He then builds the next four houses according to contract. On this analysis, it would not be possible for the employer to exercise retention in respect of the sums due for the sixth house on the basis of the incorrect glass in the first house: the breach has happened in the past and is not likely to be repeated. Moreover, the sums due for the sixth house are arguably not the counterparts of building the first house, thus contravening the doctrine of mutuality. The employer would of course have other remedies, such as damages, for the builder's breach of contract in using the wrong glass in the conservatory.

10–13   There is also an equitable dimension to retention: the court should "ensure it does not become an instrument of abuse ... in any particular case the court may exercise a discretion as to whether retention should be permitted to operate, and if so on what terms."[27] This would enable the court to prevent a party from retaining performance of a significant obligation when the breach in question was minor.

In construction contracts governed by the Housing Grants, Construction and Regeneration Act 1996, the right of retention of performance for non-payment will not be available unless notice has been served on the party in default first.[28]

Lien is a particular type of retention. It takes the form of holding on to property which should otherwise be delivered to the other party. A special lien arises when a person is employed to do work on specific goods belonging to another. For example, a garage may hold on to a car until the repairs that have been carried out have been paid for. Certain persons such as solicitors have a general lien over all documents in their hands against the balance of their account.

JUDICIAL REMEDIES

Action for payment

10–14   The most common action which arises out of contract is a simple action for the payment of money. Where the contract price is not paid, the creditor will seek payment by way of an action to recover his debt. The creditor will be entitled to interest on the sum due. The date and rate from which interest will run will depend on the terms of the contract.

If the contract does not specify a rate, interest at the judicial rate can be claimed.[29]

---

[27] *McNeill v Aberdeen City Council (No.2)* [2013] CSIH 102, per Lord Drummond Young at [30].

[28] Housing Grants, Construction and Regeneration Act 1996 s.112.

[29] In some instances, this will be governed by the Late Payment of Commercial Debts (Interest) Act 1998.

Specific implement and interdict

A person faced by breach may apply to the court to require the other **10–15**
party to fulfil his obligations under the contract. In the case of a positive
obligation, the remedy is specific implement.[30] Suppose P purchases an
antique bureau at auction. Subsequently, the seller decides that he no
longer wishes to sell the bureau and refuses to deliver it to P. P can raise
an action concluding for specific implement of the contract of sale. In the
case of a negative obligation the remedy is interdict. Take an example
drawn from the law of options: S pays G £10,000 in return for an option
to purchase G's factory on or before a date three years from the date of
payment. Should G attempt to sell the factory to J before the time limit
has expired, S may seek an interdict to prevent him from doing so.
Failure to obey an interlocutor, i.e. decree, pronouncing specific implement or interdict may amount to contempt of court and be visited by a
fine or imprisonment. Because of this there is a requirement that a decree
of specific implement or interdict must be expressed in clear terms that
leave the defender in no doubt as to what he has to do. The laws of
Scotland and England are different in relation to these remedies.[31] In the
Scottish House of Lords case of *Stewart v Kennedy*,[32] Lord Watson said:

> "I do not think that upon this matter any assistance can be derived
> from English decisions; because the laws of the two countries regard
> the right to specific performance from different standpoints. In
> England the only legal right arising from a breach of contract is a
> claim of damages; specific performance is not matter [*sic*] of legal
> right, but a purely equitable remedy, which the Court can withhold
> when there are sufficient reasons of conscience or expediency against
> it. But in Scotland the breach of a contract for the sale of a specific
> subject such as landed estate gives the party aggrieved the legal right
> to sue for implement, and although he may elect to do so, he cannot
> be compelled to resort to the alternative of an action of damages,
> unless implement is shewn to be impossible, in which case *loco facti
> subit damnum et interesse*. Even where implement is possible, I do
> not doubt that the Court of Session has inherent power to refuse the
> legal remedy upon equitable grounds, although I know of no
> instance in which it has done so. It is quite conceivable that cir-
> cumstances might occur which would make it inconvenient and
> unjust to enforce specific performance of contract of sale, but I do
> not think that any such case is presented in this appeal."

---

[30] The type of decree sought is often referred to as "decree *ad factum praestandum*".
[31] In England the terms are specific performance and injunction respectively.
[32] *Stewart v Kennedy* (1890) 17 R. (HL) 25.

10–16 The difference can be illustrated by cases, two in Scotland[33] and one in England,[34] where the facts were similar but the result reached could not have been more different:

Each case was an action brought by a landlord of a shopping centre against a tenant of the centre. In each case, the lease between the landlord and the tenant contained a clause that required the tenant to remain in the property and conduct business from the property (known as a "keep open" clause). In each case the tenant did not wish to continue to conduct business from the property but was content to pay the rent stipulated in the lease and to observe their other obligations, while the shop unit stood empty. There is a value to landlords of shopping centres in having the units occupied and trading so that the centre is popular and attracts shoppers. It is not only important to the landlord to receive rent, but to ensure the shopping centre flourishes. The landlords therefore applied to the courts for orders that would require the tenants to keep the premises open and conduct business from them.

In each of the Scottish cases the order was granted.[35] In the English case it was not. The Scottish cases adopted and relied upon Lord Watson's dictum to the effect that the innocent party was entitled to insist that the contract that they had made be performed. In the English case, Lord Hoffman restated the position there and noted that:

> "Specific performance is traditionally regarded in English law as an exceptional remedy, as opposed to the common law damages to which a successful plaintiff is entitled as of right ... [B]y the nineteenth century it was orthodox doctrine that the power to decree specific performance was part of the discretionary jurisdiction of the Court of Chancery to do justice in cases in which the remedies available at common law were inadequate. This is the basis of the general principle that specific performance will not be ordered when damages are an adequate remedy."

10–17 Although specific implement is the primary remedy in Scotland, the courts retain an equitable power to refuse the remedy:

> "It appears to me that a superior court, having equitable jurisdiction, must also have a discretion, in certain exceptional cases, to withhold from parties applying for it that remedy to which, in ordinary circumstances, they would be entitled as a matter of course.

---

[33] *Retail Parks Investments Ltd v Royal Bank of Scotland Plc (No.2)*, 1996 S.C. 227; 1996 S.L.T. 669 and *Highland & Universal Properties Ltd v Safeway Properties Ltd (No.2)*, 2000 S.C. 297; 2000 S.L.T. 414.

[34] *Cooperative Insurance Society Ltd v Argyll Stores (Holdings) Ltd* [1998] A.C. 1; [1997] 3 All E.R. 297.

[35] In a subsequent Scottish case, the pursuer sought and obtained damages for breach of a "keep open" clause: *Douglas Shelf Seven Ltd v Co-operative Wholesale Society Ltd* [2007] CSOH 3.

In order to justify the exercise of such a discretionary power there must be some very cogent reason for depriving litigants of the ordinary means of enforcing their legal rights."[36]

Lord Watson's dictum indicates that the discretion is a narrow one. In one case it was noted that: "Considerations of what is or is not reasonable are quite irrelevant."[37] The circumstances in which it might apply have been variously described as those where the decree would be "inconvenient and unjust"[38] or where the innocent party had "no legitimate interest, financial or otherwise, in performing the contract rather than claiming damages."[39] It is apparent that whatever test is applied, it is one that is difficult to satisfy.

In addition to the general equitable power to withhold the remedy there are a number of situations where it is recognised that the innocent party has no right to implement:

(a) A decree of specific implement cannot be obtained to enforce an obligation to pay money. Otherwise a debtor would be in contempt of court for defaulting in payment and liable to imprisonment.

(b) The courts will not enforce contracts involving a personal relationship. It would be an undue restraint on personal liberty to compel persons to work together. The manager of the pop group "The Troggs" could not keep his post when the group members lost faith in him and sacked him.[40] Similarly, where the boxer Nigel Benn changed management, his original manager sought to prevent the new manager from inducing a breach of the original contract.[41]

(c) The court will not grant decree if a decree could not be enforced, or if it is impossible for the party to fulfil performance under the contract.

The pursuer's right to seek implement of one clause of the contract is not lost if he has sued for damages in respect of breach of another clause.[42]

Damages

It is typically said that in Scots law every breach of contract gives rise to a **10–18** claim for damages:

---

[36] *Grahame v Magistrates of Kirkcaldy* (1882) 9 R. (HL) 91.
[37] *Salaried Staff London Loan Co Ltd v Swears and Wells Ltd*, 1985 S.C. 189; 1985 S.L.T. 326, per Lord President Emslie.
[38] *Salaried Staff London Loan Co Ltd v Swears and Wells Ltd*, 1985 S.C. 189; 1985 S.L.T. 326, per Lord President Emslie at 329.
[39] *White & Carter (Councils) Ltd v McGregor*, 1962 S.C. (HL) 1; 1962 S.L.T. 9.
[40] *Page One Records Ltd v Britton* [1967] 3 All E.R. 822.
[41] *Warren v Mendy* [1989] 1 W.L.R. 853; [1989] 3 All E.R. 103.
[42] *Douglas Shelf Seven Ltd v Co-operative Wholesale Society Ltd* [2009] CSOH 3.

"The contract and the breach of it are established. That leads of necessity to an award of damages. It is impossible to say that a contract can be broken even in respect of time without the party being entitled to claim damages—at the lowest, nominal damages."[43]

However, the Inner House has observed that this is not always the case:

"We are not persuaded that a breach of contract confers an automatic entitlement to at least nominal damages ... Much of the difficulty raised in discussions of the point arises from the distinction made in the earlier cases between 'actual damage' and trouble and inconvenience ... There could be cases, in our view, where a breach of contract was to the immediate benefit of the innocent party. In that event, it would be contrary to principle that the innocent party should be entitled to nominal damages for the mere fact of the breach."[44]

If this approach is followed, the innocent party would be unable to claim any damages in the (rare) case where he had not suffered loss and had actually benefited from the breach. However, the Inner House affirmed that where the innocent party could show that he had been "put to trouble and inconvenience" by the breach then a nominal award would be appropriate.[45]

Despite this general right to damages, in the case of minor breaches, parties will rarely wish to undergo the financial (and sometimes emotional) outlay involved in vindicating their rights in a court of law. Suppose a customer has a complaint which is not satisfactorily dealt with by personal representation at the shop. He may well seek help from a newspaper consumer column, trade association or ombudsman, rather than raise an action in the sheriff court.[46]

In assessing damages, the courts will need to measure the extent and type of the loss. There are also three doctrines which restrict the availability of damages: causation; remoteness; and mitigation.

The measure of damages

10–19 Every day, courts assess damages. However, "the assessment of damages is not an exact science."[47] It is easier to state the general principles than to determine the exact level of award in a particular case:

---

[43] *Webster v Cramond Iron Co* (1875) 4 R. 752, per Lord President Inglis at 754.

[44] *Wilkie v Brown*, 2003 S.C. 573 at 579.

[45] *Wilkie v Brown*, 2003 S.C. 573 at 579.

[46] Although there are simplified forms of procedure to deal with small claims in the sheriff court.

[47] *Koufos v C Czarnikow Ltd (The Heron II)* [1969] 1 A.C. 350, per Lord Upjohn at 425.

"... the broad general rule of the law of damages [is] that a party injured by the other party's breach of contract is entitled to such money compensation as will put him in the position in which he would have been but for the breach."[48]

It is sometimes said that contract damages are "forward looking". This means they aim to put the innocent party in the future position he would have been in if the contract had been performed.[49]

Although this rule is straightforward, there are a number of ways in which damages can be calculated. In general, damages are measured according to the loss suffered by the innocent party, not by reference to the gain made in consequence of the breach by the contract-breaker. In *Teacher v Calder*[50]:

A agreed to lend £15,000 to B to use in his business as a timber merchant under an agreement which was to last five years. B agreed to keep at least £15,000 of his own money in the business during that period. B broke the contract and withdrew sums which he invested in a distillery where they earned lucrative profits. Damages were assessed by reference to A's loss, not by reference to the (higher) profits made by B.

Three English cases have, however, adopted different bases for measuring **10–20** damages in special circumstances. First, in *Ruxley Electronics & Construction Ltd v Forsyth*[51]:

The defendant had contracted with the plaintiffs for them to install a swimming pool in his garden. The contract said that at the deep end the pool should be 7ft 6in deep. This was to allow the owner to use the pool for diving. When it was complete it was discovered that the pool was only 6ft 9in deep. This meant that the owner could not safely dive into it. This change in depth had not diminished the market value of the pool, although it did diminish the use value of the pool to the owner. If economic loss was the only measure of damages, the defendant would have got nothing despite the fact that there was clearly a breach of contract. The defendant argued that in order to reflect his loss the damages would have to be the sum it would cost to dig up the pool and reconstruct it, which was £21,560.

The House of Lords were unanimous in rejecting the defendant's claim. They did so on the basis that the cost of reinstatement would be excessive when compared to the benefit that would result. However, this did not

---

[48] *A/B Karlshamns Oljefabriker v Monarch Steamship Co Ltd*, 1949 S.C. (HL) 1, per Lord Wright at 18.

[49] In contrast, damages in delict are "backward looking", since they aim to undo the harm caused, insofar as money can.

[50] *Teacher v Calder* (1898) 25 R. 661; affirmed on this point (1899) 1 F. (HL) 39.

[51] *Ruxley Electronics & Construction Ltd v Forsyth* [1995] 3 All E.R. 268.

mean that, because there was no diminution in value, there was no award of damages. They said that apart from diminution in value and the cost of re-doing the works, there was a third means of assessing damages. This was to examine the loss of amenity that had occurred. The defendant had been denied a pleasurable amenity for which he contracted and should be compensated for that loss. The sum awarded was £2,500.

10–21   The second development occurred in *Attorney General v Blake*[52]:

> The defendant was employed in the British security and intelligence services from 1944 to 1961. During that period he became an agent for the Soviet Union and supplied secret information to them. In 1961 he was convicted of treason and sentenced to 42 years' imprisonment. In 1966 he escaped and fled to the Soviet Union. In the late 1980s he wrote his autobiography. He earned a substantial fee from the publisher. The Attorney General raised proceedings against him which ultimately came to include a claim for damages for having breached a contractual undertaking not to divulge information learned in the course of his employment. Although there had been a breach of the contractual undertaking, it could not be said that the United Kingdom Government (his employer) had suffered any loss. The issue became whether the damages could be assessed by reference to what the defendant had gained—the publisher's fee for the book. This would be achieved by requiring him to account to the Government for the fee he had made.

By a majority of four to one the House of Lords held that the Government were entitled to an accounting for profits. This is a substantial departure from the rule noted in *Teacher*. The circumstances in which this rule might apply are not clear. Lord Nicholls indicated that two conditions would have to be satisfied. The first was that the plaintiff could demonstrate a "legitimate interest in preventing the defendant's profit-making activity and, hence, in depriving him of his profit". The second was that the legitimate interest made it "just and equitable that the defendant should retain no benefit from his breach of contract". It is clear that this measure of damages will usually be applied only in exceptional circumstances.[53]

10–22   The third measure originates in an older English decision, which was resurrected by the House of Lords in *Attorney General v Blake*. "Wrotham Park" damages stem from the case of *Wrotham Park Estate Co*

---

[52] *Attorney General v Blake* [2001] 1 A.C. 268; [2000] 4 All E.R. 385.

[53] This remains the position in Scots law, where the impact of *Attorney General v Blake* has not yet been tested. However, the case was followed in a non-exceptional commercial breach situation in the English case of *Esso v Niad* [2001] All E.R. 324, Ch D.

Ltd v Parkside Homes Ltd.[54] Here, 14 extra houses were built in a development in contravention of a contractual restriction on the number of houses. Once the houses were built they could not be torn down, so the breach could not be reversed. The plaintiff suffered no economic loss, but the defendant had breached the contract and made a gain from doing so. The court awarded damages calculated according to the amount the plaintiff would have charged the defendant to release him from the obligation. This measure is therefore sometimes called the "hypothetical release" measure. It allows the pursuer to claim a sum of money which represents what he would (in theory) have charged the defender to be released from the contract.

Type of loss suffered

Breach of contract normally involves loss measurable in money terms **10–23** (pecuniary loss). The innocent party is hit in the pocket. For example, if A breaches the contract by the late delivery of a photocopier, the innocent party might wish to claim damages for (a) the cost of hiring a photocopier for the period of the delay; and (b) any lost profits if customers took their business elsewhere.[55]

As contracts are concerned with economic transactions, it was for a long time impossible to obtain damages for non-pecuniary loss. So if an employee was wrongfully dismissed in humiliating circumstances he could not recover compensation in respect of the injured feelings which he suffered.[56] Such loss was said to be too remote. He could only recover in respect of his lost wages.

In some contracts, however, the only or main loss which results is non-pecuniary. In certain circumstances such loss can be recovered. A wedding photographer who fails to turn up at the wedding to take the official photographs is liable in damages for the disappointment this causes.[57] Likewise when a holiday completely fails to live up to the claims made for it in the brochure and ruins the pleasure of the holidaymaker.[58] The principle is that where a purpose of the contract is to raise expectations of a non-pecuniary nature and breach occurs, damages may be recoverable for the disappointment and injured feelings which result. It has been extended to cover situations where it is a direct consequence of the breach

---

[54] *Wrotham Park Estate Co Ltd v Parkside Homes Ltd* [1974] 1 W.L.R. 798. Although overturned by the Court of Appeal in *Surrey CC and Mole DC v Bredero Homes Ltd* [1993] 3 All E.R. 705, the decision in *Wrotham Park* was approved and effectively reinstated by the House of Lords in *Attorney General v Blake*. It has recently been discussed by the Privy Council in *Pell Frischmann Engineering Ltd v Bow Valley Iran Ltd* [2009] UKPC.

[55] *Watts v Bell & Scott WS* [2007] CSOH 108.

[56] *Addis v Gramophone Co Ltd* [1909] A.C. 488.

[57] *Diesen v Samson*, 1971 S.L.T. (Sh Ct) 49.

[58] *Jarvis v Swans Tours Ltd* [1973] Q.B. 233; [1973] 1 All E.R. 71. This was approved by the House of Lords in *Ruxley Electronics & Construction Ltd v Forsyth* [1995] 3 All E.R. 257. See also *Milner v Carnival Plc (t/a Cunard)* [2010] EWCA Civ 389, where the couple whose expectations had been disappointed had spent £59,000 on their cruise: they were awarded £12,000.

that the innocent party will suffer trouble, distress and inconvenience. Many cases for professional negligence brought against solicitors include such a claim. Take the example of a client who alleges that her solicitor has been negligent in respect of conveyancing on his new house. One head of damage will relate to trouble, distress and inconvenience in respect of matters such as not getting into a new house on time.[59]

Causation

10–24 Before an award of damages can be made it must be established not only that there has been a breach and a loss, but that there is a direct causal link between that breach and loss. In *A/B Karlhamns Oljefabriker v Monarch Steamship Co Ltd*[60]:

> A charterparty was entered into for the transport of soya beans from Manchuria to Sweden. The contract included two clauses which provided (a) that the ship should be seaworthy, and (b) that it would not be a breach if the ship deviated, if required to do so by an order of the British Government. This second clause was inserted because the parties recognised the risk of war and thought there was a real chance that the ship might be requisitioned during the course of its voyage. Unknown to the shipowners, the ship was unseaworthy when it left port and it was delayed in both Colombo and Port Said to effect repairs. When it reached Britain it was detained by the government, the Second World War having broken out. The charterers sought to recover from the owners the extra cost of shipping the soya beans from Glasgow to Sweden. The owners defended the action on the basis that the real cause of the extra cost was the act of the British Government in requisitioning the ship. As the contract stated the Government action was not to be a breach, no claim for damages could succeed.

The House of Lords rejected this argument and found that the dominant cause of the loss was the initial unseaworthiness of the ship. Without that, the ship would in all likelihood have arrived on time and avoided requisition by the Government. Accordingly, the pursuers had established the link between their loss and the defenders' breach of contract and were entitled to damages.

Remoteness

10–25 A breach of contract may give rise to many consequences. The contract-breaker will not, however, be held liable for all that flows from the breach.

---

[59] *Curran v Docherty*, 1995 S.L.T. 716.
[60] *A/B Karlhamns Oljefabriker v Monarch Steamship Co Ltd*, 1949 S.C. (HL) 1.

Example: P, a businessman, hires a taxi to go to the airport. The taxi fails to turn up, P misses his flight and loses the opportunity to make an important business deal at his proposed destination. Subsequently P's business goes bankrupt, his house is repossessed, his wife leaves him and so on.

In this example, a causal link can be shown between the breach and all the subsequent losses. The policy decision for the law to answer is, however, how far should the contract-breaker be responsible for the consequences caused by his breach? In general, a defender is not liable when the loss is "too remote". What is remoteness? Bankton said compensation was payable in respect of loss which "proceeds immediately from the thing itself."[61] The leading Scottish case is *Balfour Beatty Construction (Scotland) Ltd v Scottish Power Plc*[62]:

In 1985 Balfour Beatty were engaged in constructing the city bypass to the west of Edinburgh. The works included the construction of an aqueduct to carry the Union Canal across the new bypass. The aqueduct was to be made of concrete. In order to mix the concrete a site was obtained nearby at a quarry near Ratho. The South of Scotland Electricity Board (SSEB) supplied electricity to the site. (Subsequently Scottish Power inherited SSEB's liabilities.) The aqueduct required a long continuous pour of concrete for the first stage of its construction, to ensure it was watertight. When the pour was almost complete, the electricity supply was interrupted. In consequence, the aqueduct had to be demolished and reconstructed. Balfour Beatty sued for breach of contract and concluded for payment of damages of £229,102.53. At first instance, Lord Clyde held (a) that SSEB were in breach of contract; but (b) that the loss claimed was too remote. South of Scotland Electricity Board were not informed nor could they have been otherwise aware that a continuous pour of concrete was required for a particular operation and that reconstruction would be required if the electricity supply failed. Lord Clyde therefore made no award. On appeal that decision was reversed by the Second Division. They held that it was not necessary for SSEB to foresee the precise damage which occurred. It was enough that the type of consequence was within their contemplation. Scottish Power appealed to the House of Lords.

In deciding the case, the House of Lords referred to the classic nine- **10–26** teenth century statement on this matter—a dictum of Alderson B. in *Hadley v Baxendale*:

"The damages ... should be such as may fairly and reasonably be considered either arising naturally, ie, according to the usual course of things, from such breach of contract itself, or such as may

---

[61] Bankton, I, 11, 15.
[62] *Balfour Beatty Construction (Scotland) Ltd v Scottish Power Plc*, 1994 S.C. (HL) 20; 1994 S.L.T. 807.

reasonably be supposed to have been in the contemplation of both parties at the time they made the contract as the probable result of the breach."[63]

Note the two branches of the test:

(1) the loss was a normal result of the breach, one involving knowledge imputed to everyone; and
(2) the parties were aware of special circumstances which made that particular loss a probable result.

In either case, the critical time for identifying what was in the knowledge of parties is the point at which the contract was made, not when it was breached.

In the *Balfour Beatty* case the House of Lords concluded that the requirement to demolish and rebuild the aqueduct were not matters within the reasonable contemplation of the electricity board. Balfour Beatty were therefore not entitled to damages reflecting the cost of these works. In deciding what could be said to have been within the contemplation of the parties, Lord Jauncey referred to a dictum of Lord Reid in *Koufos v C Czarnikow Ltd*[64]:

"I would agree ... that it is generally sufficient that that event would have appeared to the defendant as not unlikely to occur. It is hardly ever possible in this matter to assess probabilities with any degree of mathematical accuracy. But I do not find in [earlier cases] any warrant for regarding as within the contemplation of the parties any event which would not have appeared to the defendant, had he thought about it, to have a very substantial degree of probability."

10–27 This indicates that the second alternative within *Hadley v Baxendale* is a hard test to meet. A 2009 decision House of Lords on remoteness, *Transfield Shipping Inc v Mercator Shipping Inc (The Achilleas)*,[65] also supports this proposition:

The charterers of a ship (*The Achilleas*) returned it to its owners nine days late. As a result of the late redelivery, the owners were in breach of the next charter agreement. The subsequent charterers agreed to accept the ship nine days late, but took the opportunity to renegotiate the fee for their entire charter period. This saved them, and cost the owners, $1,365,000. The owners therefore sued the original charterers for the losses caused by this breach of contract. There

[63] *Hadley v Baxendale* (1854) 9 Exch. 341 at 354.
[64] *Koufos v C Czarnikow Ltd (The Heron II)* [1969] 1 A.C. 350 at 388E.
[65] *Transfield Shipping Inc v Mercator Shipping Inc (The Achilleas)* [2008] UKHL 48. This has since been discussed and applied in a number of Scottish cases, including *Ronald Henderson t/a Henderson Group Development v Edwards* [2013] CSOH 113.

were two ways of calculating the losses: (a) the market rate for the extra nine day charter, $158,000; or (b) the loss of $1,365,000 suffered by the owners on the subsequent hire.

Applying *Hadley v Baxendale*, the House of Lords awarded only the current market rate for the charter. The Law Lords agreed (by different routes) that the party in breach should only be liable for losses that he had undertaken. Lord Hoffmann stated:

> "If, therefore, one considers what these parties, contracting against the background of market expectations found by the arbitrators, would reasonably have considered the extent of the liability they were undertaking, I think it is clear that they would have considered losses arising from the loss of the following fixture a type or kind of loss for which the charterer was not assuming responsibility. Such a risk would be completely unquantifiable, because ... they would have no idea when that would be done or what its length or other terms would be."[66]

The subsequent charter agreement, and the downwards revision in fee, were not circumstances which the original charterer knew about or could have been expected to know about. There was therefore no liability for that loss.

The importance of this case lies in the emphasis it places on interpretation. This has clearly been acknowledged by the Outer House in a recent Scottish case. Lady Wise stated that:

> "It is clear from the speech of Lord Hoffmann in *Transfield* that there will be scope for discussion in many cases about whether a type or kind of loss, even if forseeable, should be excluded as being outwith those which the contracting parties intended should fall within the scope of the contractual duties ... [W]hether a given type of loss was one for which a party assumed contractual responsibility [involves] ... the interpretation of a contract as a whole against its contractual background."[67]

A case which clearly illustrates the two branches of the *Hadley* test is **10–28** *Victoria Laundry (Windsor) Ltd v Newman Industries Ltd*[68]:

> A boiler was ordered by the plaintiffs who operated a laundering and cleaning business. It was delivered 20 weeks late. The plaintiffs sought to recover damages in respect of lost business profits for the period during which they should have had the use of the boiler. The

---

[66] *The Achilleas* [2008] UKHL 48, per Lord Hoffmann at [23].
[67] *Ronald Henderson t/a Henderson Group Development v Edwards* [2013] CSOH 113, per Lady Wise at [20].
[68] *Victoria Laundry (Windsor) Ltd v Newman Industries Ltd* [1949] 2 K.B. 528; [1949] 1 All E.R. 997.

defendants knew the purpose for which the boiler was to be used. They also knew it was required as soon as possible. They were not informed specifically, however, regarding the loss of profits which might occur if there was a delay in delivery. These comprised (a) a large amount of profits drawn from the new business, "the demand for laundry services at that time being insatiable", valued at £16 per week, and (b) highly lucrative government dyeing contracts valued at £262 per week.

The trial judge held that the loss of profits was not recoverable. This decision was overturned by the Court of Appeal only to be reinstated on a further appeal to the House of Lords. This indicates the difficulty in applying this test.

Mitigation of loss

10–29   Faced by a breach of contract, the innocent party is expected to take reasonable steps to minimise his loss. He should act like a prudent person following the dictates of common sense. If possible he must attempt to stem the loss. He does not, however, have to go to great or extraordinary lengths; the onus of proof is on the contract-breaker to show that the other party has not mitigated his loss. So a person who breached a contract to ship goods to Canada was liable to pay the costs of shipping by another route at four times the cost unless he could show that another, cheaper method was available.[69] The legal principle is that the innocent party cannot recover a greater sum by way of damages than if he had taken those steps. In a contract for sale of goods, for example, if a buyer wrongfully refuses the goods then the measure of damages is, prima facie, to be ascertained by the difference between the contract price and the market or current price at the time or times when the goods ought to have been accepted.[70] So a grain merchant must attempt to sell the goods to another buyer if the original buyer under the contract refuses to pay for the goods. If the price the merchant achieves is the same or higher, only nominal damages are recoverable.

The measure of damages seen from a different viewpoint

10–30   Some writers believe that damages can be more appropriately analysed by breaking down a party's loss into three types: restitution, reliance and expectation. The case of *McRae v Commonwealth Disposals Commission* illustrates these three types of loss[71]:

> After the Second World War, McRae bought from the defendants the wreck of an oil tanker which was said to lie beside the Jourmaund Reef. He fitted out a vessel to salvage the wreck, hired a crew

---

[69] *Connal Connal & Co v Fisher Renwick & Co* (1883) 10 R. 824.
[70] Sale of Goods Act 1979 s.50(3).
[71] *McRae v Commonwealth Disposals Commission* (1951) 84 C.L.R. 377.

and proceeded to the supposed location of the wreck. No wreck was found. McRae sought damages in respect of the following losses he had sustained.

(1) The cost of purchasing the wreck from the defendants—£285 (restitution loss).
(2) The cost of arranging a vessel and crew for salvage—£10,000 (reliance loss).
(3) The profit he would have made if the wreck had been there and he had successfully salvaged it—£250,000 (expectation loss).

The court decided that the expectation loss was too speculative. Instead, it awarded McRae compensation in respect of his restitution and reliance interests. On the evidence, it decided that his actual expenditure was in the region of £3,000 rather than £10,000, and he received £3,285. Accordingly, he was not being put in the position which he would have been if the contract had been performed—only expectation loss would have done that. Instead, he was compensated for the loss to his pocket—the financial outlay he had sustained on the faith of the bargain. There has been no judicial recognition of this analysis in the Scottish courts, but it does perhaps provide a cross check against which the conventional method can be tested. Note also that the innocent party is only required to mitigate his loss if suing for damages: where he sues to implement the contract, there is no principle of mitigation.[72]

Remedies Provided by the Contract

The parties may insert terms into the contract expressly providing what **10–31** should happen in the event of breach. This provides much more certainty about the consequences of breach of that contract. One party may seek to limit his liability by means of an exemption clause. A second device which is commonly used by contracting parties is to stipulate that a determinate amount should be payable by way of damages in the event of breach. Such clauses are perfectly legitimate and enforceable so long as they constitute a genuine pre-estimate of loss. They are then referred to as liquidated damage clauses. But if the clause is intended to punish the party in breach then it is invalid and unenforceable. A clause of that type is known as a penalty clause (a clause "*in terrorem*"). The general tendency of the court is not to find that the clause is penal unless it is clearly exorbitant. However, in any case, it can only be a penal clause if it arises on breach of contract.[73]

---

[72] See the discussion below in respect of *White & Carter (Councils) Ltd v McGregor*, 1962 S.C. (HL) 1; [1961] 3 All E.R. 1178.
[73] For example, see *City Inn Ltd v Shepherd Construction Ltd*, 2003 S.L.T. 885.

Penalty and liquidated damage clauses

10–32 In distinguishing between penalty clauses and liquidated damage clauses, the courts have recourse to principles which were authoritatively set out in *Dunlop Pneumatic Tyre Co Ltd v New Garage & Motor Co Ltd* by Lord Dunedin.[74] The principles can be summarised as follows:

(1) The use of the term "penalty" or "liquidated damages" is not conclusive. In each case the court must determine whether the payment stipulated is in truth a penalty or liquidated damages.

(2) A penalty is in essence designed to punish the offending party; the essence of liquidated damages is that the sum payable is a genuine pre-estimate of loss.

(3) Whether a sum stipulated is a penalty or liquidated damages is a question judged at the time of the making of the contract, not at the time of the breach.

(4) Various tests of interpretation are used by the courts in their task:

    (a) A clause will be held to be penal if the sum in question is extravagant and unconscionable.

    (b) A clause will be penal if the breach consists only in not paying a sum of money, and the clause stipulates for a sum greater than the sum which ought to have been paid.

    (c) A clause is presumed penal when "a single lump sum is made payable by way of compensation, on the occurrence of one or more or all of several events, some of which may occasion serious and other, but trifling, damage."[75]

    (d) A sum will not be penal simply because the consequences of the breach cannot be estimated. Indeed, "that is just the situation when it is probable that pre-estimated damage was the true bargain between the parties."[76]

    (e) A contractual provision to repay a deposit or to forfeit sums already paid will not be treated as a penalty clause.[77]

The onus of proof lies on the party claiming it is a penalty clause, to show that the clause is indeed "exorbitant and unconscionable and designed to operate *in terrorem*".[78] To do so, they will need to bring evidence that the clause is penal: it will not be enough simply to assert that the provision was a penalty.[79]

---

[74] *Dunlop Pneumatic Tyre Co Ltd v New Garage & Motor Co Ltd* [1915] A.C. 79 at 86.
[75] *Dunlop Pneumatic Tyre Co Ltd* [1915] A.C. 79, per Lord Dunedin at 87, quoting Lord Watson in *Lord Elphinstone v Monkland Iron and Coal Co* (1886) 11 App Cas 332.
[76] *Dunlop Pneumatic Tyre Co Ltd* [1915] A.C. 79, per Lord Dunedin at 88.
[77] *Agri-Energy Ltd v McCallion* [2014] CSOH 13.
[78] *Hill v Stewart Milne Group and Gladedale (Northern) Ltd* [2011] CSIH 50, per Lord Brodie at [15].
[79] *Hill v Stewart Milne Group and Gladedale (Northern) Ltd* [2011] CSIH 50, per Lord Brodie at [15].

An unusual illustration of the *Dunlop Pneumatic Tyre Co* principles is provided by *Clydebank Engineering & Shipbuilding Co Ltd v Castaneda*[80]:

> Four torpedo boat destroyers were ordered by the Spanish Government from a Scottish shipyard. Substantial sums were to be paid by way of damages in the event of the vessels being delivered late. The ships were delivered many months late but the shipyard declined to pay the sum stipulated. It alleged that the sum was penal and unenforceable because (a) Navy ships were not profit making assets and accordingly there was no loss to the Spanish government, and (b) the remainder of the fleet had been sunk by the American Navy off Cuba shortly after the delivery date set in the contract. Accordingly, it was contended, no loss had been suffered: if the destroyers had been delivered when due, they would have been sunk and lost with the rest of the fleet.

Both these arguments were swiftly despatched by the court and the **10–33** Spanish Government awarded the sums claimed. Two matters were noted. First, the clause itself had been inserted precisely because the quantification of loss was so difficult. Secondly, the shipyard had fixed the terms as a means of attracting the order for the vessels. It was also stated that if the destroyers had been delivered on time, the fleet might not have sunk. Liquidated damage clauses may have the effect of limiting the liability of one party. This happens where the actual loss suffered is greater than that stipulated for in the contract. But there is a difference in the two types of clause. In a limitation clause, the sum specified operates as a ceiling on damages. If the actual loss is lower, the sum recoverable is lower. Where there is a liquidated damages clause, the same amount is recoverable irrespective of whether the actual loss is greater or less than the sum specified in the clause. Where a clause is held to be a penalty, there is Scottish authority that the actual loss is recoverable even when it is greater than the sum stipulated for in the penalty.[81] Here, the paradox is that the penalty clause is invalid because it "terrorises" the other party, yet the loss suffered is greater than that sum.

In determining whether a damages clause is indeed an unenforceable penalty clause, the courts will consider whether it was penal at the date of conclusion of contract, rather than at the date of breach.[82]

Other contractual clauses

Several other devices can be used to provide in advance what the remedy **10–34** should be on the occurrence of a certain event. Examples are

---

[80] *Clydebank Engineering & Shipbuilding Co Ltd v Castaneda* (1904) 7 F. (HL) 77; (1903) 5 F. 1016.
[81] *Dingwall v Burnett*, 1912 S.C. 1097.
[82] *Hill v Stewart Milne Group and Gladedale (Northern) Ltd* [2011] CSIH 50, per Lord Brodie at [18].

(1) acceleration clauses, where if one instalment is not paid on time, the whole price becomes immediately payable; (2) forfeiture clauses, where if there is a breach the injured party forfeits his deposit[83]; (3) non-breach clauses, where sums are stipulated to be payable otherwise than on the occurrence of breach[84]; and (4) retention clauses, where a percentage of the price is retained for a specified period to cover the cost of remedying any defective performance. In these cases, neither the rules as to penalty clauses nor the provisions of the Unfair Contract Terms Act 1977 apply. However, if the contract is a consumer contract, the term will be regulated by the Unfair Terms in Consumer Contracts Regulations 1999 (SI 1999/2083).

A common clause in leases is an irritancy clause. It provides that the landlord is entitled to irritate, i.e. terminate, the lease in the event of specified breaches by the other party. In a lease for a term of years, for example, it might be provided that if the tenant should default in his payment of the rent, the landlord should be able to irritate the lease. It is now provided by statute that the landlord's right to terminate depends upon his issuing a notice of default to the tenant.[85]

ANTICIPATORY BREACH

10–35 In many of the examples considered above, the breach has occurred where one party does not fulfil its obligations at the time that they become due. In contracts where performance is due to take place at some future date, one party may indicate in advance that he is not going to fulfil his side of the bargain. He thus repudiates the contract before the time for performance arrives. This is known as anticipatory breach. In *Miller Fabrications Ltd v J&D Pierce (Contracts) Ltd* it was reiterated that whether one party's conduct amounted to anticipatory breach was "essentially a matter of fact to be determined after consideration of the whole circumstances."[86] An attempt to suspend performance until the agreed contract terms were changed "could be said to amount to an anticipatory repudiation."[87]

Anticipatory breach leaves the innocent party with three options:

(1) To rescind the contract and immediately sue for damages.
(2) To wait until the time for performance has arrived (in case the other party changes his mind) then sue for damages.
(3) To perform his side of the bargain and claim the contract price.

---

[83] cf. *Zemhunt (Holdings) Ltd v Control Securities Plc*, 1991 S.L.T. 653.
[84] *EFT Commercial Ltd v Security Change Ltd*, 1992 S.C.L.R. 706.
[85] Law Reform (Miscellaneous Provisions) (Scotland) Act 1985 ss.4–7.
[86] *Miller Fabrications Ltd v J&D Pierce (Contracts) Ltd* [2010] CSIH 27 at [7].
[87] *Miller Fabrications Ltd v J&D Pierce (Contracts) Ltd* [2010] CSIH 27 at [15]. But note that merely proposing alternative terms may not amount to an anticipatory breach: see *Wyman-Gordon Ltd v Proclad International Ltd* [2010] CSIH 99, discussed at para.10–08 above.

The third of these options has proved the most controversial. It is worth stressing that it is only a viable option in a limited number of cases. This is because first, contracts normally require the co-operation of both parties in order for performance to take place. If, for example, X repudiates a contract to have an extension built on to his house, the builder cannot enter on to the land and commence construction without X's permission. Secondly, few parties will wish to render a performance which is no longer desired. The builder will be unlikely to try to build the extension in the teeth of X's opposition. Exceptionally, however, the innocent party will not require the co-operation of the other party to fulfil his side of the bargain and will ignore the fact that performance is no longer required. The leading authority on this issue is *White & Carter (Councils) Ltd v McGregor*[88]:

> A representative from an advertising agency called at a garage to arrange a new advertising contract which was to last for three years. Terms were agreed with the manager and the contract completed.

> Later the same day, the owner of the garage telephoned the agency to cancel the contract. The agency ignored the purported cancellation, continued with the contract and sued for the full contract price. On behalf of the garage, it was argued that the agency should have sued for damages (if any) when the cancellation was notified. By suing for a debt (the contract price) rather than for damages, the agency were thus able to avoid having to show that they had mitigated their loss.

An earlier Scottish case had held that the proper test in such situations **10–36** was: what was the "reasonable and proper course" for the pursuer to take?[89] By a narrow three to two majority, the House of Lords overruled this view and held that the agency were entitled to succeed in this claim:

> "It might be, but it never has been, the law that a person is only entitled to enforce his contractual rights in a reasonable way and that a court will not support an attempt to enforce them in an unreasonable way. One reason why this is the law is no doubt because it was thought that it would create too much uncertainty to require the court to decide whether it is reasonable or equitable to allow a party to enforce his full rights under a contract."

This is an area of law in which the approach differs in Scotland and England. This is because this third option, noted above, will, in many situations, involve the innocent party compelling the party in breach to perform their obligations under the contract. This requires either an action for payment, where money is sought, or an action of specific implement, where performance of some other obligation is sought. The

---

[88] *White & Carter (Councils) Ltd v McGregor*, 1962 S.C. (HL) 1; [1961] 3 All E.R. 1178.
[89] *Langford & Co Ltd v Dutch*, 1952 S.C. 15.

differences between the Scottish and English courts in this field have been noted above.[90] The result is that in Scotland, provided that the contract is such that the innocent party can seek decree of specific implement or payment, the option of insisting on the contract will be open.[91]

---

[90] See para.10–16.
[91] Most recently affirmed in *AMA (New Town) Ltd v Law* [2013] CSIH 61.

CHAPTER 11

TITLE TO SUE

Each party to a contract acquires legal rights against the other. However, **11–01**
the contract is a private transaction between the parties:

> "in general a contract creates enforceable rights and duties only
> between those who are party to its formation. Third parties are
> typically unaffected by the contract, whether in terms of acquiring
> rights or being subject to duties."[1]

Thus, persons who are not parties to the contract do not acquire rights or
duties under it. This is sometimes referred to as "privity of contract". In
this respect a contract can be regarded as a private legislative arrangement between the parties. And this indeed is the general principle of the
law—a transaction between certain parties cannot advantage or injure
those who are not parties to that transaction (*res inter alios acta aliis nec
nocet nec prodest*). Let us take an example: A is owed £100 by B who in
turn is owed £100 by C; A cannot sue C for the £100 because he has no
rights under the contract between B and C, and cannot gain an advantage
by it. It is not possible to sue one's debtor's debtor.[2]

There are several important exceptions to the principle that only the
parties to the contract are bound by it—agency, assignation, *jus quaesitum tertio*, and contracts transferred by operation of law.

AGENCY

Agency describes the relationship which arises when one person (the **11–02**
agent) is appointed to act as the representative of another (the principal).[3]
A variety of examples comes to mind. The owners of a house instruct a
solicitor to sell their house for them. A woman going to live abroad
appoints her daughter to conduct her affairs in Scotland during her
absence. A foreign manufacturer retains a Scottish firm to sell its goods in
the United Kingdom. In each of these cases, two different aspects of
agency arise. First, the contract of agency is created between the principal

---

[1] Scottish Law Commission, *Discussion Paper on Third Party Rights in Contract*, Scot. Law
Com. D.P. No.157 (March 2014), p.14.
[2] See *Henderson v Robb* (1889) 16 R. 341.
[3] For a detailed review of agency in Scots law, see L.J. Macgregor, *The Law of Agency in
Scotland* (Edinburgh: SULI/W Green, 2013).

and the agent. Secondly, the agent can make contracts which bind his principal. This second aspect means that the principal acquires rights and duties under a contract which he himself has not made. In other words, he becomes a party to the contract, even though he took no direct part in its formation. For this to occur, the agent must act within the four corners of the authority vested in him. If he acts without authority, then he alone is liable on the contract, unless the principal held him out as having authority or subsequently takes steps to ratify his act.

> *Example*: Joe, Don and Fay are partners in an architects' firm. Fay agrees to purchase three sports cars for herself and her partners. If the partnership deed grants Fay authority to do this, then the partnership must pay for the cars. Otherwise Fay alone is liable to pay the purchase price of the cars, unless (i) Joe and Don held Fay out as having the necessary authority, or (ii) they are prepared to ratify the purchase.

Where the agent is acting with authority, then normally only the principal acquires rights and duties under the contract. It is presumed that the other party intends to contract with the principal rather than the agent. The seller of a house intends to contract with the prospective purchasers, not the solicitor who has drafted and sent the formal offer. If the purchaser defaults in paying the price, the seller will sue him, not his solicitor. In two situations, however, the agent himself may be bound by the contract. This occurs where the agent either (a) does not disclose that he has a principal, or (b) does not divulge his principal's identity. In both cases the third party has a right of election—to sue the agent personally or to sue the principal (assuming that the latter's identity is disclosed). A bidder at an auction, for example, might refuse to state the identity of the client for whom he is bidding. If the bid is successful but the price is not paid within a reasonable time, the seller might opt to sue the bidder. The bidder will be personally liable on the contract of sale, although he has a right of recourse against his principal.

Assignation

11–03 Assignation[4] is the process by which contractual rights, and arguably contractual obligations, are transferred to a third party.[5] For instance, a person who orders a boat to be built might assign the right to receive the boat to another person or the boat builder might assign his right to receive payment. The transferor is known as the assignor (or cedent), while the transferee is known as the assignee. It is necessary to distinguish between the assignation of *rights* under a contract, and the assignation of *obligations*.

---

[4] It is called "assignment" in English law.
[5] See also R.G. Anderson, *Assignation* (ELET, 2008).

Assignation of rights

Most contractual rights are assignable when consent is given. The **11–04** question of whether or not one party can assign his rights without the consent of the other party is more difficult. Some contracts prohibit assignation. In other cases the nature of the right may make it apparent that it is not capable of being assigned. Simple debts are, however, generally assignable. Debt collection companies rely on this principle. It enables them to purchase bad debts from other businesses to pursue against the debtors.

Assignation of obligations

This is less straightforward. When a party seeks to assign a right, the **11–05** other party must perform exactly the same obligation but to a different person. Generally, this will make little difference to the party performing the obligation. If, on the other hand, a party seeks to assign his obligations, the effect on the other party can be considerable. A person who had concluded a contract with a bespoke tailor in Savile Row for a suit would be justifiably unhappy if the obligation to make and deliver the suit was assigned to a theatrical costumier.

To deal with this, it is possible for the contracting parties to include a term that assignation shall not be allowed. Even without such a term, it will not be possible to assign an obligation where it is clear that there has been a choice of specified person (*delectus personae*). This will be so where the identity of the contracting party subject to the obligation is of importance. That will depend on the obligation in question. Factors that mean that *delectus personae* is more likely to exist include the importance of any qualities of personal service within the obligation and a degree of skill of craftsmanship being required to complete the work.[6] If, on the other hand, the obligation is to supply materials or do work of a stipulated standard it is less likely. For example, the obligation of the Savile Row tailor could not be assigned but an obligation to supply 5m of a specified cloth might be capable of assignation.

The issue of whether it is possible to assign obligations at all remains a **11–06** contentious one. A party who has undertaken an obligation and wishes to transfer it to a third party may do so by novation[7] or sub-contracting. The former requires the consent of the other contracting party. The latter leaves the other contracting party with his rights against the person with whom he contracted. Assignation of obligations removes these protections. In England, the House of Lords has stated that the burden of a contract cannot be assigned.[8] In Scotland, support for the proposition that assignation of obligations is permissible is derived from *Cole v Handasyde & Co*.[9] In that case, however, the competency of assigning an

---

[6] *Cole v Handasyde & Co*, 1910 S.C. 68, *Scottish Homes v Inverclyde DC*, 1997 S.L.T. 829.
[7] Considered in Ch.13.
[8] *Linden Garden Trust Ltd v Lenesta Sludge Disposals Ltd* [1994] 1 A.C. 85; [1993] 3 W.L.R. 408; [1993] 3 All E.R. 417.
[9] *Cole v Handasyde & Co*, 1910 S.C. 68.

obligation was not the principal issue. That was whether *delectus personae* existed. Despite these doubts, modern support for the proposition that assignation of obligations is possible may be derived from *Scottish Homes v Inverclyde District Council*:

> "If on a sound construction of its terms, express or implied, a contract entitles a contracting party to substitute another in his place both as regards performance and the benefits of the contract, there is, in my opinion, no rule of Scots law which would prevent that from having effect."[10]

Form of assignation

11–07 Two steps are required to assign a contract: the assignation and the intimation. No particular form of words is required to assign a right.[11] It is enough that words are used which show that the assignor intended to transfer his particular rights under the contract to the assignee. Although assignation takes place between the assignor and assignee, it will not be complete until the other party to the contract has been told about the assignation. This is known as intimation and is extremely important in perfecting the assignee's right. If, for example, a debtor pays his debt to the original creditor because he has not been informed that the debt has been assigned to a new creditor, he will be held to have discharged his obligation.

What is the assignee's right?

11–08 He stands in the shoes of the cedent. All pleas available against the assignor are thus available against the assignee. The relevant Latin tag here is *assignatur utitur jure auctoris* (an assignee exercises the right of his cedent). Where an insured allegedly made false statements in his proposal form for life assurance and then assigned the benefit of the policy, the insurance company was entitled to seek to reduce the insurance contract.[12] The assignees had no better right to the proceeds of the policy than the insured himself. If his statements were false, he (and in consequence the assignees) had no entitlement to benefit under the policy.

> "It appears to me to be long ago settled in the law of Scotland—and I have never heard of any attempt to disturb the doctrine—that in a personal obligation, whether contained in a unilateral deed or in a mutual contract, if the creditor's right is sold to an assignee for value, and the assignee purchases in good faith, he is nevertheless subject to all the exceptions and pleas pleadable against the original creditor."[13]

[10] *Scottish Homes v Inverclyde DC*, 1997 S.L.T. 829, per Lord Penrose at 835.
[11] *Brownlee v Robb*, 1907 S.C. 1302.
[12] *Scottish Widows' Fund v Buist* (1876) 3 R. 1078.
[13] *Scottish Widows' Fund v Buist* (1876) 3 R. 1078, per Lord President Inglis at 1082.

One of the legal effects of death or bankruptcy is to transfer all assignable rights and duties automatically to the executor (on death) or the trustee in bankruptcy respectively. Accordingly, when a party to a contract dies, his rights pass to his representatives.

JUS QUAESITUM TERTIO

Jus quaesitum tertio[14] is a right acquired by a third party through con- **11–09** tract, literally "the third party has acquired a right". Scots law allows two parties to confer an enforceable *right* upon a third party who is not a party to the contract. It is not possible, however, to impose an *obligation* or duty on a third party by virtue of *jus quaesitum tertio*. The basis of the doctrine is to be found in a passage in Stair's *Institutions*:

> "It is likewise the opinion of Molina, cap. 263 and it quadrats to our Customs, that when Parties Contract, if there be any Article in favour of a third Party, at any time, *est jus quaesitum tertio*, which cannot be recalled by both the Contractors, but he may compel either of them to exhibit the Contract, and thereupon the obliged may be compelled to perform."[15]

Read literally, this passage implies that the third party's right is complete as soon as there is a provision in his favour in the contract. He can sue upon the contract as soon as it is made. It will also be seen that Stair identifies three aspects to this right:

(1) the contracting parties cannot revoke the agreement;
(2) the third party can compel the contracting parties to display the contract to him; and
(3) the third party can enforce the provision in his favour.

The courts have been somewhat reluctant to allow the third party such **11–10** extensive rights. They will do so only where that is the manifest intention of the contracting parties. This reluctance is understandable. In most instances of *jus quaesitum tertio*, the third party will be receiving a gift and there is a strong presumption against donation. The leading case is *Carmichael v Carmichael's Executrix*[16]:

> A father took out an insurance policy for £1,000 on the life of his eight year old son. The policy provided that the sum assured was to be paid on death to the son's executors, providing he attained the

---

[14] This doctrine is currently the subject of a Scottish Law Commission review and *Discussion Paper on Third Party Rights in Contract*, Scot. Law Com. D.P. No.157 (March 2014). Reform of the law may be forthcoming as a result. Chapter 2 of the Discussion Paper provides a comprehensive survey of the current state of third party rights in Scots law.

[15] Stair, I, 10, 5.

[16] *Carmichael v Carmichael's Executrix*, 1920 S.C. (HL) 195.

age of 21 years and continued to pay the premiums. If the son died before attaining 21, however, the premiums were to be repaid by the insurance company to the father. Alternatively, he could surrender the policy for whatever value it had. The father duly paid the premiums and kept the policy in his possession, never delivering it to the son. Between his 21st and 22nd birthday and before the first premium payable by him was due, the son was killed in an air accident. He left a will leaving all his property to his aunt. In an action to determine whether the father or the aunt was entitled to the benefit of the policy, the father claimed that the son had not acquired a right to the proceeds of the policy. The contract, he said, was between him and the insurance company. The son would only acquire a right after he had paid the first premium due by him, or if the father had delivered or formally intimated that policy to the son. None of these things had happened. Despite these considerations, the House of Lords found in favour of the aunt.

The decision might suggest that the court adopted a broad view of the doctrine. In fact, the reverse occurred; the speech of Lord Dunedin considerably narrowed the doctrine. He suggested that in Stair's statement, the phrase "*est jus quaesitum tertio*" should be transposed with the words "which cannot be recalled by both the contractors." In other words, the insertion of the clause in the third party's favour was of itself not enough. In addition, it had to be shown that the contracting parties could not revoke their agreement. Delivery or intimation to the other party would be ways of evincing this intention, but in other cases it would be a question of interpretation. Here, the whole circumstances of the case pointed to an irrevocable intention having been formed. The terms of the policy clearly envisaged that the father's rights ceased after the son reached majority. Thereafter, the son could elect to continue the policy, or convert it into a different type of policy, or receive a cash benefit. Irrevocability, however, was no longer a consequence of the agreement, as Stair had stipulated, but rather a condition of the establishment of the right.

11–11   The right to revoke may not be an absolute bar to establishing the existence of a *jus quaesitum tertio*. In *Love v Amalgamated Society of Lithographic Printers of Great Britain & Ireland*, a widow claimed sickness benefit in terms of her husband's trade union membership.[17] Although the right to benefit was revocable (the union rules could be altered at any time) it had not been so revoked at the time of his death. The widow was successful in her claim. This case is difficult to reconcile with *Carmichael* and is perhaps an apt illustration of the saying that hard cases make bad law, or at least law which is more difficult to state with certainty and precision. In any event it does seem just to hold that the wife's right would only have been defeated if the union rules had been altered before her entitlement arose.

---

[17] *Love v Amalgamated Society of Lithographic Printers of Great Britain & Ireland*, 1912 S.C. 1078.

What, then, are the criteria to be satisfied to establish a *jus quaesitum* **11–12**
tertio? The right must be created in a contract between two parties: a
unilateral promise by one party that the purported *tertio* will benefit
under a future contract does not create a *jus quaesitum tertio*.[18] The
parties must expressly state that the third party is to benefit. In *Morton's
Trustees v The Aged Christian Friend Society of Scotland*, the agreement
was made between a benefactor and a provisional committee charged
with the duty of setting up a charitable society.[19] The contract specifically
stipulated that the benefactor was to pay annual instalments to the
society, rather than to the provisional committee. This was described as
"a clear instance of our doctrine of *jus quaesitum tertio*". Accordingly, the
society was entitled to enforce its right to payment of the instalments
outstanding on the benefactor's death.

It is not enough for the third party to show merely that a benefit was **11–13**
incidentally conferred upon him. There must be an express provision in
his favour (*pactum in favorem tertii*). In *Finnie v Glasgow & South-
Western Railway Co*, two railway companies agreed to fix the freight rate
for the carriage of coal along a certain railway line.[20] When the railway
companies varied the rate upwards, a person who transported freight
along the line sought to enforce the companies' agreement. The action
was unsuccessful. It was not a contract made for his benefit so he had no
jus quaesitum tertio. Whether the requisite intention is present or not can
be evinced in several ways:

(1) by the nature of the original contract;
(2) by the whole circumstances of the case;
(3) by intimation or delivery of the contract.

In *Carmichael*, the son and indeed the whole family knew of the policy.
Before joining the air force, he had contacted the insurers to check that
military service was not inconsistent with the policy and he had spoken to
his lawyer about it in relation to his will.

Rights of enforcement

A *jus quaesitum tertio* can be enforced even if the original contracting **11–14**
parties no longer have an interest to sue. In *Morton's Trustees*, the provisional committee had become defunct once the charitable society had
been founded. The third party may enforce the right even where one of
the contracting parties can also sue on the contract. In *Lamont v Burnett*,
the purchaser of a hotel in Crieff, in addition to the purchase price of
£7,000, offered to pay to the seller's wife "not less than one hundred
pounds as some compensation for the annoyance and worry of the past
few days, and for her kindness and attention to me on my several visits to

---

[18] *Smith v Stuart* [2010] CSIH 29. The unilateral promise to create the *jus quaesitum tertio*
   may itself be enforceable however.
[19] *Morton's Trustees v The Aged Christian Friend Society of Scotland* (1899) 2 F. 82.
[20] *Finnie v Glasgow & South-Western Railway Co* (1857) 3 Macq. 75.

Crieff".[21] This was accepted by the seller. It was held that this extra provision could be enforced by the wife and the view was expressed that the husband might also enforce the provision.

A doubt existed as to whether the *tertius* could sue for defective performance or only for total failure to perform.[22] That question was considered in *Scott Lithgow Ltd v GEC Electrical Products Ltd*[23]:

> The Ministry of Defence commissioned Scott Lithgow's predecessors to build a new naval vessel, HMS Challenger. The electrical work was sub-contracted to GEC Electrical Products Ltd, which in turn sub-contracted some of the work to other subcontractors. Defects developed in the wiring of the electrical equipment. The Ministry claimed that they had a *jus quaesitum tertio* arising out of the contracts between GEC and the sub-contractors as they were expressly mentioned in those sub-contracts. They also claimed that they were entitled to seek damages from the "subsubcontractors" for defective performance.

11–15 After debate, Lord Clyde held that such a claim could exist and allowed the averments on this branch of the case to go to proof before answer. He stated:

> "In general I can see no reason why a third party should not be entitled to sue for damages for negligent performance of a contract under the principle of *jus quaesitum tertio*, but whether he is so entitled must be a matter of the intention of the contracting parties. That has to be ascertained from the terms of the contract."

The status of jus quaesitum tertio

11–16 There have been relatively few cases of late dealing with *jus quaesitum tertio*. However, that does not mean it is without significance in Scots law. There is good sense in giving effect to contracting parties' intention to benefit a third party, if they make that intention sufficiently clear. In England a similar right has been introduced by statute.[24]

"BLACK HOLES"

11–17 A particular problem arises where a party to a contract is not the party who suffers loss by reason of breach of that contract. This situation is known as "transferred loss". It is also known more colourfully as a

---

[21] *Lamont v Burnett* (1901) 3 F. 797.
[22] See Gloag, *Contract*, 2nd edn (1929), p.239; cf. *Cullen v McMenamin Ltd*, 1928 S.L.T. (Sh Ct) 2.
[23] *Scott Lithgow Ltd v GEC Electrical Products Ltd*, 1992 S.L.T. 244.
[24] Contract (Rights of Third Parties) Act 1999. There are, however, differences in the application of this statute to create a third party right. Further, many commercial contracting parties disapply the Act by inserting a clause to that effect in their contract.

"black hole", because the claim for damages has vanished. For example, suppose the owner of land (A) engages a builder (P) to build an office block. Once the building is completed, A sells it to B. If a problem emerges in relation to its construction then it is B who will suffer a loss. Since B has no contract with P, he cannot sue for breach of contract. A does have a contract with P so could sue P, but A has suffered no financial loss, since he sold the office block for its market value.[25]

The solution developed by the English courts allows A to recover damages on B's behalf.[26] It is not a perfect solution. Doubts remain about the way in which B can force A to disgorge the damages, and what might happen if A became insolvent after recovering damages but before giving them to B.

In Scots law, Lady Smith has rejected the use of *jus quaesitum tertio* to solve this problem since:

> "The parties to the contract must intend to benefit the particular third party ... and the third party upon whom the right to benefit is conferred must be identified in the contract."[27]

In the majority of cases, the contract between A and P will not directly confer a right upon B, who may well be unknown at the time of contracting.[28] Instead, it appears that the Scottish courts favour an approach similar to that in England. The party to the contract will be entitled to sue for breach of contract, even if they have not suffered the loss:

> "... the defenders would be entitled to raise proceedings against the pursuers for substantial damages even in respect of a loss that had been suffered by another company ... The defenders would be subject to an obligation to account for any damages recovered to such third party, but that is not a matter that concerns me in the present proceedings".[29]

While this solution does not address the relationship between A and B, it does ensure that the contract-breaker is not relieved of liability fortuitously.

---

[25] In practice, a builder may grant a "duty of care" letter to subsequent purchasers, known as a collateral warranty.

[26] *St Martin's Property Corp Ltd v Sir Robert McAlpine Ltd* [1994] 1 A.C. 85.

[27] *Marquess of Aberdeen and Temair v Turcan Connell* [2008] CSOH 183 at [47].

[28] Where B is identified in the contract as the *tertius*, then a claim in *jus quaesitum tertio* would of course succeed, in principle.

[29] *McLaren Murdoch & Hamilton Ltd v Abercromby Motor Group Ltd* [2002] CSOH 229, per Lord Drummond Young.

TRANSFER BY OPERATION OF LAW

11–18 In some instances a legal entity which has entered into contracts will cease to exist and be replaced by a new entity. An example of this occurs where local government or other public bodies are reorganised. In such a situation there is often legislation intended to transfer the rights and obligations of the body to be abolished to its successor.

In addition to these special situations which are the subject of particular rules there is at least one general set of rules which has the effect of transferring contracts of employment where a business is purchased—the Transfer of Undertakings (Protection of Employment) Regulations 2006 (SI 2006/246). The circumstances in which these regulations operate and the detailed rules that have evolved as to how they are applied are not matters within the scope of this book. It is relevant here simply to note that when the regulations apply, the effect is that one employer may be substituted for another in the contract of employment.[30]

JOINT AND SEVERAL LIABILITY

11–19 We have been examining circumstances where someone other than the parties themselves can sue upon the contract. It is convenient to discuss here the principles to be applied where more than one party is liable under a contract. A contract may involve undertakings by more than two parties. For example, if a man and woman jointly contract to purchase a flat, they will both be liable to the seller. In the event of default, the seller may choose to sue both prospective purchasers. However, suppose that the man has gone missing and cannot be traced. The seller is entitled to sue the woman alone for the whole account. This is referred to as joint and several liability. The liability is "joint", in the sense that each obligant is liable for the whole amount to the creditor. It is "several", in the sense that each has a right to seek to recover the contribution from the co-obligant. Accordingly, should the woman in the example pay the whole purchase price, she has a right of action against the man for his share, should he re-appear.[31] In many situations in Scots law, joint and several liability will be expressed by the parties or be implied by law.[32] This occurs where, for example, the words "joint and several liability" are actually used, in guarantees, in partnership obligations, and in relation to bills of exchange.

> *Example*: Lender X lends £100 to Y after receiving an undertaking that Z will guarantee the sum. Should Y default in payment, Z is bound to repay the whole £100 to X and Z would then be entitled to recover any such payment from Y.

---

[30] See further S. Middlemiss and M. Downie, *Employment Law in Scotland* (London: Bloomsbury Professional, 2012).
[31] *Moss v Penman*, 1993 S.C.L.R. 374; *McGillivray v Davidson*, 1993 S.L.T. 693.
[32] See *Wright v Tennent Caledonian Breweries Ltd*, 1991 S.L.T. 823.

If the liability of the obligants is not joint and several, each co-obligant is only bound to the extent of his own proportionate (pro rata) share.

CHAPTER 12

THE REQUIREMENT OF LEGALITY

12–01 A contract must be lawful both in its object and in its mode of performance. If either of these requirements is not satisfied, then the courts will decline to enforce the contract. Such contracts are referred to as illegal contracts (*pacta illicita*). The reference to illegality is misleading as it tends to suggest the commission of a crime, whereas the principle of contractual legality extends over a much wider field. A contract of surrogacy would not be enforced by the courts, but the making of the agreement in itself is not a criminal offence. "Illegality" in this context does not always mean a breach of the criminal law: a delictual act or some lesser degree of culpability could challenge the validity of the contract here. Indeed one of the curiosities of contract law is that the most important type of agreement classified under this heading, a restrictive covenant, is one which is frequently seen as laudable and enforced, rather than illegal and invalid.

The general principle is that no action arises out of an immoral situation (ex turpi causa non oritur actio). Neither party can enforce or claim damages for breach of an unlawful agreement. The unlawfulness does not need to be pleaded by the parties; it is the duty of the judge to take notice of an unlawful transaction.

> *Example*: A householder engages a plumber to carry out the replacement of the lead pipes and tank in his house. The works are eligible for grant assistance from the local authority. The parties agree that the plumber shall carry out various other repair works at the house and that he will artificially inflate the estimate for the lead replacement work in order to attract the maximum council grant. If a dispute arises and either party seeks to enforce the contract, they run the risk that the court will refuse to adjudicate on the matter. Both parties seek to defraud the local authority. Accordingly their contract is tainted by illegality.[1] The sheriff may even direct that the papers be sent to the procurator fiscal's office to consider whether a criminal prosecution should be brought.

---

[1] Since this example was first used in this book it has become a reality: *Taylor v Bhail, The Independent*, November 20, 1995.

WHAT CONSTITUTES UNLAWFULNESS?

Some contracts are forbidden by statute. Others are illegal at common **12–02** law. Other contracts are entirely legal in nature, but rendered illegal through unlawful performance, as in the example above. The most important categories of unlawful contracts are as follows:

Contracts to commit a crime or delict

An agreement to commit a crime is not enforceable. It may also amount **12–03** to conspiracy and be punishable under the provisions of the criminal law. Contracts to commit a delict are likewise unenforceable. It is clearly against public policy to uphold such bargains.

Contracts promoting sexual immorality

Contracts tending to promote sexual immorality are not upheld. It is **12–04** thought undesirable to associate the law with such transactions. This can be illustrated by reference to a case beloved of generations of law students, *Hamilton v Main*[2]:

> Hamilton sought to set aside a promissory note for £60 which he had granted to Main. Hamilton gave the note in payment of his account in respect of his sojourn at Main's public house. The evidence disclosed that Hamilton had resided there for seven days, together with a prostitute. During his stay they had purchased 113 bottles of "port and Madeira, besides a large quantity of spiritous and malt liquors." Hamilton claimed that he had granted the promissory note when he was intoxicated and that it had been induced by fraud and circumvention.

The First Division held that the promissory note could not be enforced. No reasons for the decision are given in the somewhat cryptic report of the case. It is probable that the bill was not enforced because such transactions were not to receive the approbation of the court. By depriving the landlord of his normal right to enforce the bill, the decision of the court deterred other landlords from countenancing such immoral arrangements. The dignity of the law should not be soiled by adjudicating upon disputes of this nature.

If there is an immoral purpose known to both parties, the courts will refuse to allow the parties to sue on the contract even where the bargain itself is perfectly legitimate. In *Pearce v Brooks*[3]:

> A firm of coachbuilders agreed to hire a brougham carriage of "intriguing design" to a prostitute. They knew she was going to use the carriage to ply her trade. She failed to pay the hire and the firm sued on the contract.

---

[2] *Hamilton v Main* (1823) 2 S. 356.
[3] *Pearce v Brooks* (1866) L.R. 1 Ex. 213.

It was held that they could not succeed. The contract indirectly promoted sexual immorality and was therefore illegal. What constitutes immorality is changing. In a more recent English case, a contract to place advertisements for telephone sex chat lines was held not to be void on grounds of public policy.[4]

Contingency fees

12–05 It has always been the law of Scotland that lawyers are not entitled to accept contingency fees (*pacta de quota litis*) for their services. In other words, lawyers cannot agree to act in a case in return for a percentage of any sums successfully recovered for their clients. It is, however, possible for lawyers to agree to act on the basis that the fees will be paid only if there is a successful outcome to the case. Such cases are referred to as speculative actions. There is no restriction on parties other than solicitors and advocates entering into contracts whereby they will be paid contingency fees.[5]

Contracts against public arrangements and justice

12–06 Arrangements which involve any element of corruption will be held unlawful. These include the purchase of honours such as knighthoods, together with contracts attempting to interfere with the processes of justice, such as an agreement to bribe a witness. When war breaks out, contracts with individuals or companies in the opposing state are in general invalidated.[6] The foreign national is then deemed to be an enemy alien and it is against public policy to assist such persons.

Contracts in restraint of trade

12–07 This is the most important type of contract presumed to be unlawful. It will be discussed later in the chapter.

Gaming contracts

12–08 Until September 1, 2007, gaming contracts were *pacta illicita* in Scotland. This meant that the winner of a bet could not enforce it against the loser or bookmaker, for example.[7] Under s.335 of the Gambling Act 2005, such contracts are now enforceable. Section 335 stipulates: "The fact that a contract relates to gambling shall not prevent its enforcement".

---

[4] *Armhouse Lee Ltd v Chappell, The Times*, August 7, 1996.
[5] *Quantum Claims Compensation Specialists Ltd v Powell*, 1998 S.L.T. 228.
[6] See *Cantiere San Rocco SA (Shipbuilding Co) v Clyde Shipbuilding & Engineering Co Ltd*, 1923 S.C. (HL) 105.
[7] *Wordsworth v Pettigrew* (1799) Mor. 9524.

DECLARING CONTRACTS UNLAWFUL

The courts have long asserted a power to declare contracts illegal at **12–09** common law. Underlying the courts' intervention in this area is the notion of public policy. Is it in the interest of the community that a particular contract be struck down? Obviously, the greater the intervention of the courts, the more they will be seen to be legislating and thereby usurping the function of Parliament. After a lengthy period of judicial creativity, particularly in the nineteenth century, there has been a tendency for the courts to avoid inventing new heads of public policy. But, as always, there are supporters and opponents of this view. For those who believe that there are no new grounds on which courts can declare contracts to be against public policy and hence unlawful, the following quotation of Burroughs J. is apt:

> "Public policy is a very unruly horse and when you once get astride it you never know where it will carry you."[8]

But with typical bravado, Lord Denning adopted a more adventurous approach:

> "With a good man in the saddle, the unruly horse can be kept in control. He can jump over obstacles."[9]

Perhaps the wisest words on this matter came from Sir George Jessel[10]:

> "It must not be forgotten that you are not to extend arbitrarily those rules which say that a given contract is void as being against public policy, because if there is one thing more than another public policy requires it is that men of full age and competent understanding shall have the utmost liberty of contracting and that when their contracts are entered into freely and voluntarily shall be held sacred and shall be enforced by Courts of Justice. Therefore, you have this permanent public policy to consider—that you are not lightly to interfere with this freedom of contract."

This statement is often cited as the embodiment of the doctrine of free- **12–10** dom of contract. That doctrine accepts that public policy requires certain contracts should not be enforced, but indicates it is of the first importance that those powers be exercised sparingly. Accordingly, it is the legislature which has had a more important role in relation to unlawful contracts in recent times. Many statutes contain provisions affecting the validity of particular contracts. Early Scottish statutes provided that contracts of usury (money lending at a high rate of interest), where the interest stipulated was above the legal rate, were null. When applying these

---

[8] *Richardson v Mellish* (1824) 2 Bing. 229 at 252.
[9] *Enderby Town Football Club v Football Association* [1971] Ch. 591 at 606.
[10] *Printing and Numerical Registering Co v Sampson* (1875) L.R. 19 Eq. 462 at 465.

provisions to individual circumstances today, the judges emphasise that their task is to construe the provision in the context of the whole Act in question and the mischief at which it was directed. Readers will also recall that when interpreting a contract if two meanings are possible, it will be presumed that the parties intended that the contract would be legal.

12–11   Where a contract is not directly prohibited by statute, it may still be alleged that it is illegal and unenforceable. This may occur, for example, if a statute imposes a penalty on a particular type of conduct. This can occur where a legal contract is performed in an illegal manner. In *St John Shipping Corp v Joseph Rank Ltd*[11]:

> A charterparty was entered into for the carriage of grain from America to Britain. Contrary to the Merchant Shipping Acts, the master overloaded the ship 11 inches beyond what was legal on the "Plimsoll marks". He was fined £1,200 for the offence. The charterer refused to pay part of the costs of carriage, claiming that it should not be bound when its cargo had been put at risk. So when the shipowners brought action for recovery of these sums, the defence was that the contract was illegal.

Devlin J. held that the sums were recoverable. Upon a true construction, he said that the statute was directed toward the prevention of over-loading, not the prohibition of contracts. Accordingly, the mere fact that there had been an illegal manner of performance did not debar the shipowners' claim. The intention of the legislature was to create a stat-utory offence for overloading, not to declare particular types of contract illegal. This case has been followed in Scotland. In *Dowling & Rutter v Abacus Frozen Foods Ltd (No.2)*[12] there was a contract for the provision of workers. When they turned out to be illegal immigrants payment was withheld. The pursuers provided the illegal workers from another agency and did not know they were not entitled to work in the United Kingdom. The claim for payment was allowed:

> "... the contract itself was perfectly legal for a legal purpose with legal aims, that is to say the provision of labour for value. If illegality supervened or entered upon the scene, it was purely by reason of the status of the workers in question in relation to the Immigration Act. This seems to me to be in a direct parallel with the position to be found in the *St John Shipping Corporation case*."[13]

---

[11] *St John Shipping Corp v Joseph Rank Ltd* [1957] 1 Q.B. 267.
[12] *Dowling & Rutter v Abacus Frozen Foods Ltd (No.2)*, 2002 S.L.T. 491.
[13] *Dowling & Rutter v Abacus Frozen Foods Ltd (No.2)*, 2002 S.L.T. 491 at [20].

THE CONSEQUENCES OF ILLEGALITY

It is not the case that any element of illegality will render the contract **12–12** unenforceable. If an action could never be brought on an illegal contract, injustice could result. A rogue could engage in an unlawful contract with an innocent party and thereby obtain money or property. If no action were allowed, then he would reap the advantage of his own pernicious dealings.

> *Example*: X agrees to supply Mongolian widgets to Y. After Y pays the price, X discloses that it is illegal to import Mongolian widgets into this country. If no action for recovery of the price was available to Y—as suggested by the maxim ex turpi causa non oritur actio—the rogue X would have successfully duped Y.

Each case turns on its own facts:

> "... it is clear that just because illegality enters into a contract, that does not necessarily make it unenforceable ... there has to be some scope for considerations of inadvertence, irrelevance, immateriality, innocence and so on to mitigate significantly or even exclude the issue."[14]

The law has devised a series of principles to deal with the consequences of illegal contracts. The difficulty is that these principles have never been fitted into a coherent scheme and that the two leading cases on the topic are conflicting. Let us begin by trying to identify the general approach of the law.

Parties equally blameworthy

If the parties are equally at fault (*in pari delicto*), the principle is that the **12–13** position of the possessor is the better one (*in turpi causa melior est conditio possidentis*). To put it another way, the loss is allowed to lie where it falls. So if a person pays money for an illegal drug, he cannot recover the money from the supplier, even if the drugs were never given to him. An illustration of this point is provided by *Barr v Crawford*[15]:

> A woman was informed that her chances of taking over the licence of a public house from her deceased husband were slender. On the strength of certain representations made to her, she made an initial payment of £8,000 to two individuals. She understood that a payment of £10,000 would secure the transfer of the licence at the next meeting of the district licensing board. Later, she sought to recover the money from the two individuals.

---

[14] *Dowling & Rutter v Abacus Frozen Foods Ltd (No.2)*, 2002 S.L.T. 491 at [19]. See also *Parkingeye Ltd v Somerfield Stores* [2012] EWCA Civ 1338.
[15] *Barr v Crawford*, 1983 S.L.T. 481.

It was held that the payment was a bribe and the transaction was an illegal one. The pursuer did not offer to prove that she was not *in pari delicto* and accordingly the judge dismissed the action.

Parties not equally blameworthy

12–14 Where parties are not equally blameworthy, a distinction is drawn between the rights of the guilty party and the rights of the innocent party. By "innocent party" in this context we mean a person who has been induced to enter the unlawful contract as the result of some unfair advantage having been taken of him by the other party. The courts do not weigh the relative turpitude of two guilty parties against one another.

(a) The guilty party

12–15 The guilty party can never sue on the contract. "No court will lend its aid to a man who founds his cause of action upon an immoral or an illegal act", said Lord Mansfield. It should, however, be remembered that where there has been an illegality in performance and not in the object of the contract, the party who has transgressed the statute may recover.[16]

(b) The innocent party

12–16 The innocent party can enforce the contract if he has made a mistake regarding the illegality alleged to taint it. In *Archbolds (Freightage) Ltd v S Spanglett Ltd*[17]:

> The defendants contracted to carry the plaintiff's whisky in their van. Unknown to the plaintiffs, the van was not licensed to carry goods by the defendants and the carriage therefore amounted to an offence. The whisky was stolen. The plaintiff's action for recovery of the value of the whisky was defended on the ground of illegality. The Court of Appeal held the plaintiffs entitled to recover the value of the whisky as the measure of damages for breach of contract. A mistake as to the existence of the licence did not deprive the plaintiffs of the right to enforce the contract. It was only the method of performance which was illegal rather than the making of the contract itself.

Apart from mistake, two other grounds which may protect the innocent party have been developed in English law.

(1) If the contract itself is illegal, the innocent party may enforce a collateral warranty.
(2) If there has been fraud then, even though the contract cannot be enforced there may be damages for fraud.

---

[16] *Dowling & Rutter v Abacus Frozen Foods Ltd (No.2)*, 2002 S.L.T. 491.
[17] *Archbolds (Freightage) Ltd v S Spanglett Ltd* [1961] 1 Q.B. 374; [1961] 1 All E.R. 417.

It is difficult to know how far such grounds might be accepted in Scot- **12–17** land. Scots law has, arguably, a more fully developed concept of unjus- tified enrichment than English law. There are, accordingly, circumstances where a party may recover when a contract has failed through illegality. In addition, there may be recovery upon a quantum meruit basis (pay- ment for work done). If it is shown that a statute was designed to protect a particular class, and an innocent party has been prejudiced as a result of an illegal contract, then he may be granted a remedy. Accordingly, where a contract of loan was made with an unregistered moneylender, the borrower could recover property deposited with the moneylender. This was because the Act which required the moneylender to be registered was for the benefit of borrowers as a class.[18]

There are two leading Scottish authorities on the consequences of statutory illegality. In *Cuthbertson v Lowes*[19]:

> Two fields of potatoes were sold by the Scots acre. This was contrary to the Weights and Measures Act, which declared null and void any contract using local or customary measures. It was held that the seller was entitled to recover the market value of the potatoes.

Lord President Inglis said that the seller was not suing upon the contract **12–18** but was in effect pursuing a claim for recompense under the principles of unjustified enrichment. The decision was distinguished in the subsequent case of *Jamieson v Watt's Trustee*,[20] where a joiner did work in excess of the amount he was authorised to do by licence under the Defence Reg- ulations. It was held that the proprietor did not have to pay for the excess. There has been a tendency to regard *Cuthbertson* as wrongly decided or, at best, to be binding only on its own special facts. For instance, Gloag draws a distinction between agreements which the law will not allow to operate as contracts and contracts which are contrary to law.[21] That is a difficult distinction to understand or apply. It seems rather that the consequences of illegality depend on two factors: the degree of turpitude involved and the requirements of public policy. It was not particularly heinous to sell potatoes according to an old measure. But there were strong grounds of public policy for preventing joiners from doing work without a licence shortly after the Second World War, when a number of economic restrictions were in force.

The courts often approach the question of illegality on an equitable **12–19** basis depending on the particular circumstances which have occurred. This can be seen in the recent case of *Malik v Ali*.[22]

The pursuer refused to deliver a disposition which she had executed for a property in Glasgow. The defender claimed that the property had been bought by him, in the pursuer's name, and that she had agreed to deliver

---

[18] *Phillips v Blackhurst*, 1912 2 S.L.T. 254.
[19] *Cuthbertson v Lowes* (1870) 8 M. 1073.
[20] *Jamieson v Watt's Trustee*, 1950 S.C. 265.
[21] Gloag, *Contract*, 2nd edn, 1929, p.550.
[22] *Malik v Ali*, 2004 S.L.T. 1280 (IH).

the disposition to him at a later stage. The reason the property had been bought in the pursuer's name was to help ensure that her fiancé in Pakistan was granted a visa to enter the United Kingdom. The basis of the contract was therefore illegal, since it was to deceive the immigration authorities. The pursuer argued that she was not obliged to deliver the disposition, since she had only agreed to do so under an illegal contract. Her claim failed.

The Inner House stated:

> "It may be that when the nature of the illegality in the formation or execution of a contract is clear or agreed, and central to the parties' arrangements, the court will not interfere, and the estate would be left to lie where it falls ... [However] there may be questions of equity to be taken into account ... if the [pursuer]'s position is sustained, she will obtain decree for recovery of a heritable property, for which, on the basis of her own averments, she has paid nothing, and in respect of which, again in terms of her own averments, she accepts that, if she has not paid the purchase price, she is under an obligation ... to deliver a signed disposition of the subjects to the [defender]. Such a situation is quite unsatisfactory and could in the event prove to be fundamentally inequitable."[23]

RESTRICTIVE COVENANTS

12–20 Restrictive covenants are clauses which limit a party's liberty to practice his trade or profession. They are sometimes referred to as clauses in restraint of trade. Such clauses are frequently found in contracts of employment, partnership, and sale.

Examples:

(1) Chop agrees to buy Loin's butcher shop. In terms of the agreement, Loin undertakes not to set up in business as a butcher within five miles of the shop for a three-year period.

(2) Amp works for the Plug Electric Co. His contract of employment stipulates that if Amp leaves the company he shall not join a rival company within the United Kingdom for 12 months after his employment with Plug ceases.

Courts dealing with restrictive covenants have a difficult balance to strike. On the one hand, they wish to uphold contracts. They are reluctant to release a party from an obligation freely entered into. To do so destroys the security of contractual engagements. It tends to make parties less likely to abide by their contracts in future. However, the courts also

---

[23] *Malik v Ali*, 2004 S.L.T 1280 (IH) at [11]. The relevancy of equitable considerations was also discussed and approved in *Dowling & Rutter v Abacus Frozen Foods Ltd (No.2)*, 2002 S.L.T. 491.

wish to uphold individual liberty. A person ought to have the right to earn a livelihood. It is in the public interest that competition be encouraged. Persons should not be allowed to abuse a superior bargaining position to secure an unfair trading advantage. Accordingly, the balance is between:

> *Freedom of Contract v Freedom of Trade*[24]
> *The Right to Bargain v the Right to Work or Trade*

The ground rules

Over the years, a number of principles have been developed to determine **12–21** whether or not a restrictive covenant is valid. The principles are essentially five in number:

(1) Restrictive covenants are prima facie void and unenforceable.
(2) Restrictive covenants will only be upheld if they are reasonable:

    (i) as between the parties, and
    (ii) in the public interest.

(3) Restrictive covenants are most readily enforced in contracts of sale of a business.
(4) In employment cases, an employer cannot protect himself against competition alone. He must demonstrate some exceptional proprietorial interest, e.g. a trade connection or trade secret.
(5) The restriction must go no further than is reasonably required.

The classic statement of the law occurs in the speech of Lord Macnaghten in *Nordenfelt v Maxim Nordenfelt Guns & Ammunition Co Ltd*[25]:

> "The public have an interest in every person's carrying on his trade freely: so has the individual. All interference with individual liberty of action in trading, and all restraints of trade of themselves, if there is nothing more, are contrary to public policy, and therefore void. That is the general rule. But there are exceptions: restraints of trade and interference with individual liberty of action may be justified by the special circumstances of a particular case. It is sufficient justification, and indeed it is the only justification, if the restriction is reasonable—reasonable, that is, in reference to the interests of the parties concerned and reasonable in reference to the interests of the public, so framed and so guarded as to afford adequate protection to the party in whose favour it is imposed, while at the same time it is in no way injurious to the public."

---

[24] Specific reference to this is made in *Cyrus Energy Ltd v Stewart* [2009] CSOH 53, per Lord Woolman at [25].
[25] *Nordenfelt v Maxim Nordenfelt Guns & Ammunition Co Ltd* [1894] A.C. 535 at 565.

12-22 In determining reasonableness, regard will be had to a number of factors, including the nature of the restriction imposed, its duration, and the spatial area over which it is imposed. At one time it was thought that a general restraint, which prevented a person from working anywhere in the world, was unenforceable. This is illustrated by the facts of *Nordenfelt* itself:

> In 1886, Nordenfelt sold his arms business to a limited company which was formed for the purpose of purchasing it. He received a large sum for the sale and it was agreed he would act as the new company's managing director for five years after its formation. Two years later, the company amalgamated with another company. At the time of the transfer Nordenfelt entered into a restrictive covenant with the company similar in terms to one he had agreed to on the sale of the business in 1886. It was stipulated that for a 25-year period he should not "engage except on behalf of the company either directly or indirectly in the trade or business of a manufacturer of guns, gun-mountings or gun powder explosives or ammunition."

When he attempted to breach this undertaking, the company sought to enforce the covenant. Nordenfelt contended that the restraint was wider than was required to protect the company's legitimate interests and that: "It cannot be the law that a man should be prevented from earning his living in any part of the wide world." The House of Lords rejected this contention and upheld the covenant. In view of the fact that it was a worldwide business ("He had upon his books almost every monarch and almost every State of any note in the habitable globe") and that he had received a very good price for his transfer, the restraint was reasonable.

Contracts of sale of a business

12-23 When a business is sold as a going concern, one part of the purchase price will be in respect of the goodwill of the business. The goodwill comprises the customers and reputation of the seller, in other words, the seller's trade connection. If the purchaser could not insert a restrictive covenant into the contract to restrict competition by the seller, the goodwill would be valueless. The seller could immediately set up in the same business again and attract his customers to the new premises. Accordingly, such restrictions will be enforced when they provide protection to the purchaser's legitimate interests. In one case, the Privy Council stated that such clauses do not come within the operation of the doctrine of restraint of trade, "provided that the degree of interference does not exceed the accepted standard."[26] This is another way of saying that in contracts of sale of a business, the presumption has shifted in favour of such covenants being upheld. The power of the court to intervene is still present, but it will only be exercised when the restraint is demonstrably excessive

---

[26] *Bridge v Deacons* [1984] 2 All E.R. 19.

or against the public interest.[27] Nevertheless, the Outer House has held that where such a restraint is challenged, the onus will be on the company to demonstrate that the extent of the restraint is justified.[28]

While it is open to the purchaser to restrict competition by the seller, the converse proposition does not hold. In one case, the seller of a men's hairdressing business sought to prevent the buyer from engaging in ladies' hairdressing in competition with the seller.[29] The restriction sought was refused. The reason given by the sheriff in this novel situation was that the restraint was not designed to protect the seller's legitimate interest, but simply to stifle competition.

Contracts of partnership

Where a restrictive covenant is inserted in a partnership deed, the question will again turn on the legitimate interests of those who rely upon the term for protection. In the first reported Scots decision on restrictive covenants, the court upheld a covenant involving a bookselling partnership in Glasgow.[30] If all the partners accept the same restriction there is a definite presumption that the term is enforceable. Otherwise it is impossible to give a precise guide to which covenants will and which will not be enforced. Two cases will suffice as illustrations. Interdict has been granted to prevent a doctor from exercising the profession of a general practitioner in a small country town on the basis of covenant. No argument seems to have been led regarding the public interest in securing the best possible medical provision in the particular area.[31] But public interest was a factor of some importance when a large Hong Kong firm of solicitors sought to enforce a covenant against a partner who had left the firm.[32] The firm was departmentalised, which meant that the covenant went well beyond the individual partner's role in the firm. Nevertheless, the public interest in facilitating the assumption of new partners by established solicitors' firms was accepted by the Privy Council. If a partner was not bound by such a provision, it would deter firms from assuming partners, because once the partner had acquired clients through the firm, he might set up on his own taking the clients with him. However, if the restriction sought is too wide, it will be struck down. A covenant which sought to prevent a solicitor from practising within 20 miles of Glasgow Cross was thought to be excessive and interim interdict refused.[33] Counsel for the respondent had submitted that the area probably included about half the law firms in Scotland.

12–24

---

[27] See *George Walker & Co v Jann*, 1991 S.L.T. 771.
[28] *Cyrus Energy Ltd v Stewart* [2009] CSOH 53 at [31].
[29] *Giblin v Murdoch*, 1979 S.L.T. (Sh Ct) 5.
[30] *Stalker v Carmichael* (1735) Mor. 9455.
[31] *Anthony v Rennie*, 1981 S.L.T. (Notes) 11.
[32] *Bridge v Deacons* [1984] 2 All E.R. 19.
[33] *Dallas McMillan & Sinclair v Simpson*, 1989 S.L.T. 454.

Cartels, etc.

12–25 Apart from covenants involving individuals, freedom of trade can also be prejudiced where manufacturers or traders combine together to regulate the availability of certain commodities, or to fix prices. Suppose, for example, all the manufacturers of widgets agreed together to fix a price for widgets well in excess of production costs. That would greatly enhance their profits to the detriment of the public interest. This area is now largely covered by statute and the competition laws of the European Union. The rules that apply are detailed and are outwith the scope of this book.

Employment

12–26 In contracts for the sale of a business, the seller receives something in return for his agreement to the restrictive covenant, viz. the value of the goodwill. This is not true in the case of employees. They may only be persuaded to sign a contract containing a covenant to ensure that they obtain the job and therefore a means of livelihood. The consequences of a restrictive covenant may be more oppressive in the case of an employee. It therefore requires closer scrutiny. However, it may be that the first task for the court is to determine if the contractual relationship is one of employment or not. In doing so, it is not helpful to classify relationships "too rigidly". Where the defenders are directors who also have a significant shareholding in the company then it may be that "the transaction was closer to that end of the spectrum occupied by the sale of a business" such that it is "inapt to bracket [them] with normal employees".[34]

In employment cases, a restrictive covenant is "a *pactum illicitum* only if the restriction imposed is wider than is necessary to protect the legitimate interests of the master".[35] Plainly, the two crucial phrases in this passage are "wider than is necessary" and "legitimate interests." What do they mean? Let us begin by looking at the term "legitimate interests." It unpacks into two separate but overlapping categories:

(a) trade secrets and confidential information; and (b) preservation of business connection.

Legitimate interest (1)—trade secrets and confidential information

12–27 With good reason the area covered by trade secrets and confidential information has been described as "somewhat nebulous and ill-defined." This is because true trade secrets will normally be protected by intellectual property rights such as patents and copyrights. Moreover,

---
[34] *Cyrus Energy Ltd v Stewart* [2009] CSOH 53 at [25].
[35] *Scottish Farmers' Dairy Co (Glasgow) Ltd v McGhee*, 1933 S.L.T. 142, per Lord President Clyde at 145.

independent of any express contractual term, there is an implied term in contracts of employment that an employee will not disclose confidential information to other parties.[36]

The relevant principles are as follows:

(1) The parties' obligations are prima facie determined by the contract of employment.

(2) The question of the use and disclosure of information is the subject of implied terms.

(3) The duty of good faith and fidelity during the employment which is implied by law depends upon the nature of the employment. The duty is broken if the employee copies or memorises customer lists.

(4) After the employment ceases, the duty of good faith is more restricted in scope. It only covers information of a type amounting to a trade secret.

Whether or not information is so confidential as to amount to a trade **12–28** secret depends upon the whole circumstances of the case. Relevant factors are (a) the nature of the employment; (b) the nature of the information; (c) whether the employer impressed the confidentiality of the information upon the employee; and (d) whether the information can be easily isolated from other information which the employee possesses. Prices and customer lists can constitute trade secrets. Restrictive covenants cannot, however, extend the employer's rights to protect information which would otherwise be the subject of implied terms.

A difficult issue concerns the employer's general business methods and organisation. Does this constitute a trade secret or confidential information? In *SOS Bureau v Payne*, which involved an employee who sought to leave an employment agency where she had worked, the sheriff upheld a covenant in order to prevent disclosure of the employer's "system of work, presentation of the service to the customer and in particular fee charging policy."[37] This statement would effectively cover most employees. If an employee does not know about the employer's system of work, he is more likely to be looking down the wrong end of an unfair dismissal barrel than worrying about the validity of a restrictive covenant. The more persuasive line of authority can be traced back to Lord Atkinson. He accepted that information about business organisation and methods was naturally acquired by the employee and stated that:

"... he violates no obligation express or implied arising from the relation in which he stood to the [employers] by using in service of some persons other than them the general knowledge he has acquired of their scheme of organisation and methods of business."[38]

---

[36] *Faccenda Chicken Ltd v Fowler* [1987] Ch. 117; *Harben Pumps (Scotland) Ltd v Lafferty*, 1989 S.L.T. 752.

[37] *SOS Bureau v Payne*, 1982 S.L.T. (Sh Ct) 33.

[38] *Herbert Morris Ltd v Saxelby* [1916] 1 A.C. 688.

His words were echoed in a later case by Lord Pearson, who stated that the employer's scheme of organisation and methods of business are not to be counted as trade secrets.[39] Lord Ross has accepted Lord Pearson's view as a correct statement of the law.[40]

12–29   An illustration of the continuing importance of restrictive covenants where issues of trade secrets and confidential information are concerned is provided by *Bluebell Apparel v Dickinson*[41]:

> In January 1977, D was taken on as a management trainee by Bluebell Apparel, manufacturers of "Wrangler" jeans. By June 1977, D was in sole charge of their Kilwinning factory but in August he intimated that he was leaving to take up a position with Levi Strauss and Co. Bluebell Apparel sought an interdict to prevent this on the basis of an agreement which D had signed when he joined them. It provided that except with the written permission of the employers, D would not, for a period of two years after the end of his employment with them, perform any services, either as owner, partner, employee, or consultant for any person or business entity in competition with Bluebell Apparel.

The First Division upheld the covenant on the basis that D possessed confidential information about Bluebell Apparel. Accordingly, D was prevented from working for a competitor anywhere in the world in any capacity for a period of two years. His knowledge after only eight months regarding Bluebell Apparel's pricing policy and customers was thought sufficient to justify a two-year long, worldwide restraint.

Legitimate interest (2)—preservation of business connection

12–30   Employers are not entitled to protection against competition alone. Competition is the very essence of the market. Where there are no trade secrets or confidential information to protect, the presumption is that the employee is freely entitled to practise his trade or profession. However, there are certain qualifications to that general approach. An employer does have a legitimate interest in preserving his business connection, which can be enforced in certain circumstances.

Let us first deal with non-solicitation of clients. Prohibitions against active attempts to poach clients for a limited period are frequently upheld. It is thought reasonable by both sides that the employee will not seek to undermine the employer's business in this manner. After all, what reasonable employer intends to train industrial spies to steal business out from under his nose? But when it is simply a case of competition, either by joining a competitor, or by setting up in business on one's own, the general principle is that the employee cannot be shackled.

12–31   Secondly, a reasonable restraint will be enforced when there is some

---

[39] *Commercial Plastics Ltd v Vincent* [1964] 3 All E.R. 546 at 551.
[40] *Bluebell Apparel Ltd v Dickinson*, 1980 S.L.T. 157 at 158.
[41] *Bluebell Apparel Ltd v Dickinson*, 1980 S.L.T. 157.

intimate relationship between the employee and the customers of the business such that he acquires a degree of influence over them. In *Scottish Farmers Dairy Co (Glasgow) Ltd v McGhee*, a milk-roundsman was the only contact between the business and the customers. His contract contained a covenant which prevented him from setting up in competition with the company for a period of two years within a one-mile radius of his employer's place of business.[42] It was held that he should not be allowed to take advantage of the position his job gave him vis-a-vis the customers. This would be unfair competition with the employer. Accordingly, the covenant was upheld:

> "... the preservation of his business connection is a legitimate interest of every trader; and if, to protect that interest, a prohibition against competition by the servant is made necessary by the particular nature and circumstances of the master's business, the law of Scotland recognises the prohibition as an enforceable term of the contract of employment."[43]

If the employee did not have an opportunity to exercise influence over clients or customers, it is difficult to see why he should be prevented from competing under this head.[44]

No wider than is necessary

In considering how wide the restriction is there are three matters to consider: the time for which it operates; the area over which it operates; and the content of the restriction imposed. On the following pages are some examples of spatial and temporal restrictions which have been held to be valid. It will be seen that a great range of different restrictions have been enforced, from a quarter of a mile to the world in extent, from six months to life in duration. Where trade secrets are concerned, then the ambit of the restriction can be very wide as in the "Wrangler" case. In employment contracts, however, area covenants are in general looked upon with disfavour. This is because they appear to be simply an attempt to stifle competition. There is Court of Appeal authority in England to the effect that they will not be enforced where a lesser, more precise restriction would have adequately protected the employer's interests.[45] One recent case concerned an attempt by the employer to impose a variable "quarantine" period on the employee. The contract stated that when the employment was terminated the employer would notify the employee of a quarantine period of up to 12 months during which time the employee could not compete. Although the clause was not upheld, the ground for rejecting it was because the employer failed to exercise the

12–32

---

[42] *Scottish Farmers Dairy Co (Glasgow) Ltd v McGhee*, 1933 S.C. 148; 1933 S.L.T. 142.
[43] *Scottish Farmers Dairy Co (Glasgow) Ltd v McGhee*, 1933 S.C. 148, per Lord President Clyde at 153.
[44] *Hinton & Higgs (UK) Ltd v Murphy*, 1989 S.L.T. 450; *Office Angels v Rainer Thomas* [1991] I.R.L.R. 214.
[45] *Office Angels v Rainer Thomas* [1991] I.R.L.R. 214.

option properly, since it did not specify a fixed quarantine period.[46] The prospect thus remains open that a variable restrictive covenant could be upheld if exercised properly. However, it is suggested that such clauses are prejudicial to the employee, by virtue of lack of certainty when the contract is concluded. Consequently, they should be treated with caution.

12–33   The restriction contained in the covenant should be directed at the legitimate interest which the employer is entitled to protect. If the clause is drafted too widely, it will be unenforceable and the employer will lose even the protection that he was entitled to seek. Determining the scope of legitimate interest requires consideration of the job which the employee did. In *Rentokil Ltd v Hampton* the restrictive covenant sought to prevent the employee from being involved with the "marketing, sale or supply of products or services" in competition with Rentokil.[47] As he was a timber infestation surveyor, the restraint was held to be wider than was required and declared invalid. It prevented him from competing, not only in respect of his own area of work, but in respect of new areas. Similarly there was no legitimate interest in preventing him from dealing with persons with whom he had no connection during the period of his employment. If the legitimate interest is preservation of business connection by preventing contact with customers, a clause which would prevent contact with customers in relation to business other than that of the former employer is too wide.[48] Generally, however, a non-solicitation clause is more likely to be enforced than a non-compete clause.

Where the legitimate interest at stake is the preservation of confidential information it is very difficult to draft an effective clause that deals with that and nothing else. The nature of confidential information makes it difficult to specify what is to be protected. It is also difficult effectively to police any such prohibition on disclosure of such information. The courts therefore accept that, in some situations, the only effective means of obtaining protection for legitimate interests will be a prohibition on employment by the employer's rivals or contact with customers.[49] Accordingly, the manager of a Wrangler jeans factory could not take employment even as a doorman in Nicaragua for Levis or Lee Cooper.[50]

Severability

12–34 Frequently, a restrictive covenant will consist of several separate restrictions. If each restriction is truly independent of the others, then the invalidity of each will not affect the validity of the others. Accordingly, a reasonable restriction will be enforced even where the unreasonable restriction falls. So where a salesman agreed not to canvass his employer's customers and also not to carry on business as a traveller in a particular area, the former provision was upheld but the latter rejected as too

---

[46] *Seabrokers Ltd v Riddell* [2007] CSOH 146 at [31].
[47] *Rentokil Ltd v Hampton*, 1982 S.L.T. 422.
[48] *Aramark Plc v Sommerville*, 1995 S.L.T. 749.
[49] *PR Consultants Scotland Ltd v Mann*, 1997 S.L.T. 437.
[50] *Bluebell Apparel Ltd v Dickinson*, 1980 S.L.T. 157.

wide and too vague.[51] The divisibility of the clause can be the subject of express stipulation in the contract.[52] If there is no such stipulation the court can only sever an unreasonable part of the clause if it can be done by simple deletion.[53] The courts will not, however, re-write the restriction so as to make it enforceable. That is to confuse the function of the parties in making the contract with that of the courts in interpreting it.[54] The parties cannot exclude the jurisdiction of the courts by declaring that the terms of the covenant are reasonable.[55]

Remedies for breach of covenant

The preferred remedy for an employer is to seek an interdict preventing **12–35** breach. If that is not possible, the employer may seek damages from the employee to compensate for any losses sustained by the breach of the covenant.

Court procedure is of critical importance in covenant cases. Frequently, the matter comes before the court at an interim stage. Accordingly, the decision is made on the pleadings as they then stand, together with such statements as are made by the parties' representatives at the bar of the court. There is a two-stage approach. First, the petitioner must make out a prima facie case. Secondly, he must demonstrate that on the balance of convenience, the interim interdict should be granted.[56] A prima facie case is one which has a seeming cogency. It is sometimes said that the pleadings disclose a case to try. The balance of convenience broadly speaking relates to the relative prejudice which will be suffered by the parties if the interim interdict is granted or refused. Among the considerations which the court will take into account are the following:

(1) When was the action brought?
(2) How long does the covenant have to run?
(3) What is the prejudice to the employer?[57]
(4) What is the prejudice to the employee?[58]
(5) Will the employee be deprived of his livelihood?
(6) Is there a remedy in damages?[59]
(7) Is the loss quantifiable?[60]
(8) Is the employee being paid to accept the covenant?[61]

---

[51] *Mulvein v Murray*, 1908 S.C. 528.
[52] *Hinton & Higgs (UK) Ltd v Murphy*, 1989 S.L.T. 450.
[53] *Living Design (Home Improvements) Ltd v Davidson*, 1994 S.L.T. 753.
[54] *Hinton & Higgs (UK) Ltd v Murphy*, 1989 S.L.T. 450.
[55] *Hinton & Higgs (UK) Ltd v Murphy*, 1989 S.L.T. 450.
[56] *Toynar Ltd v Whitbread & Co Plc*, 1988 S.L.T. 433, per Lord Ross.
[57] *Cyrus Energy Ltd v Stewart* [2009] CSOH 53 at [36].
[58] *Cyrus Energy Ltd v Stewart* [2009] CSOH 53. Note that "post-covenant" factors are unlikely to prevent the covenant being enforced.
[59] *Group 4 Total Security Ltd v Ferrier*, 1985 S.C. 70; 1985 S.L.T. 287.
[60] *Rentokil Ltd v Kramer*, 1986 S.L.T. 114.
[61] *Agma Chemical Co Ltd v Hart*, 1984 S.L.T. 246.

There are two other remedies which may be available to employers faced with apparent loss of confidential information. First, the information may be covered by intellectual property rights under the law relating to patents and copyrights. Secondly, if it is reasonably thought that the employee has removed trade items, customer lists, schedules of prices and the like, these may be recovered by a "dawn raid" carried out by a commissioner under s.1 of the Administration of Justice (Scotland) Act 1972. This can be an effective—but very expensive—manner of proceeding.

Where the employer seeks damages, he must be able to prove loss and causation. For example, he may show that he has lost profit as a result of the ex-employee soliciting clients from him. Failure to show loss or causation will result in no award, even if there has been a breach of a restrictive covenant.[62]

---

[62] *Dunedin Independent Plc v Welsh* [2006] CSOH 174 at [66]–[71]. Although Lady Clark held that the restrictive covenant clause was not enforceable, she proceeded to deal with issues of causation and loss.

Examples of Spatial Restrictions

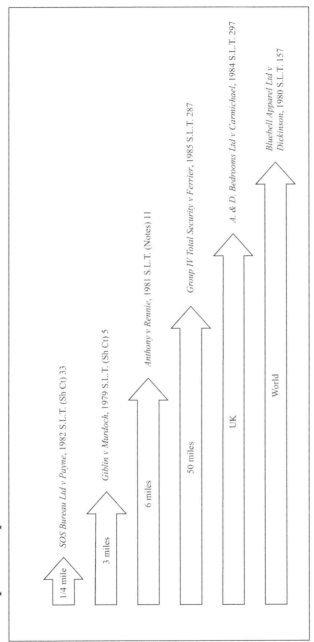

1/4 mile — *SOS Bureau Ltd v Payne*, 1982 S.L.T. (Sh Ct) 33

3 miles — *Giblin v Murdoch*, 1979 S.L.T. (Sh Ct) 5

6 miles — *Anthony v Rennie*, 1981 S.L.T. (Notes) 11

50 miles — *Group IV Total Security v Ferrier*, 1985 S.L.T. 287

UK — *A. & D. Bedrooms Ltd v Carmichael*, 1984 S.L.T. 297

World — *Bluebell Apparel Ltd v Dickinson*, 1980 S.L.T. 157

Examples of Temporal Restrictions

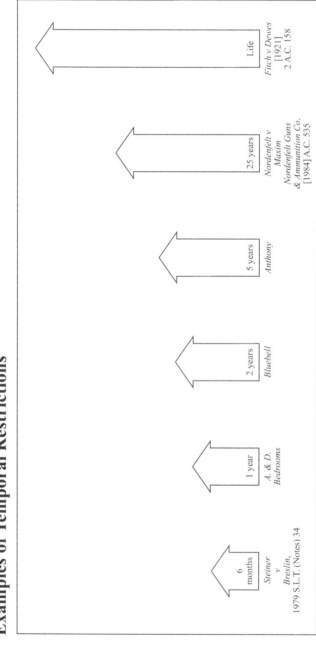

CHAPTER 13

THE EXTINCTION OF OBLIGATIONS

TERMINATION

When does a contract come to an end? In most instances, contractual **13–01** obligations are extinguished when both parties have fully performed their respective sides of the bargain. A contract for the sale of goods, for example, is normally completed when the item is delivered in return for the correct price. The parties owe no further duties to one another under the contract. Similarly, in unilateral obligations, once the person who has made the promise fulfils his undertaking, the obligation is at an end. So if a businesswoman promises to pay a law student £100 if he comes first in an essay competition, the obligation will be discharged on her paying him the money if he wins the competition. Apart from performance, however, there are several other methods by which contractual obligations can come to an end.

Discharge by consent

The parties may agree to release each other from their respective con- **13–02** tractual obligations without performance. Put simply, the contract is cancelled by mutual agreement. Where a creditor agrees to release the debtor, this is known as "acceptilation". If, for example, A owes B £50 in respect of a quantity of towels which B has delivered to him, B may agree to waive the debt (perhaps because A has done him a favour). If such a release is not granted in the course of a business, it might qualify as a gratuitous unilateral obligation with the result that in order to be effective it would require to be in writing.[1]

Novation and delegation

An obligation is extinguished when it is agreed that a fresh obligation by **13–03** the debtor be substituted for it (novation) or when a new obligation by another debtor is substituted for it (delegation).

> *Example*: Ben owes Sid £50. Ben suggests that if Sid lends him a further £50 he will give him a new receipt for £100 (novation). Alternatively, Ben may suggest that as Alf owes him (Ben) £50, a

---

[1] Requirements of Writing (Scotland) Act 1995 s.1(2)(a)(ii).

new obligation should be entered into under which Alf owes Sid £50 (delegation). If Sid accepts either proposal, the original obligation by Ben will be extinguished.

There is a presumption that a new obligation is additional to an existing obligation. Accordingly, a debtor should always ensure that he obtains an express discharge of the original debt.[2]

Compensation

13–04 Where each party owes the other a sum of money, the one debt can be compensated or set off against the other.

> *Example*: Ralph and Zeke are grain merchants who have constant dealings with each other. Ralph owes £50,000 in respect of a wheat consignment he bought from Zeke yesterday. Zeke in turn owes Ralph £120,000 for oats which he bought from him a week ago.

The two debts can be set off against each other resulting in an obligation by Zeke to pay Ralph the difference, that is £70,000. The effect of compensation is accordingly to cancel Ralph's obligation. There are some conditions which must be satisfied before the right of set-off can be used. First, both claims must be liquid, which means they must be readily ascertainable in money terms. If one of the claims is illiquid, then no right of set-off exists. A claim for damages is illiquid because until a precise figure is put upon the claim by a court, the sum is not ascertained. Secondly, the debts must be presently due. There is no right of set-off in respect of future debts. Finally, both parties must be creditor and debtor to each other in the same legal capacity. Suppose a solicitor is owed £2,000 by a client in respect of professional fees. The client cannot claim set-off on the basis that the solicitor is the trustee of an estate which is due to pay him a sum of money. But the client could claim a right of set-off if he was a joiner who had done work for the solicitor who has not paid for it.

13–05 Set-off must be distinguished from retention. The aim of set-off is to extinguish part or all of the obligation. Retention, on the other hand, is about securing performance by the other party by lawfully withholding one's own obligations under the contract.

Confusion

13–06 A person cannot be under an obligation to himself. If company A owes company B money and subsequently B were to assign all debts owed to it to A, then the obligation has been "confused" and the debt is extinguished.

Two further methods by which contractual obligations are

---

[2] Liability will turn on the interpretation of the terms of the new agreement, where relevant: *Blyth & Blyth Ltd v Carillion Construction Ltd*, 2002 S.L.T 961.

extinguished require more detailed discussion. The first is prescription, the second frustration.

The principle of prescription governs the length of time for which obli- **13–07** gations subsist. The need for such a rule is clear. Rights cannot exist forever. A creditor must exercise his right to enforce the debt within a reasonable time. It would be unfair if someone were to remain silent about a debt for 10 years and then seek to take action against the other party. Further, as time elapses, it becomes increasingly likely that evidence will be lost. Witnesses' memories will be dimmed. They may go abroad or die. Accordingly, the law presumes that after a period of time has elapsed without a claim having been pursued, the creditor must be deemed to have abandoned that right. The right is then said to have "prescribed".

Before 1973 the law regarding prescription was in a confused and chaotic state. On the basis, however, of work done by the Scottish Law Commission, the Prescription and Limitation (Scotland) Act 1973 was enacted, which signally improved and simplified this branch of the law. It deals with three different categories: positive prescription, negative prescription and limitation. Our main interest lies with the second of these categories.

Negative prescription

There are two periods of negative prescription, (a) a short negative pre- **13–08** scription of five years, and (b) a long negative prescription of 20 years. Most contractual obligations are extinguished at the end of five years.[3] So if a car is sold and the price not paid within five years, the debt is thereafter extinguished. The main exceptions concern those obligations which relate to land.[4] In such cases, the 20-year period applies.[5]

Computation of prescriptive period

The prescriptive period commences running on the date on which the **13–09** obligation becomes enforceable.[6] In respect of a claim for breach of contract, the action must be brought within five years of the date of the loss, injury or damage which occurred as a result of the breach.[7] In *Greater Glasgow Health Board v Baxter Clark & Paul* the following circumstances occurred[8]:

---

[3] 1973 Act s.6.
[4] The 1973 Act has been amended by the Title Conditions (Scotland) Act 2003 in relation to the negative prescriptive period where it relates to real burdens.
[5] 1973 Act s.7.
[6] 1973 Act s.6(3).
[7] 1973 Act s.11(1).
[8] *Greater Glasgow Health Board v Baxter Clark & Paul*, 1992 S.L.T. 35.

Between 1969 and 1972, a firm of architects supervised works which were undertaken at Yorkhill Hospital in Glasgow. Some physical damage in the form of cracks manifested in 1972. In 1978 a document was signed between the parties where the architects accepted that there were faults but not that they were liable. No action was raised until 1982. It was held that the action had prescribed. The prescriptive clock had commenced ticking in 1972. Accordingly, by the time the action was raised the obligation had prescribed.

Where there is a series of transactions between the parties, the prescriptive period commences on the date on which payment for the goods last supplied or the services last rendered became due.[9] In the case of a loan or deposit of a sum of money, the period commences on the date stipulated for repayment in the contract or, if no such stipulation is made, the date on which a written demand for repayment is made.[10] So far as obligations to pay money or execute work by instalments are concerned, the date of commencement is that on which the last of the instalments is to be paid or executed respectively.[11]

13–10   Prescription stops running when a relevant claim is made by the creditor or a relevant acknowledgment is given by the debtor. What does this mean? A relevant claim is made if the creditor has taken steps to pursue his right, either by raising a court action or referring the matter to arbitration.[12] Both courses of action clearly indicate that he has not abandoned his claim. The same principle applies if he contests any claim inconsistent with his own alleged right. For example, if he stated his right as a defence to an action brought against him by the debtor.[13] Conversely, a debtor's actions may amount to acknowledgment if they clearly indicate that he regards the claim as still subsisting. This might occur, for example, if he made part-payment of a debt allegedly owed by him.

Mora, taciturnity and acquiescence

13–11   There is an older, common law principle by which a claim may be time-barred. This is known as "*mora*, taciturnity and acquiescence". Translated into modern language, this means delay, silence and consent. Even if a right has not prescribed, a person may nevertheless be personally barred because he has taken an unreasonable length of time to vindicate the right.

> *Example*: Ted and Alice sign an agreement regarding the sale of widgets. Nothing follows on from the agreement but four years and eight months after it is concluded, Ted seeks to enforce it. Although

---

[9] 1973 Act Sch.2 para.1(4).
[10] 1973 Act Sch.2 para.2(2).
[11] 1973 Act Sch.2 para.4(2).
[12] 1973 Act s.9.
[13] 1973 Act s.10.

the prescriptive period has not yet elapsed, Alice may argue *mora*, taciturnity and acquiescence. If the plea is successful, Ted's claim will fail.

By and large, this principle is redundant in the law of contract.

FRUSTRATION

Few people claim to be able to predict future events. Fewer can actually **13–12** do so. After a contract has been concluded, events may occur which are not the fault of either party, which are unforeseen and which have a dramatic effect on the rights and obligations of the parties. In response to this problem the doctrine of frustration has been developed. Where it operates both parties will be released from their contractual obligations. The circumstances necessary to bring about frustration of a contract were summarised in *Paal Wilson & Co A/S v Partenreederei Hannah Blumenthal (The Hannah Blumenthal)* as follows:

> "The first essential factor is that there must be some outside event or extraneous change of situation, not foreseen or provided for by the parties at the time of contracting, which either makes it impossible for the contract to be performed at all, or at least renders its performance something radically different from what the parties contemplated when they entered into it. The second essential factor is that the outside event or extraneous change of situation concerned, and the consequences of either in relation to the performance of the contract, must have occurred without either the fault or default of either party to the contract."[14]

In some cases, the courts have discharged the parties from their obligations on the basis of an implied term.[15] This approach is artificial. How can the courts imply a term on the basis of giving effect to the parties' intentions when the event is one to which, by definition, they have not directed their minds? A graphic refutation of the implied term theory was provided as long ago as 1922 by Lord Sands:

> "A tiger has escaped from a travelling menagerie. The milkgirl fails to deliver the milk. Possibly the milkman may be exonerated from any breach of contract; but, even so, it would seem hardly reasonable to base that exoneration on the ground that 'tiger days excepted' must be held as if written into milk contract."[16]

---

[14] *Paal Wilson & Co A/S v Partenreederei Hannah Blumenthal (The Hannah Blumenthal)* [1983] 1 A.C. 854, per Lord Brandon.
[15] For example, *Taylor v Caldwell* (1863) 3 B. & S. 826.
[16] *James Scott & Sons Ltd v R&N Del Sel*, 1922 S.C. 592; affirmed 1923 S.C. (HL) 37.

Types of frustrating event

13–13 Impossibility is the primary ground on which the doctrine of frustration proceeds. If one party dies and a degree of *delectus personae* is present, then frustration operates. For example, a portrait painter dies in the middle of a commission. Likewise if there is destruction of the subject matter. Changed circumstances can make performance of the obligations impossible or at least extremely impracticable. The terrorist attacks on the World Trade Center in September 2001 rendered contracts frustrated where the contracting party's offices had been destroyed. Natural disasters, such as Hurricane Katrina, can also render contracts impossible to perform. Impossibility may affect the rights that are enjoyed under the contract as well as the obligations.

Apart from actual impossibility, there is also legal impossibility:

Example: A makes a contract with B to deliver rare Scottish heather to Liberia. After the contract is made, the government passes a law forbidding the export of Scottish heather.

Although it is not physically impossible to deliver the heather, it is legally impossible. Clearly, A can no longer perform the contract. Otherwise he would be guilty of an offence. Accordingly, the parties are discharged from their respective obligations. The leading case on this branch of the law is *James B Fraser & Co Ltd v Denny Mott & Dickson Ltd*[17]:

In 1929 a timber yard was let and it was agreed that the lessor should purchase all his timber from the lessee and that the lessor should have an option to purchase. On the outbreak of war, certain legislation was passed which meant that further trading between the parties could not continue. The lessor sought to exercise the option to purchase the yard.

It was held by the House of Lords that the whole agreement, including the option clause, was terminated when the relevant legislation was passed. The legislation had effectively frustrated the agreement. Another similar example of legal impossibility occurs when war breaks out between two countries. A contract between persons in two opposing states automatically falls on the outbreak of war. Thus in a contract for the supply of marine engines between an Austrian and Scottish company, the outbreak of the First World War terminated the contract.[18] Thereafter, the Austrian company was an enemy alien with whom it was illegal to do business.

13–14 There remains for consideration a third type of supervening event which we might loosely call "commercial impossibility". In such cases, performance of the contract is not physically or legally impossible, but circumstances have changed to such a marked extent that the venture is no longer that which the parties originally envisaged. The original

---

[17] *James B Fraser & Co Ltd v Denny Mott & Dickson Ltd*, 1944 S.C. (HL) 35; [1944] A.C. 265.

[18] *Cantiere San Rocco SA (Shipbuilding Co) v Clyde Shipbuilding & Engineering Co Ltd*, 1923 S.C. (HL) 105; [1923] A.C. 226.

purpose of the contract has been frustrated: can one party be released from its obligations as a consequence? It is firmly established that frustration does not occur simply because performance has become more onerous or expensive for one of the parties. In *Tsakiroglou & Co Ltd v Noblee Thorl GmbH*[19]:

> A charterparty was entered into to carry freight to Britain. It was assumed by the parties that the ship would proceed through the Suez Canal although nothing was expressly stated in the contract. The Suez Crisis of 1956 intervened and the canal was closed and the ship would have had to undertake its voyage round the Cape of Good Hope.

It was held that the charterparty was not frustrated. Although the voyage was longer and more expensive to perform than envisaged at the time the contract was made, and the profits would consequently be lower, that was not a ground for discharging the parties from their obligations. The court indicated, however, that if the freight had been perishable and if it were to be damaged or to perish as a result of the longer voyage, then the contract probably would be frustrated. Another example is provided by *Davis Contractors Ltd v Fareham Urban District Council*, where inflation had caused the cost of a particular building contract to increase dramatically.[20] This would have meant the contractor would have made no profit on the contract price as originally agreed. Nevertheless he was held bound to his contract. The extra cost was no reason to invoke the doctrine of frustration. Today, building contracts are usually drawn up on special standard forms which contain provisions designed to deal with escalating costs which may arise in respect of a number of specified contingencies.

The most radical example of "commercial frustration" is provided by **13–15** the English case of *Krell v Henry*[21]:

> Rooms overlooking Pall Mall were hired at a high price to view the processions which were to take place in connection with Edward VII's coronation. Because the King had appendicitis, the coronation had to be postponed.

It was held that the contract for the hire of the rooms was terminated by frustration. The basis for the claim was that the whole rationale or purpose of the contract, the bedrock on which it was founded, had disappeared. The hirers did not want to see the Mall in its usual livery with its usual array of pedestrians and carriages. They had paid a high price to see the procession.

It has been suggested that *Krell* would not be followed in Scotland. **13–16** Lord Cooper, founding on Professor Gloag, doubted whether it is good

---

[19] *Tsakiroglou & Co Ltd v Noblee Thorl GmbH* [1962] A.C. 93.
[20] *Davis Contractors v Fareham Urban DC* [1956] A.C. 696; [1956] 2 All E.R. 145.
[21] *Krell v Henry* [1903] 2 K.B. 740.

authority north of the border.[22] Even south of the border its authority is in some doubt. It was decided only a few weeks apart from another "Coronation case," *Herne Bay Steam Boat Co v Hutton*[23]:

> A pleasure boat was hired to view the naval review which was to take place off Spithead in connection with the coronation celebrations. When the review was cancelled, it was argued that the contract for the hire of the boat was frustrated.

The same court which decided *Krell* held in this case that the contract was not frustrated. What are the distinctions between the two cases? Clearly, there is very little to choose between them. The operative distinctions appear to be first, that the owners of the pleasure steamer were in the business of hiring out their craft. It was not their purpose to inquire into the reasons for the hire. Just as a taxi driver might know his vehicle was being hired to go to Musselburgh, but did not know that it was to see the races, so the boat owner could not be expected to inquire into the motives for every contract of hire into which they entered. By contrast the owner of the flat in Pall Mall was hiring it out on a special "one-off" basis.

Secondly, there was actually something to see in Herne. The distinguished jurist, Sir Frederick Pollock, went to view the British fleet assembled at Spithead and declared it to be a very impressive spectacle.[24] There was unlikely to be any special attraction in watching the usual pedestrian and vehicular traffic in Pall Mall.

13–17   It remains true, however, that distinguishing between the two cases is decidedly tricky. In Scotland, it is more likely that the presumption would be in favour of the contract being upheld if all that had occurred was the non-occurrence of an expected event as opposed to the occurrence of an unexpected event. In *Hong Kong & Whampoa Dock Co Ltd v Netherton Shipping Co Ltd*[25]:

> Shipowners sought to cancel a contract which they had made with a Hong Kong company to repair one of their ships. The shipowners claimed that it was "commercially impossible" for them to deliver the ship at Hong Kong within a reasonable time. This was because the ship lay at Singapore and the authorities there had stipulated that extensive preliminary repairs had to be carried out. Accordingly, the ship would not be ready to set out before the typhoon season, when it was dangerous for her to be at sea. Nevertheless the contract was upheld. All three judges in the Inner House expressed their unease over extending the width of the concept of commercial impossibility.

---

[22] Cooper, "Frustration of Contract in Scots Law" (1946) 28. J. Comp. L. 1.
[23] *Herne Bay Steam Boat Co v Hutton* [1903] 2 K.B. 683.
[24] Pollock, "Notes" (1904) 20 L.Q.R. 4.
[25] *Hong Kong & Whampoa Dock Co. Ltd v Netherton Shipping Co Ltd*, 1909 S.C. 34.

The event must be unforeseen

If the parties have foreseen a particular event and have provided for the **13–18** event in their contract, then the doctrine of frustration is not brought into play. So if there is a danger that war will break out and the parties make provision for such a contingency in their contract, the term of the contract will govern the legal relations of the parties if war does indeed break out. A clause which is intended to provide for future unexpected events is known as a "force majeure" clause. Where there is such a clause, it must define the categories of event that it refers to, such as *damnum fatale* (acts of God), acts of war or terrorism, and natural disasters. If the frustrating event is not covered by the specific force majeure clause, then the clause does not apply and the common law rules on frustration will be relevant. Where the clause does apply, it operates to suspend performance until the frustrating event is at an end. The contract is therefore not terminated, but the parties are released from their obligation to perform until the event is over or until either party terminates the contract in terms of the clause.

Neither party at fault

As frustration is an equitable doctrine, it has no role to play if the cir- **13–19** cumstances disclose that one of the parties was at fault. Where, for example, it was known that there was a war zone and one of the parties caused a ship to enter that zone, he could not thereafter plead frustration.[26] It was his act which caused the detention of the ship. So it was not possible to claim that a supervening event had occurred without fault of either of the parties. Accordingly, the obligation was not discharged. Self-induced frustration is, in fact, no more than breach of contract.

> *Example*: An opera singer is engaged to appear with Scottish Opera for five weeks. If she loses her voice accidentally through illness, the contract is frustrated. But if she chooses to enter the European Women's Open Yodelling Championship and thereby loses her voice so that she cannot perform, that is breach of contract.[27]

Effect of frustration

Where frustration applies, both parties to the contract are released from **13–20** their future obligations. The losses are said to lie where they fall. Injustice could clearly arise from this if one party had performed all or part of their obligation and found themselves unable to exact any performance in return. This result is avoided by rules on unjustified enrichment under which the disadvantaged party may claim against the other.[28] However,

---

[26] *Ocean Tramp Tankers Corp v V/O Sovfracht (The Eugenia)* [1964] 2 Q.B. 226; [1964] 1 All E.R. 161.
[27] cf. *Poussard v Spiers & Pond* (1876) 1 Q.B.D. 410.
[28] *Cantiere San Rocco SA (Shipbuilding Co) v Clyde Shipbuilding & Engineering Co Ltd*, 1923 S.C. (HL) 105; [1923] A.C. 226.

liability for any breach or failure which occurred prior to the frustrating event will not be lost, and the parties will retain any accrued rights under the contract.

Risk—the alternative to frustration

13–21 Where the subject matter of the contract has been destroyed the alternative to discharging the contract through frustration is to determine who must bear this loss. In early Scottish cases concerning this situation the question asked was: on whom should the risk fall? So if a horse was hired and then stolen whilst in the possession of the hirer the question was: who should bear the loss of the horse, the owner or the hirer?[29] Similarly, if goods were damaged in transit, should the owner or the carrier be liable? Out of these cases, certain rules were established regarding the passing of risk in the most common contract—sale. In a contract for the sale of goods, risk is presumed to pass when property (ownership) in the goods passes, unless the parties have agreed otherwise.[30] In a sale of heritage it has been established that risk passes when the missives are completed. In *Sloans' Dairies v Glasgow Corp*, premises were sold under missives.[31] Before the disposition had been delivered, the subjects were badly damaged by fire and had to be demolished. It was held that the risk was the purchasers' and they therefore had to bear the loss which had occurred.[32] In either case the parties may specify when the risk of destruction passes from one to the other. Such a provision would mean that the rules on frustration would not apply.

The operation of these rules regarding the passing of risk in sale reduces considerably the problem of supervening events. In such cases, it is up to the person who bears the risk to take whatever steps he can to minimise or insure against the risk.

The position of leases

13–22 From earliest times, Scots law has taken the view that a lease, like any other contract, can be frustrated. In English law this is not the case, partly because a lease constitutes a separate estate in land, partly because of the belief that a person who enters a contract for a period of years must assume the risk of whatever contingencies occur in those years. Not everything can be foreseen, but it is at least likely that a variety of incidents will occur in the course of a long time. It has been stated that while it is untrue to say that a lease can never be frustrated in English law it is

---

[29] See *Trotter v Buchanan* (1688) Mor. 10080.
[30] Sale of Goods Act 1979 s.20. Special protection is given to consumers: risk remains with the seller until the goods are delivered to the consumer, s.20(4), as amended.
[31] *Sloans' Dairies v Glasgow Corp*, 1977 S.C. 223.
[32] In Scottish Law Commission, *Report on the Passing of Risk in Contracts for the Sale of Heritable Property* (HMSO, 1990), Scot. Law Com. No.127, a change in the law was recommended, but no legislative action was taken. However, it is standard practice to insert a clause in missives to assert that risk remains with the seller after conclusion of missives, until the disposition is delivered.

true to say that such a situation will hardly ever occur.[33] Scots law is so far different in this respect that not only do we allow frustration of a lease in the event of actual destruction of the subject (*rei interitus*), but we also hold a lease frustrated in the event of constructive destruction. So where the tenants in a 19-year lease of salmon fishings were unable to take advantage of the lease when the area came to be used by the Royal Air Force as an aerial gunnery and bombing range, the lease was held to have terminated.[34] A similar decision was reached in *Mackeson v Boyd*, where a mansion which had been let was requisitioned by the authorities during the war, 14 years into a 19-year lease.[35] Despite the relatively short proportion of the lease still to run and the uncertainty, in 1940, of how long the requisition would last, the lease was nevertheless held terminated by constructive total destruction of the subject matter and the legal eviction of the tenants. Lord President Normand said in the course of his opinion:

> "In the chapter of leases of heritage, and I think also in the chapter of *rei interitus*, our law is by no means the same as the law of England, and, to quote Lord Justice-Clerk Hope, if we were to attempt to apply that law in these cases, we should run the greatest risk of spoiling our own by mistaking theirs."[36]

---

[33] *National Carriers Ltd v Panalpina (Northern) Ltd* [1981] A.C. 675; [1981] 1 All E.R. 161.
[34] *Tay Salmon Fisheries Co Ltd v Speedie*, 1929 S.C. 593.
[35] *Mackeson v Boyd*, 1942 S.C. 56.
[36] *Mackeson v Boyd*, 1942 S.C. 56 at 63.

APPENDIX

FURTHER READING

GENERAL

Gloag, W.M., *The Law of Contract: a Treatise on the principles of contract in the law of Scotland,* 2nd edn (Edinburgh: W. Green, 1929).

McBryde, W.W., *The Law of Contract in Scotland,* 3rd edn (Edinburgh: SULI/W. Green, 2007).

von Bar, C., Clive, E., and Schulte-Nölke, H., *Principles, Definitions and Model Rules of European Private Law: Draft Common Frame of Reference,* (Munich: Sellier, 2009) (also available online at *http://ec.europa.eu/ justice/contract/files/european-private-law_en.pdf* [Accessed February 25, 2014]).

The Scottish Law Commission's Discussion Papers and Reports are available at: *www.scotlawcom.gov.uk/publications/*

CHAPTER 2: FORMATION OF CONTRACT—CONCLUDING AN AGREEMENT

Lubbe, G., "Formation of Contract", in Reid, Kenneth and Zimmermann, Reinhard (eds), *A History of Private Law in Scotland* (Oxford: Oxford University Press, 2000), Vol.II, "Obligations".

Hogg, M. and Lubbe, G., "Formation of Contract" in Reid, Kenneth, Zimmermann, Reinhard and Visser, Daniel (eds), *Mixed Legal Systems in Comparative Perspective: Property and Obligations in Scotland and South Africa* (Oxford: Oxford University Press, 2004).

CHAPTER 3: FORMATION OF CONTRACT—ENFORCEABLE AGREEMENTS

Black, G., "*WS Karoulias SA v The Drambuie Liqueur Company Ltd*—An Analysis" (2006) 10 Edin. L.R. 132.

Black, G., "Formation of contract: the role of contractual intention and email disclaimers" (2011) Jur. Rev. 97.

CHAPTER 4: PROMISE

Macqueen, H. and Sellar, W.D.H., "Scots law: *Ius quaesitum tertio*, promise and irrevocability" in Eltjo Schrage (eds), *Ius Quaesitum Tertio* (Berlin: Duncker & Humblot, 2008).

Hogg, M., "Promise: The Neglected Obligation In European Private Law" (2010) 59(2) I.C.L.Q. 461.

Hogg, M., *Promises and Contract Law: Comparative Perspectives* (Cambridge: Cambridge University Press, 2011).

Hogg, M., "Three recent cases of promise" (2012) 16 Edin. L.R. 430.

Swain, W., "Contract as promise: the role of promising in the law of contract. An historical account" (2013) 17 Edin. L.R. 1.

CHAPTER 5: CAPACITY AND FORMALITIES

Gretton, G.L. and Steven, A.J.M., *Property, Trusts and Succession* (Haywards Heath: Bloomsbury Professional, 2013), Ch.30.

CHAPTER 6: GROUNDS OF INVALIDITY

Mcbryde, W.W., "Error", in Reid and Zimmermann (eds), *A History of Private Law in Scotland*, (Oxford: Oxford University Press, 2000), Vol.II.

Hogg, M., "The continuing confused saga of contract and error" (2009) 13 Edin. L.R. 286.

Macleod, J., "Before Bell: The Roots of Error in the Scots Law of Contract" (2010) 14 Edin. L.R. 385.

Reid, D. and Macqueen, H., "Fraud or error: a thought experiment?" (2013) 17 Edin. L.R. 343.

CHAPTER 7: TERMS OF THE CONTRACT

Peden, E., "Policy Concerns Behind Implication of Terms in Law" (2001) 117 L.Q.R. 459.

Clive, E., "Interpretation, implied terms and interference with conditions" (2008) 12 Edin. L.R. 283.

CHAPTER 8: CONSTRUCTION OF THE CONTRACT

Clive, E., "Interpretation", in Reid and Zimmermann (eds), *A History of Private Law in Scotland*, (Oxford: Oxford University Press, 2000), Vol.II.

Macgregor, L.J. and Lewis, C., "Interpretation of Contract" in Reid, Zimmermann and Visser (eds), *Mixed Legal Systems in Comparative Perspective: Property and Obligations in Scotland and South Africa* (Oxford: Oxford University Press, 2004).

Lord Bingham of Cornhill, "A New Thing Under the Sun? The Interpretation of Contract and the *ICS* Decision" (2008) 12 Edin. L.R. 374.

Cabrelli, D., "Interpretation of contracts, objectivity and the elision of the significance of consent achieved through concession and compromise" (2011) Jur. Rev. 120.

Macgregor, L.J., "Long-term contracts, the rules of interpretation and 'equitable adjustment'" (2012) 16 Edin. L.R. 104.

Richardson, L., "When interpretation is not enough: rectification of contracts" (2014) 18 Edin. L.R. 125.

CHAPTER 9: STATUTORY CONTROL OF CONTRACT TERMS

Thomson, J.M., "Judicial Control of Unfair Contract Terms" in Reid and Zimmermann (eds), *A History of Private Law in Scotland* (Oxford: Oxford University Press, 2000), Vol.II.

Ervine, W.C.H., *Consumer Law in Scotland*, 4th edn (Edinburgh: W. Green, 2008).

Cabrelli, D. and Zahn, R., "Challenging unfair terms: some recent developments" (2010) Jur. Rev. 115.

CHAPTER 10: BREACH OF CONTRACT AND REMEDIES

McBryde, W.W., "Remedies for breach of contract" (1996) Edin. L.R. 43.

Macgregor, L.J., "The Expectation, Reliance and Restitution Interests in Contract Damages" (1996) Jur. Rev. 227.

Johnston, D., "Breach of Contract" in Reid and Zimmermann (eds), *A History of Private Law in Scotland* (Oxford: Oxford University Press, 2000), Vol.II.

Smith, A., "Specific Implement" in Reid and Zimmermann (eds), *A History of Private Law in Scotland* (Oxford: Oxford University Press, 2000), Vol.II.

Black, G., "A New Experience in Contract Damages? Reflections on *Experience Hendrix v PPX Enterprises Ltd*" (2005) Jur. Rev. 31.

Macgregor, L.J., "Specific implement in Scots law" in Smits, Jan, Haas, Daniel, and Hesen, Geerte (eds), *Specific Performance in Contract Law: National and Other Perspectives* (Antwerp: Intersentia, 2008).

Lord Hoffmann, "*The Achilleas*: Custom and Practice or Foreseeability?" (2010) 14 Edin. L.R. 47.

Godfrey, A.M., "Mutuality, retention and set-off: *Inveresk plc v Tullis Russell Papermakers Ltd*" (2011) 15 Edin. L.R. 115.

CHAPTER 11: TITLE TO SUE

MacQueen, H.L., "Third Party Rights in Contract: *Jus Quaesitum Tertio*" in Reid and Zimmermann (eds), *A History of Private Law in Scotland* (Oxford: Oxford University Press, 2000), Vol.II.

Anderson, R., *Assignation* (Edinburgh: Avizandum, 2008).

Macgregor, L.J., *The Law of Agency in Scotland* (Edinburgh: SULI/W. Green, 2013), Ch.12.

CHAPTER 12: THE REQUIREMENT OF LEGALITY

Sutherland, P.J., "Contractual Restrictive Covenants" in Reid and Zimmermann (eds), *A History of Private Law in Scotland* (Oxford: Oxford University Press, 2000), Vol.II.

Macgregor, L.J., "*Pacta Illicita*" in Reid and Zimmermann (eds), *A History of Private Law in Scotland* (Oxford: Oxford University Press, 2000), Vol.II.

Thomson, J.M., "Illegal Contracts In Scots Law", 2002 S.L.T. (News) 153.

MacQueen, H.L. and Cockrell, A., "Illegal Contracts" in Reid, Zimmermann and Visser (eds) *Mixed Legal Systems in Comparative Perspective: Property and Obligations in Scotland and South Africa* (Oxford: Oxford University Press, 2004).

CHAPTER 13: THE EXTINCTION OF OBLIGATIONS

Macgregor, L.J., "The effect of unexpected circumstances in contract law in Scotland and Louisiana" in Reid, Elspeth C. and Palmer, Vernon V. (eds) *Mixed Jurisdictions Compared: Private Law in Louisiana and Scotland* (Edinburgh: Edinburgh University Press, 2009).

Woolman on Contract

ENGLISH CONTRACT LAW

Treitel's Law of Contract, edited by Edwin Peel, 13th edn (London: Sweet & Maxwell, 2011).

Chitty on Contracts, edited by H.G. Beale, 31st edn (London: Sweet & Maxwell/Thomson Reuters, 2012).

McKendrick, E., *Contract Law*, 10th edn (Basingstoke: Palgrave Macmillan, 2013).

INDEX